HIKING
NORTH AMERICA'S GREAT WESTERN
VOLCANOES

Also by Tom Prisciantelli

SPIRIT OF THE AMERICAN SOUTHWEST
Geology/Ancient Eras and Prehistoric People/Hiking Through Time

HIKING
NORTH AMERICA'S GREAT WESTERN
VOLCANOES

Tom Prisciantelli

SUNSTONE PRESS
SANTA FE

© 2004 by Tom Prisciantelli. All rights reserved.

No part of this book may be reproduced in any form
or by any electronic or mechanical means including information storage
and retrieval systems without permission in writing from the publisher,
except by a reviewer who may quote brief passages in a review.

Sunstone books may be purchased for educational, business, or sales promotional use.
For information please write: Special Markets Department, Sunstone Press,
P.O. Box 2321, Santa Fe, New Mexico 87504-2321.

Library of Congress Cataloging-in-Publication Data:

Prisciantelli, Tom, 1946–
  Hiking North America's great Western volcanoes / Tom Prisciantelli.
    p. cm.
  Includes bibliographical references and index.
  ISBN 0-86534-432-9 (pbk.)
  1. Hiking–West (U.S.)–Guidebooks. 2. Volcanoes–West (U.S.)–Guidebooks.
  3. West (U.S.)–Guidebooks. I. Title.
  GV199.42.W39P75 2004
  917.8–dc22
                                                    2004003333

Published in SUNSTONE PRESS
POST OFFICE BOX 2321
SANTA FE, NM 87504-2321 / USA
(505) 988-4418 / *ORDERS ONLY* (800) 243-5644
FAX (505) 988-1025
WWW.SUNSTONEPRESS.COM

CONTENTS

PREFACE: Appointment With a Volcano / 7

1. Considering Volcanoes and Hike Preparations / 11
2. The Earth and Volcanoes Through Geologic Time / 19
3. What Drives a Volcano / 31
4. Destruction and Construction: Eruption Types, Volcanic Formations and Rocks / 46

THE HIKES:
5. Hiking New Mexico's Volcanoes
    Capulin Volcano National Monument / 64
    Valles Caldera National Preserve / 77
    El Malpais National Monument and Mt. Taylor / 101

6. Hiking Arizona's Volcanoes and the Yellowstone Caldera
    Chiricahua National Monument / 120
    San Francisco Mountain and Volcanic Field
       (including, Sunset Crater) / 139
    Yellowstone National Park / 154

7. Hiking the Cascade Range
    Mount Lassen (Lassen Volcanic National Park) / 167
    Crater Lake National Park (Mount Mazama) / 179
    Mount St. Helens / 193

INDEX / 209
GLOSSARY / 213
SUGGESTED READING / 219

PREFACE

Appointment With a Volcano

Thursday, June 27: We're driving head-on through a hard rain. All week on the road and as we get closer to our destination we seem to be farther away. The first day, Sunday, brought us to Tonopah, Nevada and a reunion with Route 6. I had hitch-hiked Jack Kerouac's one-red-line across America thirty years ago and hadn't been back to this section of Route 6 since. Truckers and road-people know it well. Tonopah has a lot of history and is the main theme of great travel-songs, made famous by singers and groups like the Grateful Dead. Nice visit. Then on to Mt. Lassen National Park in northern California—one huge and beautiful volcanic dome. Wednesday at Crater Lake, a grand volcanic hole filled with water. With all this excitement you'd think we'd lose sight of our final destination. But it was out there, farther north, waiting. It's been 1,200 miles and still we seem to be great distances from our big debut on Friday. Come Thursday the road gets wet. The rain looks like dark sheets tinted by the pine forests in the background. Southern Washington— should have known. You can't drive through Washington without getting wet at least once. So here's our dose under the clouds and it was slowing us down. In retaliation, I drove faster. My wife worried. We balled up Interstate 5, then east on Route 12, finally moving in the direction I had longed for—directly at Mount St. Helens. I knew she was out there, brooding in the shroud. Maybe letting off a little steam from the lava dome welling up inside the crater. Maybe rumbling the ground from lava still moving up in her throat. And I knew she was there, daring me to get close and I couldn't even see her. Damn rain! We drove faster and by late afternoon cruised into the town of Randle, Washington, northeast of the mountain and directly in the path of her 1980 fury. Even though Mount St. Helens was named after a man, the mountain is too unpredictable to be considered a "he". Mount St. Helens is "she" through and through.

Once known as the "Fujiyama of America", when it stood over 9,600 feet high before the eruption that lowered her head, Mount St. Helens is one great volcanic mountain. Over the last few thousand years it has been the most active of volcanoes in the United States (at least the lower 48). It returned to life in the early spring of 1980. How did geologists define her reawakening? There were several strong earthquakes located directly under the mountain; the quakes most probably caused by magma (liquefied rock) forcing its way up through bedrock deep below the surface. Eruptions of steam and ash soon followed from the summit crater. Through March and April, the activity continued. Then the bulge appeared. First seen by geologists at the end of April, it was an ominous sign. The bulge, a huge sore almost 2 miles in diameter and 200 feet high, swelled on the mountain's north flank. And it was active—growing nearly 6 feet per day. Earthquakes were more frequent and gas emissions pointed to a future climax. The reality of the danger was recognized by geologists who started warning authorities at the same time they themselves wanted to get closer to monitor the bloated sore. David Johnston of the US Geological Survey had to get closer. An expert in volcanoes with a chance to learn more, he located his monitoring station north of the volcano with a birdseye view of the bulge. The ridge where he perched and the observatory now located at that spot are named after him—a fitting memorial to someone who wanted to learn more and did.

On the morning of May 18, 1980, I was home and unaware of what was happening, reading an article in the New York Times about the preliminary events at Mount St. Helens. At 8:32am pacific time, a significant earthquake jolted the area—more magma trying to rise to the surface. David Johnston must have known his fate in that split second. The quake loosened the bulge, sending it in a massive slide downhill while releasing all the gassed-up pressure below. In all, more than 50 people (mostly campers) would be burned and buried. Harry Truman and his lodge at Spirit Lake were about to be buried by a burning explosion of mud, trees and rocks. In a few minutes, he and his lodge would be at the bottom of the lake. Rivers were damned from all the dead trees uprooted by the debris avalanche, which charged down the mountain at interstate speeds. As the bulge started to slide downhill, a fracture opened on the north flank releasing pressure within the mountain. From the fracture, a hot blast chased the avalanche downhill ripping trees from their roots within a 230 square mile swath north of the erupting volcano. A cloud of ash rose 15 miles into the sky. The jet stream carried it east and what didn't remain aloft, dropped and covered communities in a blanket of ash that resembled dirty snow. When it was all done—relatively speaking since there would be more activity in the months to come—the mountain was missing 1,300 feet from its top and side. Up to 60,000 acres of trees would eventually be known as the Blow-down Forest. So for me, on this day of our debut in 2002, I am humbled, in awe and without past experiences to prepare myself.

In the rainy town of Randle, I asked for divine intervention. We've come all this way and our meeting was imminent. She's out there and I can't see her. We stopped in the ranger station and the young lady holding down the front desk told me it was a bad time to be visiting: "supposed to rain straight through the weekend". Thanks for the encouragement. Our audience with her majesty is tomorrow and I don't care if we get a tornado. I'll drive through that too. Almost 1,600 miles and everything and everyone seemed to be conspiring to cancel our meeting with the mountain. And the next morning it rained even harder.

Since it was too wet to camp, we spent the night at a nice little motel right in the middle of the rainy woods of Randle. On the morning of our big day, Friday, we were awakened by a peacock pecking at our door. The motel was like a game park, animals everywhere and all we could do was sleep. We checked out at 8am and headed south on Forest Service Road 25. The rain poured down harder, clouds shrouded everything. We were alone on the dark road all the way to our destination at Windy Ridge, where the rain finally let up but it got windy and the clouds moved west to east covering everything. The car rocked from the gusting winds as we pulled into the parking lot at Windy Ridge. Windy indeed! We loaded up our daypacks, prepared the cameras and bent our determination into the wind, walking south. And then it happened. A break in the clouds and there she was. I was dumbfounded, numb. The beautiful Mount St. Helens presented herself in a way I can never describe and won't even try.

From the main parking lot at Windy Ridge, we headed south on Trail 207, also known as the Truman Trail. I'm assuming it was named after Harry Truman, the old guy who refused to leave his home at Spirit Lake prior to the eruption of 1980. He's now somewhere at the bottom of Spirit Lake along with his lodge and every tree and rock between the lake and the north side of

Mount St. Helens. We took Harry's trail south, then west on Trail 216 and as it turns out, I remember very little from those first 4 miles. My wife informed me later that I took off from the parking lot like someone possessed and never stopped until I was staring straight into the volcano's open throat, now known as The Breach. Most of the north side is gone, down in the lake or beyond. The clouds had opened and our great debut was of a time and place I'll never forget and never be able to share in real terms for it was surreal. And for many months now I've reviewed our pictures and still can't find one that truly shows her majesty and power. This is my goal—to share what I've experienced in ways pictures can't and words will never explain. It can only be seen and felt on the trail. Mount St. Helens is one of many (active, dormant or extinct) volcanoes in North America but, in my mind, the one that best shows the remains of a violent eruption. We stood right at ground zero on the north side and felt her brooding, sensed her energy still welling up from below and stared in awe. And so the great adventure to the western volcanoes begins. Each one has a special message. You can only hear it by getting close enough to listen.

Mount St. Helens from Windy Ridge.

1

Considering Volcanoes and Hike Preparations

Approaching Volcanoes

Researching my first book, *Spirit of the American Southwest*, helped me better understand geologic processes. I realized then that to truly learn something, you should write about it, teach it or preach it. During my research, I was often distracted—drawn more toward the distraction than the main subject. It wasn't until after finishing the book that I sensed the great distraction was volcanic. Terms jumped out of text and drew my attention. Geology is more than a descriptive science, particularly in the area of volcanoes. It's a whole new language and one with definitions that stir the imagination. A type of lava named Aa is considered clinkery, Pahoehoe lava is ropy. Convergent and subductive behavior is most often associated with orogenies. Exotic terrains attach themselves as the crust dives down. The west coast grew outward in this manner. The east coast was wounded and the Appalachian Mountains were the result of converging with Europe, South America and Africa. Mountain building at it's best. Below it all the god of the underworld, Pluto, builds plutons—plutonic rock. Discordant and concordant dikes, sills, batholiths, stocks and laccoliths are symptoms. Lava domes could be resurgent and stratovolcanoes are most certainly composite. Ash can fall but you'd better run if it flows. If it's hot enough, it will weld. If it's loose, stay away from it. Roof pendants hang from the ceiling in the master batholith. The island of Vulcano, off the coast of Sicily, is the forge of the blacksmith of the Roman gods. Volcanic eruptions can be Vulcanian, Strombolian, Vesuvian or Hawaiian. The worst is Plinian. Mount St. Helens had most Plinian symptoms. There are smokers in the water. At mid-ocean rifts, hydrothermal vents puff away heat from the fever below. You could find schist in the scarp. If it's not schist, it could still have schistosity. Lava that cools fast when it reaches the surface is fully quenched. Volcanic islands sit behind an ocean's trench like volcanic arcs hug the coastline. There's hot rock, fever down below. The terminology never ends.

Approaching This Book / What's the Game Plan?

Our effort is primarily about finding great hiking trails in the west. And more! When hiking with friends, I've noticed that they may focus on the trees along the trail. Is that a Cottonwood or Sycamore? Or, a bird may catch their eye. What bird has a red wing patch like that? Only on rare occasions do they inquire about the rocks. Except maybe to note a cliff is steep or that mountain has an odd shape. There's much to appreciate about the geologic features surrounding the trail; hence, this book. And, an interesting sideshow to geology—when you're looking for geologic features, you come across archaeological features. Then things really get interesting. Hopefully this work combines all of the most interesting elements of geology and archaeology along the trail and presents them in a manner that adds to the enjoyment of hiking.

Before we begin, a quick aside about my writing style. This is a book about hiking and the geology of volcanoes. Geology can be highly technical and at times not exactly a light read. To enhance the process of understanding technical material but not beat it into the ground, I have a tendency to repeat some elements of a particular subject. The intent is to reinforce the material and prepare the reader for another layer of information about that subject. There is also a bit of repetition in the hikes' section since some readers tend to read the hikes first without going through the earlier, introductory chapters. So please bear with me if I seem to be repeating myself on subjects like subduction, tectonic plates, magma or even the Hawaiian Islands. They are all critical to understanding volcanoes and what we're about to see on the trail.

Our hikes are going to follow the Pacific plate east to west under North America. We'll review tectonic plate theory in chapter three but for the current discussion consider that a slab of rock, once the deep floor of the Pacific Ocean, sits miles below the southwest. The slab was jammed under North

America when it collided with the Pacific oceanic plate and didn't end its dive under the continent until it ran into the deep, hard basement rock of the Great Plains—the old footings of North America. At that time, the slab was nearly horizontal under the continental plate where friction may have had something to do with slowing it down. Why do we care about the remains of a tectonic plate below North America? To geologists the answer is simple: follow the plate and you'll find the volcanoes.

Scientists theorize that over 200 million years ago the continents were very active. Young North America had slipped around equally youthful South America and collided with northwest Africa. North America and South America had a history. They collided often, only to separate and try it again. Around the same time, in geologic time that is, North America collided with Europe. Then most of the continents came together forming a mega-continent named Pangea. Pangea would eventually break up, sending North America on a journey west. During the trip, the Atlantic Ocean would form in the continent's wake. And North America would begin a long battle, a collision with the Pacific's oceanic plate. The war continues today. As the wet oceanic plate moved under the continent, it created volcanic activity which progressed from west to east. As the plate dove below the crust of the continent, it entered the hot mantle, which cooked the slab to molten rock called magma. The magma was then pressured up through the crust to the surface. Volcanoes grew along the coast first, above where the plate entered the mantle. Then the slab appeared to move inland at less of an angle, closer to the continental plate above. It went almost horizontal all the way to eastern New Mexico where the plate's movement seemed to reach a dead end. Geologists believe the plate may have changed its direction of movement and then began to dip again at a steeper angle back into the hot mantle. The deeper the dip, the more hot rocks are pressured toward the surface. With the plate now deep in the upper mantle, and seemingly moving away from eastern New Mexico and the western Great Plains, the volcanoes again appeared. But this time moving back west as the plate dipped deeper below the upper crust. In a particularly violent period, called the Mid-Tertiary Orogeny, southwest New Mexico, southeast Arizona and Nevada experienced considerable volcanic activity. The deeper the plate dipped into the mantle and seemed to regress back toward the west, the more violence came out of the ground.

It seems strange that although the activity migrated back toward the west coast, New Mexico has some of the youngest volcanic rock in the southwest. In fact, there's still hot rock under New Mexico so it's not over. The volcanic rocks at Capulin Volcano National Monument can be considered infants. Capulin itself is only about 60,000 years old. Very young in geologic time. Some geologists believe a hot spot (aka hotspot or mantle plume) may exist under northern New Mexico. Add to that the fact that the Rio Grande River basin is a rift valley, similar to the East Africa Rift. As the basin rifts (pulls apart), the crust thins making it easier for more hot rocks in the mantle to find surface exits. Subsurface volcanic activity, a result of the Rio Grande River valley rifting near Socorro, is proof of such activity. Another factor to consider is a long zone of crustal weakness that runs from east-central Arizona up through the northeastern corner of New Mexico. It's called the Jemez Lineament (aka linament). Along the entire stretch, the crust is believed to be thinner than usual as the lineament follows deep earth fractures that date to ancient geologic time. Capulin is at the northeast end of the zone. The Jemez Mountains, the Zuni-Bandera volcanic field and Mt. Taylor are related. They all sit on the lineament. With the lineament, the possible presence of a hot plume under northern New Mexico and the river valley rifting, geologists may have found the culprit(s) for the southwest's recent volcanic activity. We'll discuss these features on our first hike at Capulin Volcano National Monument, not far from where the Pacific plate reversed course. The hikes start there and continue west, along the lineament, where various volcanoes of various ages explain the plate's movement and follow those areas of weakness. We'll also consider some interesting contradictions, some relating to hot spots. The journey will end at Mount St. Helens where a renegade plate has started the action all over again, creating the Cascade Range. A fractured chunk of the northeast corner of the Pacific plate, known as the Juan de Fuca plate, is diving under Oregon, Washington and western Canada much like the Pacific plate did under the southwest. An even smaller renegade plate, the Gorda, is heating up northern California. So we'll end the hikes at Mount St. Helens where volcanism is so young, so current in fact, that we may see some action from the mountain. We'll follow the slab west from northeastern New Mexico and we'll adhere to tectonic plate theory that established the preliminary rules of plate movement and volcanism. But with modifications to any theory and our game plan, we'll look into the thinning crust of the west, the rift valley of the Rio Grande and hot spots—all responsible for the hot rocks below and their move to the surface. There are many interesting lessons on the road, following the volcanoes. Lessons of how the west is changing, probably more so than the rest of North America.

  The best approach to using this book and enjoying the hikes is to take your time reading through the first four chapters. Spend some quality time understanding the innards of a volcano, how they form, what they look like, the various rock types and the structures they produce. A background in how the earth was formed helps, along with the earth's makeup, tectonic plates and how processes deep below the crust influence all volcanic activity. As you read, other sources of information can help fill in the blanks. Use the Internet for additional research or read other books to learn more—some books and web sites are listed in the Suggested Reading section. Take your time in the beginning and get comfortable with the basics. Then move on to planning your trip to the first volcano. Starting with chapter five the hikes will be listed by state or location of the country. Chapter five will cover the New Mexico volcanoes, followed by other states (chapters) from Arizona to the northwest. Each hike will be followed by a section titled: On the Road to the Next Hike, where we'll discuss some interesting road experiences and features that will present themselves on the road between hikes. We'll start our hikes at Capulin Volcano National Monument in New Mexico. Wherever you start, planning is critical. Do you want to camp? Stay in a hotel? Hike? As for hiking and local conditions, contact ranger stations and visitor information centers. Contact the national and state parks and request material you can review before the trip. Make notes about the most important features you're interested in seeing and which trails get you to those features. Also, jot down in your notes the key features to look for such as rock formations and areas where the volcano affected the countryside. The more notes, the better. Then prepare for some powerful and educational experiences. And some of the best hikes you've ever taken. An awareness of what surrounds you on the trail tends to change your hiking habits.

Zen Approach at the Trailhead

Let's assume you've read the material and are minutes from the hike. You've prepared well with plenty of notes. You may have done some research on the Internet or read a brochure at the visitor center about the local geology. In any case, you're well prepared and ready to go. You've filled your pack with the necessary gear and just finished drinking some water before hitting the trail. The next logical step is to start hiking.

Before taking that first step, it may be helpful to find a spot to sit and think. Off the trail, on a rock, under a tree, wherever you can find some solitude. Clear your mind, relax, take a few deep breaths, close your eyes and try to comprehend what happened at this location. Call it the Zen of the hike, or meditation. It's nice to find some peace and comprehend the events responsible for such scenery. Let's say you're about to hike at Mount St. Helens. Imagine Mount St. Helens when it was a snow-covered mountain, thousands of years after its last eruption. Now it's 1980 and the magma chamber deep below the surface is rumbling again with molten rock being pressurized toward the surface. The magma is seething through cracks and joints, breaking the country rock below with such force earthquakes are felt many miles away. Feel the pressure building within the mountain and the earthquakes being recorded by observers. As the eruption approaches, the mountain is surrounded with a frenzy of what to do—escape or watch it? Then the eruption, the release of pressure—gas, ash, blobs of lava, fiery debris climbing into the sky. If you were sitting on the dock at Spirit Lake, you could see a wall of burning ash, a glowing cloud, streaming in your direction at hundreds of miles per hour. The boiling hot flows and avalanches would be carrying every tree between the mountain and the lake. Huge fir trees, some with their roots still attached, fly by you as if they were twigs in a dark cloud. If you went along for the ride, you'd be swept up with the rest of the landscape it was carrying, driven up the north ridge beyond the lake and maybe dumped on the other side. Or, you might slosh back into the lake when the fury of that initial blast was spent. At that point, everything that was once above water at Spirit Lake would now be under it with a thick layer of trees floating on the surface. Try to understand what happened at this site—the power of a volcano as it processes through the eruptive cycle. First the rumblings, then the emission of gases from the vent, then the eruption, ash blown miles into the sky, fiery debris flowing down the mountain, ash settling in thick sheets, then maybe lava begins to ooze from the vent. If you look at Mount St. Helens you might imagine it coming from the huge hole blown from the north flank of the mountain. It's difficult to picture what happened until you open your eyes to the reality of mother nature. Feel how hard the ground is. The flank of Helens was at least that hard and now it's gone in one great blast. Feel the energy still brewing within the mountain. The time of hiking is at hand.

Trail to Mount St. Helens as it must appear to small animals you may see on your hike.

Considerations and Precautions / Before the Hike

Some of the hikes are in fairly remote country. Proper planning is essential. Always notify someone of your plans including the location, estimated time you'll be gone and what to do if you don't return at the planned time and location. Always bring a compass and a map and know how to use them. The best maps are the US Geological Survey topographic 7.5-minute quadrangles, 1:24,000 scale. They can be purchased online at the USGS site at:
   www.mapping.usgs.gov
or, another site with a wide variety of maps:
   www.topozone.com
If you're hiking in a national forest or at a national monument, forest service maps and trail guides can be purchased at the visitor centers or the forest ranger station in that area. Most of our hikes are in national forest. As part of the planning process, call the national forest office and specifically ask the following questions:

1) Is the forest open? Are there any restrictions?
2) Are the trails open?
3) Are the roads to the trailheads open?

Drink lots of water before starting the hike and bring plenty with you. Pack some food or energy bars. And since some of the hikes are in the southwest, sunglasses are a must. Take a first-aid kit, a knife and matches. These days many people have a cell phone. Bring it. If it's a long hike, extra clothing or a change of clothing may come in handy. Also, rain gear should be considered, like a poncho that takes up little space in a pack. This book can't prepare you for the local conditions. You have to check the weather report and contact the local ranger station or visitor center for road and trail conditions. My last trip to a national monument was a dud. I inquired about the trail conditions and was told they were fine. The snows had melted and all trails were open. They neglected to tell me the road to the trailhead of my planned hike was closed. So you have to ask all the necessary questions. Don't assume anything, particularly when it may effect your completing the hike alive and happy.

2

The Earth and Volcanoes Through Geologic Time

The Universe and The Beginning

To understand the machinations of a volcano, first we have to look at what exists below them. To understand what's below, we have to go deep within the earth, to its mantle and its core. And to understand the earth, we'll dig deeper into the basics of earth's beginnings and the universe. It's a humbling tale.

Around 15 billion years ago, a time frame that a truly focused mind can somewhat comprehend, energy and matter were highly concentrated. An event that scientists are still trying to nail down, maybe an exploding star, sent matter hurtling through space. It was a massive, incomprehensible explosion that started it all. In untypically simple, scientific parlance, they call it "The Big Bang". Out of this chaos, atoms formed, elements were next. Remember the Periodic Table of the Elements chart on the wall in science class. From the elements chemicals are identified. The physical processes, atoms, elements and chemicals would eventually construct the universe as we think we know it. Stars and planets would form in the process. Those of a specific astronomical science, cosmology, speculate that this growth went on for nearly 10 billion years before our solar system came to be, around 5 billion years ago. Dust, gas and planets formed. Gravity brought it all together and while it was sorting out the mess, heat and pressure were building in the middle of the mass. Our earth would be born of this material, with intense heat and pressure acting as an internal oven for our new planet. Heavy elements were attracted to the middle of the earth by gravity and light elements migrated out to the perimeter. The lighter elements eventually became the minerals of earth's outer crust. The heavier minerals built the furnace walls within the earth's core. Above it all gases formed our atmosphere, producing moisture the flora needed in order to grow so the fauna could, billions of years later, eat. Geologists estimate that most of our continental crust was formed around 500 million years ago. Not bad given that only half of it had formed two and a half billion years ago.

The Universe / Milky Way Galaxy / Earth

Earth is one of nine planets. Moving away from the sun, itself a star, the space traveler will encounter Mercury, Venus, Earth, Mars, Jupiter, Saturn, Uranus, Neptune and Pluto. All orbit the sun along with moons, asteroids and comets. This is our Solar System and combined with much dust and gas and probably more than 100 billion other stars we are all part of the Milky Way Galaxy. What is not known, and what could add more drama to the future of life on earth and elsewhere, is that of the 100 billion other stars out there, many probably have their own solar systems. Not bad odds on a bet for extraterrestrial life, or something similar to what we know as life. To get a handle on the size of our galaxy, consider that light travels at 186,000 miles per second. Our galaxy, a flat disk not unlike a spinning frisbee, is 80,000 light-years across. Convert years to seconds, then start multiplying. It's quite a trip for light to cross the Milky Way, let alone the Space Shuttle. As for other galaxies, there may be 10 billion or more scattered throughout the universe. I remember one night gazing at the constellation Pegasus—an extremely large horse. In one of its hind legs the beautiful and massive Andromeda Galaxy shines, a neighbor to our galaxy. Scientists have recently discovered within Andromeda a huge globular star cluster, usually a suspect area for black holes and they believe they've found at least one there. Our sun, a red-hot glowing ball of gas, is something like a million times the volume of our earth. That black hole in the Andromeda star cluster is 20,000 times the mass of the sun. The universe, the galaxies, black holes, our solar system—we humans on earth are still trying to understand our place within it all. One can't help but feel small, insignificant, like standing at attention before Mount St. Helens—a great lesson in humble pie.

While writing this section, we were fortunate to see a lunar eclipse. It occurred in the claws of Scorpius. Called the Night of the Scorpion Moon, the event brought another numeric figure I find hard to believe. The heart of Scorpius is a giant red star called Antares. Scientists have calculated its size to be equal that of 14 quadrillion of our moons. Go figure!

The bottom line for our purposes–the earth formed with heat in the center (the core) and rock as the outer shell (the crust). Somewhere in between is the layer (the mantle) that mixes the heat with rock to provide the fuel (magma) for volcanoes.

Geologic Time and the Maturing Earth

Many processes over geologic time were very influential in the volcanic uprisings the west has experienced in the most recent time. A quick review of geologic time will demonstrate that the changing earth and the movement of tectonic plates have been building to a crescendo of volcanic activity. It's not over, the earth will continue to change, move and erupt, forever it seems. However, looking at geologic time takes geologists down the road to understanding. Beginning with the Precambrian Era, the earth was forming and volcanic events had much to do with that process. Eighty percent of the earth's crust had volcanic origins. The next era, the Paleozoic, was the time of fishes. Water covered the continents, volcanoes quieted a bit and the oceans took over. The continents were on the move, forming new alliances with other continents. The fish thrived. Then came the Mesozoic Era, the time of reptiles and the great dinosaurs. The oceans receded (regressed), there was more land above water. Much of the activity occurred on land (aka continental events)– lakes, swamps, streams, rivers and wind had a great influence on the west. Toward the middle of that era, North America started its epic journey west. The continent would experience many orogenies (mountain building episodes), many of them involving volcanoes. Now, let's consider geologic time and events that lead to the west's more recent volcanic activity.

Precambrian Era (Earth forms – The earth's interior heats up):

Hadean Eon	4.6 to 4 billion years ago.
Archaen Eon	4 to 2.5 billion years ago.
Proterozoic Eon	2.5 billion to 550 million years ago.

Geologists group the eons (Hadean, Archaen, Proterozoic) into a very general time frame, while in no way minimizing the importance of the ancient history of our earth, they call it simply the Precambrian Era. As for earth, geologic time begins about 4.6 billion years from the present. Hadean time is the time of Hades (the underworld ruled by Pluto). The earth, too hot for land or water, finds its place in the solar system, while assuming a particular form and matter. It isn't until Archaen time, 4 billion years ago, that the earth's crust begins to form. Like a card dealer shuffling and resorting a deck, the light cards (the crust) made it to the top, the heavy cards (the metals) underneath. The concentric layers (the crust, mantle and core) are coming together in a not so chaotic process. Acasta Gneiss (pronounced NICE), the oldest known rock in the world and located in northern Canada, is dated at almost 4 billion years. For there to be rocks, there must have been crust—the basement rock of North America. That early foundation now known as the North American Craton extended from Canada and the Great Lakes to Wyoming and northern Colorado. Beyond that was water. The southwest did not exist as a solid entity nor was it attached to anything. It was loose and unconnected sand, muck and volcanic debris sloshing around in shallow seas. As the continental basements of the world take shape, the atmosphere forms from gas belched by the earliest volcanoes, then water appears but no life, not even bacteria.

Between the end of the Archaen Eon and the beginning of the Proterozoic Eon, 2.5 billion years ago, signs of life appear—all in water and now fossils in the rock record. They include Prokaryotae, Bacteria, Cyanobacteria (blue-green algae), Stromatolites frozen in rock deep within the Grand Canyon, Protoctista (simple organisms) and Eukaryotes (organisms with a cell nucleus). The earliest plants, through photosynthesis, are exhaling oxygen to the atmosphere. Volcanism is very active. Huge chambers of hot molten rock deep below the surface create fluids, which in turn drop minerals in rock fractures. Prospectors a few billion years later will find these valuable ore deposits (bonanzas) in rock cleavages throughout the west. The North American Craton grows outward by sucking in terrains along its margin. Volcanoes add more land, erosion breaks it down, mountains appear, then are deroofed and in many cases ground down to a flat plain. Sediments are carried by wind and water to shallow offshore seas. Toward the end of the Proterozoic, a billion years ago, simple plants, fungi and animalia appear. Young North America sits near the equator, in the middle of a not-so-large continent surrounded by future Australia, Antarctica, South America and Africa. Volcanic activity subsides. Mountain building continues as the young continental plates ram into each other. North America flattens to a barren landscape and things get quiet.

Paleozoic Era (Age of Fishes — The continents start moving):

Cambrian Period	550 to 500 million years ago.
Ordovician Period	500 to 435 million years ago.
Silurian Period	435 to 410 million years ago.
Devonian Period	410 to 360 million years ago.
Mississippian Period	360 to 320 million years ago.
Pennsylvanian Period	320 to 290 million years ago.
Permian Period	290 to 250 million years ago.

The Paleozoic Era (the Age of Fishes), 550 to 250 million years ago, ushers in many episodes of continental collisions with mountain building as a result and the advance of seas over the landscape. Geologists have excellent fossil records of this era—all reporting from limestone, shale and sandstone formations throughout the world. The rocks also report that much of the west had been formed by the early Paleozoic. North America, still near the equator, was separated from a huge southern continent (Gondwanaland) by the Iapetus Ocean—the future Atlantic. Much of the west was mostly a continental shelf on the North American margin. Seas were piling thick sediments along the shoreline. Invertebrates first, then the vertebrate fish and amphibians were dying, leaving their shells and skeletons. The fossil-loaded muck would harden, emerge from underwater, and form the stacked layers of fossilized rock throughout the west. Structurally, the Grand Canyon may be the best in the west in terms of layered history and it was constructed when the Canyon area (the Colorado Plateau) was as deep a basin as it is now a high plateau.

Beginning 450 million years ago, a series of mountain building events (known as orogenies) created the ancestral Appalachian Mountains, a Himalayan-size range. Northern Europe, a separate landmass, and northwest Africa, part of a huge landmass to the south, would collide with North America squeezing the Appalachians to great heights. There would be other events shoving the Appalachians around, which at one time stretched from southern North America up through Canada, Greenland and Scandinavia to the British Isles. Around 300 million years ago, the ancestral Rocky Mountains rose, also affected by the massive continent to the south. The collision with Gondwanaland (the southern culprit) drove up other mountains along the Texas and Oklahoma line. That event would cement South America to the North American plate. The Rockies would eventually erode to a nub. When the Paleozoic Era was over, only one huge continent existed. Called Pangea, it was one and by itself, with the Appalachians forming the central spine of the landmass. The Iapetus Ocean was swallowed in a trench where the continents met. Pangea sat alone, centered on the equator, surrounded by ocean. One continent, looking like a dinosaur's jaw, stretched across the globe.

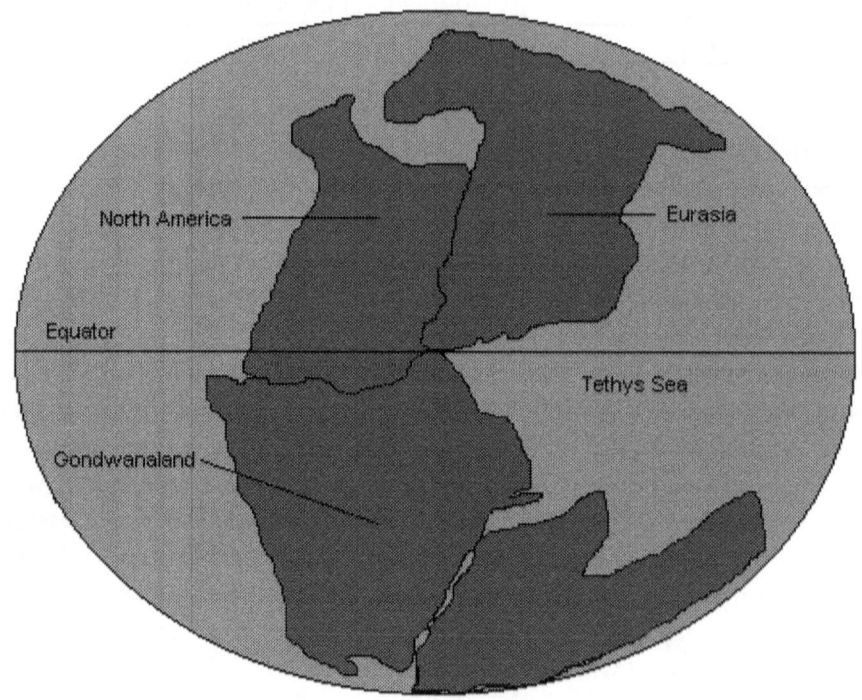

Pangea.

Many millions of years later Pangea would split and the Appalachians would be worn to a flat plain but would rise again in more recent time. At the end of the Paleozoic Era, the Permian Extinction occurred, in Permian time. The atmosphere was drier. The advances of seas slowed; huge sand-duned deserts appeared. Volcanoes were active because of all the continental collisions. Big cracks in the earth's thin crust were developing across the globe allowing lava to flow like floods. In Siberia, massive lava flows called flood basalts covering a million square miles poured over the land and sulfuric fumes poisoned the atmosphere. The added lava weight of the Siberian Traps, as they were later called, caused the earth to wobble on its axis. At the same time, an immense object from space hit the earth, further poisoning the atmosphere. The two events may have been related. Perhaps the space object's impact caused the volcanic activity. The world essentially became uninhabitable. Taken together, geologists call these events the Permian Extinction and they estimate that 90% of sea-dwellers and 70% of land animals died, ending the Paleozoic Era.

Mesozoic Era (Age of Reptiles – North America collides with the Pacific plate):

Triassic Period	250 to 205 million years ago.
Jurassic Period	205 to 145 million years ago.
Cretaceous Period	145 to 65 million years ago.

Coelophysis (See-Low-Fy-Sus) was a nasty little dinosaur; small compared to the later Jurassic monsters. Born in the Triassic Period, it was mean enough and fast enough to dominate during its time in the west—the early Mesozoic Era, the Age of Reptiles. In time, as the monster dinosaurs of the Jurassic appear and Coelophysis must hide, the supercontinent Pangea begins to split along fractures that eventually separated North America, South America and Africa. With lava pouring from cracks where the continents parted, along with the convection currents below the crust, the new North American plate is pushed west, on a collision course with the Pacific plate. As it sails on the lubricated upper mantle, the Atlantic Ocean fills the void left behind. The fracture in the crust that started it all became known as the mid-Atlantic spreading center, a rift in the ocean geologists call a mid-ocean ridge. As lava pours up through deep cracks at the spreading center, high mountains form on each side of the rift. Huge parallel ridges (mountains) forming on each side of the rift split the deep ocean floor. The mountains taper off away from the spreading center as the tectonic plates on opposite sides of the rift travel in opposite directions. The mid-Atlantic spreading center is still processing the North American plate today as it did 200 million years ago. The once active plate boundary on the east coast that spawned the early Appalachians quieted and trailed the westward moving plate like a caboose. Mountain streams carried the sediments from the eroding Appalachians eastward toward the Atlantic coastal plain. The large continental shelf that formed off east coast beaches is piled high with this sediment deep below the waves. Take a walk out from Jones Beach at low tide; you could go for miles on the remains of the early Appalachian Mountains. In the west, large sand dunes were forming. These Sahara-size dunes would eventually present themselves as the beautiful Entrada Sandstone cliffs in New Mexico along Interstate 40 and, in Zion National Park, the Navajo Sandstone mountains of the formerly massive Jurassic Navajo Desert.

By the middle of the Mesozoic, with the North American plate in full collision with the Pacific plate, the oceanic slab begins to dive under the west coast of North America. Geologists call this process subduction. Volcanism increased along the coastline above the subduction zone. An arc of volcanoes extended along the entire coast from south to north, eventually encircling the Pacific Ocean. Inland lakes, swamps and streams dominated the landscape—the Painted Desert and Petrified Forest owe their beauty to the high amounts of oxygen in the atmosphere at this time. The colors are the result of oxygenated sediments laid down along coastal streams and lakes. These Triassic Redbeds run clear across the continent. In Cretaceous time subduction along the coastline intensified. The North American plate was in full override, forcing the Pacific plate down into the hot mantle. This violent episode, known as the Laramide Orogeny, begins in the Cretaceous Period, continues into the Cenozoic Era and will be responsible for much of the mountain scenery throughout the west—now known as the Western Cordillera. The Laramide Orogeny will be unique throughout the world for its destruction and construction of the west. The Laramide's preoccupation with mountain building and volcanic activity will last from 80 to 50 million years ago, ending only when the Pacific plate could no longer be consumed under the continent. Volcanoes quieted when the oceanic plate completed its dive as far inland as the western Great Plains.

The end of the Mesozoic marked the end of the dinosaurs, the great reptiles. Between the destructive attitude of the Laramide Orogeny and, at least, one immense space object (meteorite or asteroid) hitting the earth with the calculated energy of a hundred million hydrogen bombs, life on earth was at best tentative. Firestorms burned and clouds shrouded the earth. The dinosaurs died, the mammals and some fish survived. Just like the Permian Extinction, but not as extensive in its destruction, the Cretaceous Extinction set forth a new period of earth's history.

Cenozoic Era (Age of Mammals — Mountain building and volcanoes dominate the west):

Tertiary Period:	Paleocene Epoch	65 - 55 million years ago.
	Eocene Epoch	55 - 35 million years ago.
	Oligocene Epoch	35 - 25 million years ago.
	Miocene Epoch	25 - 5 million years ago.
	Pliocene Epoch	5 - 2 million years ago.
Quaternary Period:	Pleistocene Epoch	2 million years - 10,000 years ago.
	Holocene Epoch	10,000 years ago - the present.

The Laramide Orogeny ended about 50 million years ago. From it and the more recent Basin and Range Orogeny, we have the great mountain ranges of the west and the rich ore deposits that were discovered in the 1800s from Alaska to Mexico. During the volcanic activity of the Laramide, hot fluids picked up rich ore minerals and aggregated them in cracks and fractures in bedrock deep within the earth. They crystallized to valuable ores of gold, silver, copper and other bonanzas in the western mountains. Most of these rich veins remained hidden underground until the Basin and Range Orogeny that began about 15 million years ago. The west was being stretched beyond the breaking point from plate activity along the coast and from plumes of hot magma trying to get to the surface from the mantle. The tectonic plate margin along the west coast had changed from subduction to a transform boundary—the oceanic plate was no longer diving below the continental plate but was, instead, sliding by it. The western edge of the North American plate, still being powered by the Atlantic's mid-ocean spreading center, was now moving more toward the south while the Pacific plate was moving northwest. As the plates slide by each other, earthquakes shake the ground along the coast and in the interior the crust is stretched beyond its mechanical limits. The stretch marks are very young in Nevada telling geologists it's still active. This stretching caused huge blocks of crust to sink along normal faults and mountain blocks to rise on the opposite sides of the sinking block. The blocks that came up brought into view the rich ore veins. They also put a final signature on the major mountain ranges of the west adding to the autograph of the Laramide Orogeny. Even the Colorado Plateau took its final shape at this time. As the crust was stretched more, the entire plateau turned clockwise on its side to accommodate the dynamics of earth being torn to the breaking point. The scenery we see today was essentially in place by the end of the orogeny. Millions of years of erosion would follow, chiseling the peaks to their current elevations while filling basins with debris.

Many of these prior events set the stage for the creation of the western volcanoes. The most explosive, prolonged, volcanic activity known to man began in the Oligocene. Termed the Mid-Tertiary Orogeny, it brought new volcanic activity to the west, particularly the southwest. Chiricahua National Monument in southeast Arizona reports the evidence of violent outbursts of lava and ash that occurred. So much ash flew into the air that once it settled it killed and covered everything. The landscape appeared to flatten as valleys filled with volcanic debris and mountains seemed to merge with the flat plain. The land remained flattened for millions more years until the Basin and Range Orogeny moved huge blocks of crust in opposite directions, generally up and down. Large basalt floods flowed over the west at the same time, coming from many fissures in the thinning crust. These lava floods covered eastern Washington and Oregon along with parts of Idaho and California. Around the same time, the Rocky Mountains were buried in their own debris—a thick combination of the erosional material from their decapitated peaks along with the volcanic ash that spewed forth during this time. The Rockies at one point looked like a high flat plain with just the highest mountains peaking above ground. The volcanics of the west continued for many millions of years, still caused by movement of the subducted oceanic plate. Some geologists believe that the plate's angle flattened, no longer dipping deep into the mantle. This brought the lower plate closer to the upper plate, the continental crust. The movement under the west caused friction between the plates and compression of the crust. Like pushing two sides of a piece of paper together, the middle rises as did the mountains of the west. Then the plate's angle changed. It dipped deeper into the mantle and appeared to recede back toward the coast. Volcanoes followed it all the way to Nevada. The Cascade Mountains that extend from northern California to Canada began to rise about 7 million years ago and would experience many episodes of volcanic eruptions to the present. They would erode, explode, erode some more and then be covered by the massive glaciers that covered the area during the Ice Age of the Pleistocene.

About 2 million years ago (the Pleistocene epoch), San Francisco Peaks of Arizona and the Jemez Mountains of New Mexico exploded, leaving a gapping hole in the northeast flank of San Francisco Peaks and a circular depression or caldera (Spanish for cauldron or kettle) where the Jemez volcano once stood. Other huge volcanoes were also active at this time. In the area that is now Yellowstone Park, a tremendous volcanic eruption produced thousands of times more volcanic material than Mount St. Helens. There were subsequent eruptions. One about 600,000 years ago created the great caldera in which the entire Yellowstone Park sits. In the first series of eruptions alone, about 2 million years ago, more than 500 cubic miles of magma and debris were ejected from the magma chamber at Yellowstone. Compare that to the great eruptions in the Chiricahua Mountains of southeast Arizona, which ejected 100 cubic miles of material. Mount St. Helens, a breathtaking event in our time, produced a mere one cubic mile of debris. The Yellowstone caldera is 50 miles long and 30 miles wide. Contrast that to the large Jemez caldera in New Mexico and the Turkey Creek Caldera in the Chiricahuas, both 12 miles across, and you'll understand the power brewing under Yellowstone.

Yellowstone Lake sits within the southeast corner of the caldera walls, with the Absaroka Range to the east.

Currently, the area of Yellowstone is being domed up by a large bubble of swelling magma below ground. These deep underground (mantle) plumes or hot spots appear in places around the world. There may be two hot spots in the west at the present. The biggest and most dangerous is the one under Yellowstone. The tourists who watch Old Faithful blow off steam probably aren't aware of the volcanic time bomb underground. Fortunately, the geysers and other vents throughout the park relieve some of the building pressure. In areas of the west, the debris that settled out of the sky from the May 1980 eruption of Mount St. Helens can be measured in inches on the ground. But just below that thin layer, the eruption debris that blasted from Yellowstone (600,000 years ago) measures 50, 60, 70 or more feet. As Yellowstone moves over the hot spot more eruptions are certain. The North American plate continues to move and the location of the hot spot can be tracked as the plate moves west. Since the North American plate moves about 2 centimeters a year, about the rate of growth of a fingernail, it will be sitting under the Yellowstone area for some time. The Hawaiian Islands are forming in the same way. The oceanic plate carrying the islands in a northwest direction is slowly passing over a hot spot, like a car driving over a subway grate. If you're on top of it, you feel the heat. New volcanoes will form new land on the trailing, southern edge of the islands as the plate slides over the plume.

During the Pleistocene Epoch, the Ice Age glaciers came and went, many times. The evaporation of seawater sucked up by the earlier ice sheets allowed prehistoric man, the Paleo-Indians, to cross the Bering Strait into North America. Their artifact remains have been dated in the southwest to 11,000 years ago. Eastern New Mexico was a very comfortable place for them at the time. Compared to the dry climate of today, it was moist and swampy with plenty of vegetation for the animals. They followed the Woolly Mammoths for food and for water, knowing the mammoths needed water to survive. Clovis and Folsom Man discoveries along New Mexico's eastern border were the first associating man with the mammoths. Spear points were found in mammoth bones. The Clovis people are considered the earliest (oldest) on our continent followed by the Folsom. Prehistoric people witnessed volcanic activity across the west during their time. Geologists assure us that what they saw will continue.

3

What Drives a Volcano?

The Earth

Our world is composed of three concentric zones or layers. They are: the Crust, the Mantle and the Core. At the center of the earth is the core, a hot solid ball of nickel and iron, with a temperature of roughly 3,700 degrees Centigrade. It's close to the size of the moon and approximates the sun's surface heat. The outer edge of the core is composed of dense, semi-molten rock but the inner core is hard because intense pressure maintains it as a solid. The more molten outer edge transforms to the next layer (middle zone), the mantle.

The highway mileage from Phoenix to Atlanta equals the distance through the mantle. Almost 2,000 miles thick, the mantle is considered semi-molten and nearer its outer edge, with a decrease in pressure, it becomes somewhat mushy—less solid and more molten. As we will see with volcanoes, pressure has much to do with rocks or solids turning to semi-liquid, molten blobs. As the pressure decreases toward the outer layers of the earth, solid material can change to molten rock or magma—the lifeblood of volcanoes. Volcanoes get their heat and molten rock from down deep within the mantle. Rising columns of heat create currents that stir the upper mantle. These currents move the earth's tectonic plates about. Like cooking soup—if you don't stir it, a film will form on the top and will move about the pan. Not good for soup,

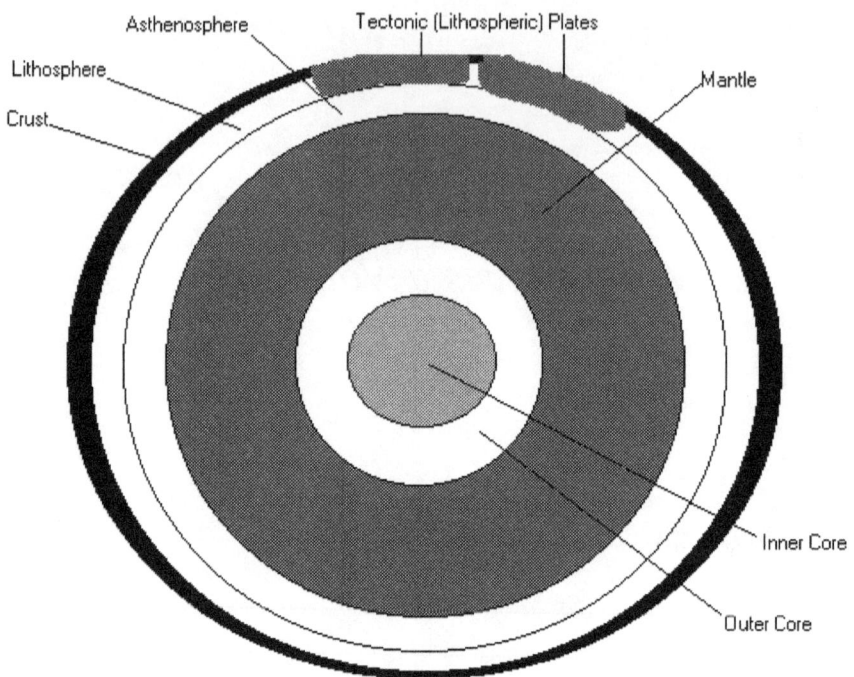

The Earth.

but perfect for tectonic plates of the earth to move and meet. The North American plate is an example and we're still moving on the soup-like mush below.

Outside the mantle is the crust—the continental crust on land and the oceanic crust underwater. The crust is thin under the oceans, averaging about 4 miles in thickness, straight down. Under the continents the crust thickens to about 20 miles but under mountain ranges it can exceed 40 miles. While the core's composition is mostly nickel and iron (the heavies), the mantle is less dense than the core, but more dense than the crust. The mantle is composed mostly of iron and magnesium. Silicon is also present, which is the main element of the earth's crust. So as we approach the surface, the heavy metal groups give way to the lighter ones—the silicate minerals. Granite and granitic-type rocks which dominate the continental crust are composed mostly of the silicates. The oceanic crust is made up of predominately basaltic-type rock. We'll discuss minerals and rock types in chapter four.

The earth's outer layer (continental and oceanic crust) is coupled with a section of the upper mantle to form stiff tectonic plates. Coupled together they are known as the lithosphere and are approximately 90 miles thick. You may have heard of the term lithospheric (tectonic) plates. If not, you will eventually. Under the lithosphere is an intermediary layer within the mantle called the asthenosphere (a "no strength" section). This is the less stiff, molten, churning, somewhat plastic layer upon which the lithospheric plates move. Or better said, boil on their way across the face of the globe. Heat rising from within the earth creates convection currents, which churn the plastic asthenosphere upon which the crustal plates ride. As the heated convection currents cool, they sink into deep trenches along subduction zones, to be heated again and sent back up to continue their work. To sum up, the core provides the heat, the mantle provides more heat along with molten rock and the plastic layer upon which the tectonic plates sit and move.

As mentioned, the upper section of the mantle, aside from providing the stiff layer that couples with the crust to form lithospheric plates, also acts as a source for heated, churning convection currents that speed the plates along. While melting solids (rock) for the churning and convection process, it also sends this molten mix to the crust in the form of magma. Pressure created by gas and surrounding rock deep below the crust force molten rock through cracks in the crust, which act as a passageway to the top. Some cracks in the crust dead-end underground. The molten material may suspend its movement to the surface and take a long time to cool, forming granitic type rocks. But if fractures are found all the way to the surface, the magma may erupt or quietly flow. One type of magma that flows freely has the chemical composition of the rock basalt—it's very hot and loaded with gas and magnesium. Basaltic rock dominates the oceanic crust. It comes up at spreading centers (rifts) in the ocean where oceanic plates are separated and moved in opposite directions. Since this process is continual, oceanic rock is fairly young rock. Basalt can also be found on land at rifts in the crust such as the Rio Grande River valley. The plateau that faces Taos, New Mexico is all basalt. It happens to be split by the Rio Grande rift.

On the other hand, if the molten rock is stiff (viscous), cooler and high in silica, flow is restricted and the big eruptions may occur. Below ground geologists call it magma, near the surface or erupted onto the surface it's called lava. If it's the explosively gas-rich thick lava, the resulting eruptions will eject ash, large blobs of glowing lava, small pieces of rock to large boulders. As gas moves to the top of a magma chamber before eruption, a hot froth brews and adds to the pressure below. When it erupts and cools, the froth will form a rock known as pumice—holes created by the escaping gas make it very lightweight, so much so this rock floats. Violent volcanic eruptions will often times eject a lateral blast of hot froth and ash. Glowing with heat it streams down the flanks of the volcano. The mixture will eventually cool and harden, or weld, to what geologists call tuff. Lava flows may follow. The critical factors are the pressure from below, the conduit to the surface, the amount of dissolved gas and the type of molten material (the chemical elements and minerals). By its nature, basalt flows freely and has a somewhat quiet way of releasing its gas. But other more pasty, viscous magma flows like honey out of a jar, often times doming or plugging the volcanic vent. Pressure builds within the vent and more violent eruptions can be expected. The rock types that result from the more viscous magma are rhyolite, dacite and andesite. Mount St. Helens has a huge dome forming within its crater that can be seen from the Johnston Ridge Observatory north of the mountain. At times visitors will see smoke curling up from the crater. The smoke, actually gas, is coming from the lava dome clogging the vent. The conduit is literally choking on the viscous lava sticking in its throat. Once the mountain clears its throat and releases its gas, look out!

Geologists have many ways of studying and understanding the earth's internals. As objects from space, like meteorites, bombard the earth, their composition can be analyzed. Since they believe much of this material was generated at the beginning of it all (the Big Bang), when the earth was forming, these objects are most likely the earth's building blocks. Also, sound waves sent through the earth report much about its internals because waves travel at different speeds depending on the density and temperature of the rock. Another interesting method geologists employ is to analyze other rocks magma brings up as captives during the trip from the mantle. As molten rock is pressurized upward through cracks, pressure from the movement and expansion will break off country rock (mantle and crustal bedrock). The broken chunks that come up within a basaltic-type magma are of interest to geologists. We know that basalt is generated deep within the mantle. So the pieces it brings, called xenoliths, provide clues to what's down there. Rocks that are transported in the basaltic lava as xenoliths contain minerals such as pyroxene and olivine.

These minerals are hard-messages from the mantle of the rock found along the magma's route.

Tectonic Plates and Volcanoes / More About Plates, Subduction and Magma

When thinking of tectonic plates, picture a cracked hard-boiled egg where each piece of shell is a plate. Opinions vary but, in general, there are anywhere from seven to twenty or more tectonic plates circling the globe (our egg). The North American plate is one, while part of the Pacific's crust that faces North America is another. The dividing lines, the not-so-demilitarized zones, that separate the plates are where the action starts. Plate boundaries are critical locations for volcanic activity. Where plates come together, such as at a subduction zone, they are considered convergent. Where they separate, like at spreading centers, they are divergent. We know that plates move about the globe, bubbled along by convection currents from the mantle. Since there are many plates and they are apparently moving, who or what plays traffic cop? That's the problem! There are no rules at convergent plate boundaries, only collisions where plates grind past, at or under each other. Those that grind past each other cause food to fall off store shelves in California. Ask the people living near the San Andreas Fault on the west coast. The North American plate is moving south along its boundary with the Pacific plate, which is moving north. Pressure builds at the intersection as they struggle to get by each other. The pressure is released when they break free, causing an earthquake. When two continental plates confront each other head-on, they collide and great mountains are formed at the continental margins where the plates meet—the Himalayas and the Urals come to mind. Both of which became high interior ranges as two continents collide and merge. If one plate moves under another, the diving plate, usually an oceanic one, reaches the mantle and is cooked, melted and sent back toward the surface as magma. Volcanoes erupt along the subduction zone. The Cascade Range, from northern California through Canada, is an example. But wait! Aren't the plates on the west coast grinding by each other, causing earthquakes? Yes but along the northwest coast, a small plate (the Juan de Fuca) radicalized, separated from the Pacific plate and dove under the northwest. It wanted one more shot at North America—a sort of plate jihad. The Juan de Fuca oceanic plate is subducting below the continent and continues to dive into the mantle. Mount St. Helens of the volcanic Cascade Range was the response and geologists know there's more to come.

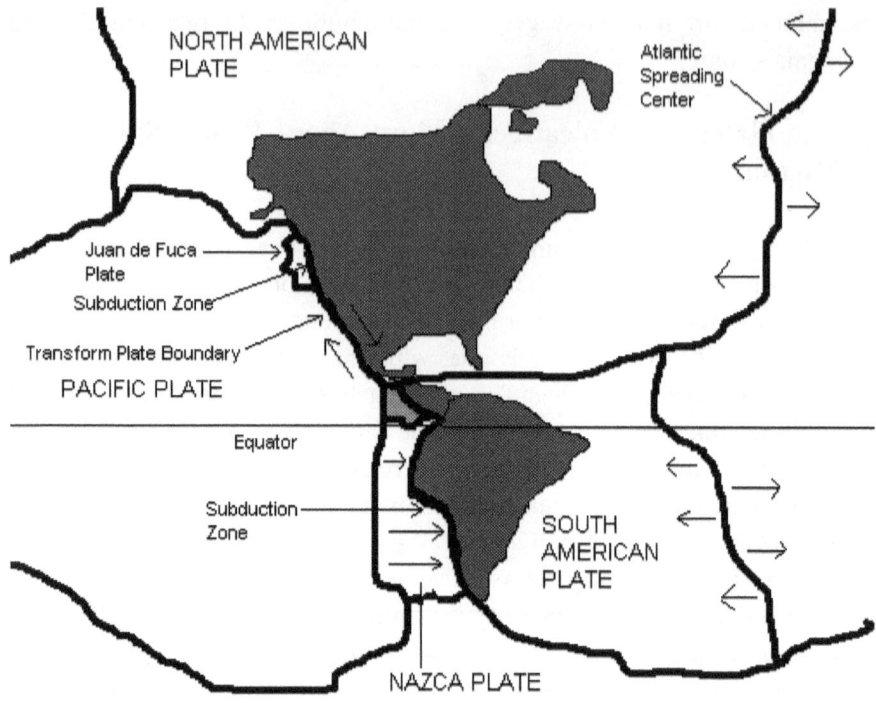

Tectonic Plates and Plate Boundaries.

We've already discussed the fact that the oceanic plate under the Pacific Ocean has challenged the North American plate before. During the age of dinosaurs, North America broke away from the megacontinent Pangea and was traveling west. The Pacific plate was traveling east and brought with it microcontinents, volcanic islands, sediment and rocks strewn across the ocean floor. As the Pacific plate dove under the young North American plate, the microcontinents and volcanic islands riding on the oceanic plate, like a conveyor belt, were scraped off and attached to the continental plate. As these chunks of land, called Exotic Terrains, mashed into the edge of the receiving plate, they were often driven inland with such force that they now appear great distances from our current coastline. Roadcuts on Interstate 80 in Nevada beautifully display the twisted remains of rock once carried by the oceanic plate. These terrains added land to North America along the coast and inland.

Alaska, western Canada, Washington, Oregon, Idaho and parts of California were written on the map in this manner. The subduction of the oceanic plate and accretion of land to the continent lasted until about 80 million years ago. The accretion process took millions of years since plates move at the ramming-speed of only a few centimeters a year. Yet there was more land still to be altered in North America. Remember the Laramide Orogeny mountain building event? Geologists believe that the oceanic plate rose from its steep dive into the mantle to a shallower angle and drove much farther inland, under the continental plate. The stress and friction, like rubbing one rock over another, squeezed the heated crust. The compression caused mountains to rise out of the ground. They're called Laramide Structures and they dominate the western landscape. Volcanic activity accompanied these mountain building events. Many volcanoes and mountains we will be visiting on our trips experienced their first episode of activity during the violence of the Laramide.

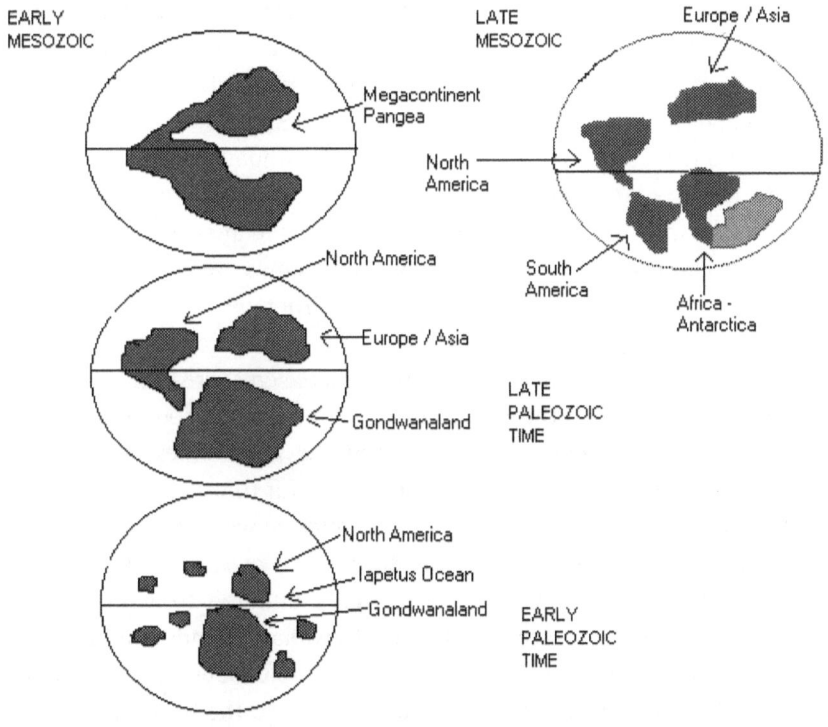

Earth's Tectonic Plates / From the Age of Fishes (Paleozoic) through the Age of Reptiles (Mesozoic).

What's a Volcano? How Does It Form?

The dictionary defines a volcano as a vent in the earth's crust through which magma escapes and some sort of related structure on the surface. The surface structure could be anything from a long line of fissures or cracks in the earth, to a small or very broad hill to a plateau or a huge mountain. The process the magma goes through as it reaches the surface along with the gas and mineral composition of the magma control the eruption and the resulting structure. It is both a thermal and dynamic process.

We already know that some volcanic activity may be caused by a plume of magma just below the crust and the resulting hot spot. Geologists are still debating the dynamics of plume theory. It's a very interesting story. In some cases the crust is thin, releasing the pressure that holds the plumes of magma down. Visitors to Yellowstone Park marvel at the eruptions of geysers. There's hot rock down there, boiling water to steam. But plate tectonic theory doesn't completely provide the answer. That is, unless you speak with a plume theorist. As it turns out, Yellowstone is nearly a thousand miles from the nearest plate boundary where volcanism usually occurs. Plume theory defines Yellowstone as an example of how plumes, and their surface hot spots, force magma up to the crust without a subducted plate in the neighborhood. There's still much studying to be done on mantle plumes before an agreement can be reached but scientists are tracking hot spots all over the globe to answer questions that plate tectonics can't. We know that the Hawaiian Islands are near the center of an oceanic plate, nowhere near a plate boundary. Then why does Hawaii have active volcanoes? Plume theorists postulate that as the Pacific plate moves northwest, the plume below forces magma through the crust creating the islands. And although it appears that the islands are developing to the southeast, they're actually developing and moving northwest as the plate slides over the hot spot. A plume will either dome the earth above or, if it finds fractures through the crust, will erupt lava. As the Hawaiian Islands move northwest on their tectonic plate, the plume sends up lava through the oceanic crust. Volcanic islands first form on the ocean floor, eventually building to a point above water. Geologists call them Seamounts. The Hawaiian Islands are known as the Emperor Seamount. Some of the Hawaiian volcanoes are the highest structures in the world, from the ocean floor bottom to the fiery summit. The plate continues to move and each new volcano will, in due time, become dormant as it passes beyond the hot spot. It will remain a huge land mass resisting erosion for millions of years until it eventually sinks below the waves.

Scientists continue to study the presence and effect of hot spots (mantle plumes) and how they relate to the theory and reality of plate tectonics.

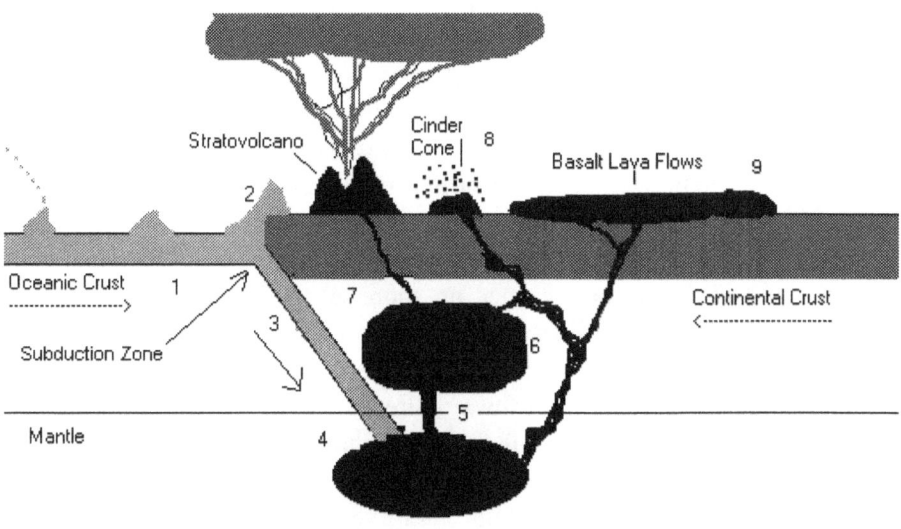

Plate subduction starts the volcanic process.

Throughout the globe, most volcanic activity occurs along subduction zones, with or without hot spots. Using the illustration above, we can follow the volcanic process from the point where the heavy and wet oceanic plate approaches and collides with the lighter continental plate (number 1). Composed mostly of basalt, the oceanic plate pays the price for its weight problem. A continental plate being very thick but composed of lighter granitic rock, lighter than basalt and its relatives, overrides the oceanic plate. The wet plate dives into a deep trench along a subduction zone. Oceanic trenches can reach six to seven miles below sea level. We know that an oceanic plate brings a lot of spare baggage along for the ride. And as it dives under the continent, like a conveyor belt, it brings with it crust and other chunks of land (exotic terrains), even volcanic islands, some still spewing ash and lava from their vents. All of this material—sand, mud, limestone, underwater mountains, volcanoes—is scraped off the oceanic plate and attached to the continent's edge, the coastline. Eventually mountains of this material form at the continental margin (number

2). Or, in the case of the coastlines of North America, are shoved hundreds of miles inland. In this manner, continents tend to grow in the direction of the subduction zone and beyond. They may even swallow the entire oceanic plate and part of the spreading center that was pushing it. The North American plate added more land in this manner, growing to the west, south and east. On the west coast in particular, the North American continent grew outward from a beach front near present day Wyoming a billion years ago to today's beach front along the California, Oregon and Washington coasts. Much of the northwest came to be as these exotic terrains were brought onshore and accreted (attached) to the continent.

Geologists see in the mountain ranges along the coast the remains of sea floor and exotic terrains carried on shore by the invading plates. Some rock in the northwest, particularly Oregon and Washington, compares favorably with rock in Alaska. At times, the oceanic plate smeared these terrains, like cream cheese on a bagel, in a northward direction along the coast. On the east coast, some of the rocks of the Appalachian Mountains have the same mineral makeup, composition and age as those of Europe and northwest Africa. And to add more ammunition to tectonic plate theory, similar plant and animal fossils can be found in rock formations at these same scattered locations. Geologists believe these organisms did not have the ability or navigation skills to swim the Atlantic. They must have been in the same place at the same time, probably somewhere on the megacontinent Pangea during the dinosaur's time. When it broke apart midway through the Mesozoic Era, and the North American plate sailed west, similar species and rocks were separated at the spreading center and now appear at different locations around the world.

Back at our subduction zone, the deeper the angle of dive the faster the oceanic plate will reach the mantle and the sooner the melting process begins (number 3). It may have to travel hundreds of miles down before melting begins but it will arrive at its heated destination, within the mantle. Destination may not be the best word to describe the plates arrival location. At some point within the upper mantle, no specific destination, the wet crust heats to the point where melting can occur (number 4). Because the crust is water soaked, steam forms along with various gases—nitrogen, sulphur, hydrogen, carbon dioxide and carbon monoxide are a few. This volatile mix along with the melting rock will become the molten blobs geologists call magma. As the heat increases with depth, mineral bonds in rock break down, releasing ions. Ions facilitate the change from a solid to molten, semi-liquid state. However, because of the extreme pressure at this depth, the mix cannot totally liquefy. The rocks will remain somewhat solid. Through pressure and the fact that liquids or even semi-liquids will find their own path, fractures in the overlying rock are exploited by the molten mix (number 5). Steam continues to build pushing the expanding molten mass up. Some pressure will be relieved during the journey and the magma's composition may change. Geologists call these huge molten bodies Plutons—Pluto being the god of the underworld, it seemed an appropriate name. Continuing its drive toward the surface, the mix expands even more as pressure is released at shallower depths.

A number of things can happen at this point. The pluton may find, or create, a huge chamber miles below the surface where the released pressure and lower heat allow minerals to form (crystallize). Some of the minerals that did not break down during the heating process may have dropped out of the mix. These are generally the heavier, metallic minerals. They may eventually line the walls of the magma chamber to create a specific type of rock. The magma, now with less metallic minerals, begins to change character. Lighter minerals dominate the mix as the silica content increases. Existing country rock penetrated by the magma will be broken off by the pressure and friction of the surging molten mix. As large chunks break off, they are incorporated in the flow. Over time, sometimes millions of years, the magma will cool and harden sufficiently to form huge chambers of granitic rock deep below the surface. Granitic rock can be anything from granite to granodiorite, or even diorite. Diorite, containing more metallic minerals and less silica than granite, often times forms near the walls of the chamber. Because the magma took a long time to cool, large crystals form. Look at a piece of granite or even a granite counter top. The large grained texture is obvious. Quartz, feldspar, amphibole, mica and other minerals form as fairly equal size crystals within the rock. Quartz is usually the last to crystallize at a much lower temperature than most minerals. It fills the cavities between the already solid minerals cementing the mix to form a granitic rock. Once this great mass solidifies to granite and other Plutonic rocks (number 6), through faulting and millions of years of erosion, it may be exposed at the surface as mountain ranges or batholiths. The Sierra Nevada, a great batholith of granodiorite rock, is a striking example.

The picture, however, is not complete. Some of the magma may continue to pressure its way toward the surface through more fractures (number 7). The closer the surface the more fractures are available. The magma may still be high in gas content, including steam. If it makes it to the surface with this volatile mix still incorporated in the magma, eruptions occur. Not necessarily an explosion by combustion, an eruption is actually the sudden release of pressure as the dissolved gases are freed like expanding bubbles. Shake a soda bottle and pop the top, gases are freed and out pours the foaming liquid. If the magma mixture still contains water or has migrated through moist rock, the water will flash to steam. Steam discharge from a volcanic vent is a symptom that an eruption is near. And finally the eruption occurs, ejecting blobs of lava, rock, pulverized ash and gas through the volcano's vent. Now airborne, the ash and rock fragments, called tephra, rise in a gas filled column above the volcano. Back inside the volcano, still not relieved of its pressure, more magma continues to move up from the magma chamber through the conduit to the crater's vent while released gas continues to push more ash up into the sky. High in the air, the plumes of smoke, actually gas and ash, often display lightning from cloud to cloud. Lightning is the result of electrical discharges between particles in the air. Ash can be carried into the stratosphere and circulated around the globe. Some of the ash will fall to the ground as ash-fall and will form a rock called tuff or ash-fall tuff. Eventually the eruption cloud above the volcano will collapse under gravity and a lack of gas pressure from below. Much of the material once suspended in the cloud will sink into the crater and flow down the side of the volcano. Other dangerous flows containing pieces of shattered lava, rock and gas may be blasted laterally from the vent, rushing downhill at hundreds of miles per hour. These are called pyroclastic flows. The debris in the flow is pyroclastic rock. The flows eventually settle and solidify to create massive volcanic formations like those at Chiricahua National Monument. As the eruption progresses, pasty lava flows may follow, slowly oozing from the vent into the crater. Most of the lava at this point is high in silica and is considered viscous (thick) and doesn't flow well. This lava may form lava domes in the crater as the thick magma pushes its way through the vent but doesn't flow far. It just piles up in a dome shape, eventually plugging the vent and forming a plug dome. Many volcanic craters contain domes. Mount St. Helens has a beauty right in the center of its fractured crater. Mount Lassen is a dome. Looking at Lassen one can imagine the size of the volcano that once stood there since the dome itself is a mountain. The Cascade Range in general is a wonderful example of volcanism, composed mostly of young volcanoes, very young in geologic age—just a few million years old. The northern Cascades are older but those below the Canadian border are progressively younger to the south and more likely to continue their activity given their youthful demeanor.

Like many of the Cascade Range, the huge volcanic mountains that exhibit this violent behavior are called stratovolcanoes or composite volcanoes. They are composed of alternating layers of rock, ash and lava flows that accumulate around the vent, eventually constructing a cone the size of a mountain. More than a few of the stratovolcanoes of the west have a good part of the cone missing. In many of these violent (Plinian) eruptions, part of the cone that had developed over time may have been removed by a summit or sideways blast. Pliny the Elder described how the Vesuvius Volcano erupted and buried Pompeii in 79 AD. Geologists named these violent eruptions Plinian. Mount St. Helens is an example, as are Mt. Taylor in New Mexico and San Francisco Peaks in Arizona. Strangely enough all three blew out to the north. In some cases, the entire volcanic cone may collapse. As an eruption progresses, large volumes of gas and magma may be discharged from the magma chamber. As the chamber empties, its roof and the cone above can no longer be supported. The volcanic structure, with the vacated magma chamber below, weakens and may collapse inward leaving a huge basin surrounded by the remaining walls. This is called a caldera. In northern New Mexico, just outside Los Alamos, stands the remains of a former volcano that erupted and collapsed almost 2 million years ago. The Jemez Mountains are one huge volcanic pile. And within these beautiful mountains the Valles Caldera reports the remains of violent eruptions. The caldera is about 12 miles across and now contains a green meadow, a favored location for elk. The caldera at Oregon's Crater Lake, 5 miles across and 4,000 feet deep, is filled with clear, blue water. Once a very large mountain, known as Mount Mazama, it erupted around 7,000 years ago. The lake is contained within the former walls of the volcano and along its steep flanks you can see the remnants of how the mountain was constructed. Thick lava and pyroclastic flows are frozen in time on cliff faces high above the lake. When the cone collapsed, like a partially demolished building, the layers of earlier hardened flows were cut in half as the walls dropped and are now exposed at many locations around the lake.

Crater Lake.

Back to our illustration, there are occasions where eruptions are not so violent. Some magma from the mantle may have found its way to the surface more directly through fractures in the crust. Basaltic magma is very fluid and has had a chance to release much of its steam during its move to the surface. Gases are present but the eruption is less violent. In these somewhat milder eruptions, small blobs of magma are shattered and flung into the air and partially solidify before landing on the surface. The dark debris accumulates around the vent to form a conical hill called a cinder cone (number 8). Driving east on Interstate 40, just outside Flagstaff, Arizona, cinder cones dominate the landscape north of the highway. Many have been excavated for the cinder. In other situations, the basaltic magma will flow out of the vent onto the surface as lava, often times travelling great distances (number 9). These lava flows can be massive, covering many thousands of square miles. The depth of some flows can be measured in miles. Sixteen million years ago flood basalts covered large parts of Washington and Oregon filling the Columbia River Valley with basalt lava. Along the valley, these flows stacked up like stairs—one flow hardens, another flows right on top of the previous one and hardens. Driving in eastern Washington and Oregon, the eye follows the road up these plateaus for many miles but the mind may find it hard to comprehend the dark source for such beautiful scenery.

4

Destruction and Construction Eruption Types, Volcanic Formations and Rocks

Types of Eruptions

Like most geologic processes and their interpretations, not all volcanic activity fits into neat patterns. There are variations to every theme. Over time, through the study of recent volcanic activity and piecing together the messages left in rocks, geologists have provided us with some guidance. It is defined in the behavior of an eruption.

We've already mentioned Plinian eruptions. They are the most explosive, the most dangerous to plant, animal and human life because of their intensity and acreage affected. These eruptions can be counted on to destroy some or all of the summit and crater, maybe even the cone itself (outer walls or flanks). In Plinian eruptions, large volumes of magma and accompanying debris are ejected from the vent. The inner magma chamber that feeds the vent may have passed up so much magma, gas and broken rock that it weakens. The vacated chamber may then deflate like a balloon. All that remains above the chamber, including the summit and flanks, weaken and collapse inward. The resulting cavity, surrounded by the remaining walls of the volcano, often many miles across, is called a caldera. This is standard Plinian destructive behavior—eruption, destruction, then collapse. Calderas typically have specific rock and ash types— rhyolite and dacite are two—that were ejected during the eruption along with pieces of country rock blown from the vent. Once again, country rock is the rock strata that the rising lava squeezed through, broke off and brought up during its journey. Rocks found at the surface tell us what was deep below feeding the vent. At Chiricahua National Monument, a volcanic disneyland, the first eruptions were of rhyolite in the form of pyroclastic chunks, to pieces of lava and ash. Once the ash settled and hardened, future lava flows followed many years later. This lava, of somewhat different composition, had been sitting in the bottom of the magma chamber and started moving up after the rhyolitic material had been ejected. The lava, which eventually hardened to a rock called dacite, filled many valleys of older volcanic landforms carved by erosion. Over time, the older rock eroded away, leaving the hardened dacite that once filled the valleys sitting as ridges above the rest of the terrain. In the Chiricahuas, on top of Sugarloaf Mountain, there are pieces of dacite scattered around a lookout tower. This is an excellent spot to get a view of the remains of the caldera created by the eruption. The caldera is not that obvious but the view is of the higher elevations in the Chiricahua range—part of the caldera—so the original volcano must have been enormous. In many cases, calderas are destroyed over millions of years by erosion or mountain building. But geologists can discover and map a caldera by the faults in the neighborhood and the rock and ash layers found locally and at great distances from the main event. Some calderas are obvious when you see them. Others are buried and destroyed by geologic processes. Our caldera hikes will be to the most obvious and most spectacular.

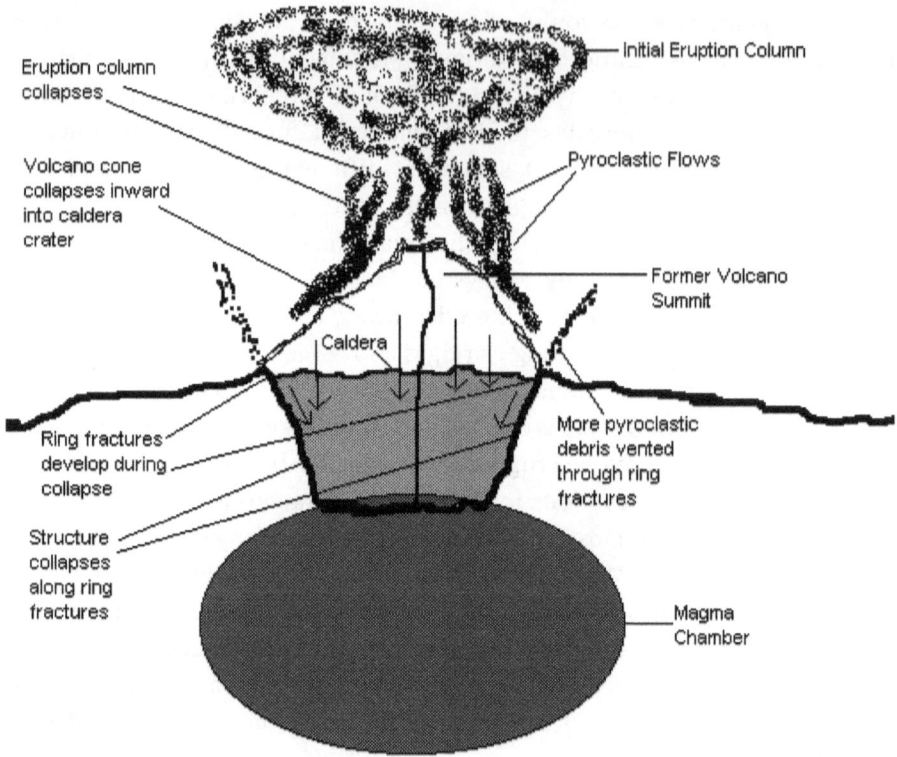

Formation of a caldera.

The lava of Plinian eruptions is the highly viscous (thick) variety and does not flow freely. Gases expand within the magma and when released, all hell breaks loose. In the initial phase of a Plinian eruption, a giant gas-charged ash column (eruption column) climbs high in the sky above the volcano. As the billowing ash rises, the forces of gravity may bring it back down (column collapse) in huge clouds that drive downhill at great speeds. This ash will eventually accumulate and harden to tuff. Pyroclastic flows of gas, rock and ash may be ejected from the vent laterally. Many of these gaseous flows look like a burning cloud and are referred to as Nuee Ardente (glowing cloud), which travel at high speeds down the hill and are very destructive. In many cases, lava flows will follow, intermixing with the settling debris. If the volcano collapses resulting in a caldera, the periphery of the caldera will be lined with fractures from the breakup and collapse. These are called ring fractures and they line the outer walls of the caldera. Ash and gas will continue to escape from these fractures. The great composite or stratovolcanoes of the world are the result of the intermixing and building of layer upon layer of rock, ash, tuff and lava into huge structures that stand above all else. These mountains are likely candidates for destruction during the volcano's next period of eruptions. To study the effects of a Plinian eruption, the lesson starts at Valles Caldera in New Mexico and continues in the Chiricahuas in Arizona, Yellowstone in Wyoming, with additional sessions at Crater Lake in Oregon and Mount St. Helens in Washington—all five on our hike list.

Vesuvian eruptions, which can be as destructive as Plinian, are known for their huge billowy clouds of ash and gas that form high above the volcano. The most dangerous result of these eruptions is the ash that can cover and smother everything below as it did at Mount Vesuvius in Italy in 79 AD. Vesuvius has continued to erupt almost every century since then. A Vulcanian eruption (named after the Roman god's blacksmith, Vulcan) is similar to Vesuvian and tends to form a light colored cloud above the peak, often times covering it like any weather cloud that hovers above a peak. A Pelean eruption is yet another similar destructive type. The name comes from the early twentieth century Mount Pelee eruption that along with a Pelean eruption in the Philippines many years later caused major destruction and loss of life. Pelean eruptions are associated with what appear to be cloud-like burning flows that race down the mountainside. These nuee ardente (glowing cloud) flows form when huge volumes of lava, ash, rocks and gas are blown from the vent and with gravity fall back along the flanks. As opposed to just settling on the flank of the volcano, it forms huge glowing tongues that from a distance appear like a glowing avalanche accelerating down the mountain to hundreds of miles an hour. Again, these pyroclastic or nuee ardente flows can be just as destructive as that of any eruption type.

And from the peaceful islands of Hawaii, comes a less destructive eruption type, appropriately called Hawaiian. From one or many vents (fissures) in the earth's surface, lava pours out and covers large areas. The lava is thin with much gas; it flows freely and solidifies quickly. When it hardens, the resulting rock is usually basalt. Eruptions, though not as destructive as Plinian, can be dramatic, sending lava flowing for miles in all directions. Tourists love them. Glowing lava spurts from a vent like a burning arc, sometimes hundreds of feet in the air. Some lava will pour out of other fissures joining up to form red-hot rivers. Often the flows create a broad sloping landform—known as a shield volcano. They look like a warrior's shield laying flat on the ground. The big ones in Hawaii, like Kilauea, are shield volcanoes. They are the result of Hawaiian eruptions.

For our purposes, we won't get too hung up on the various types of volcanic eruptions. We will mention them during the hikes but will focus more on the characteristic landforms of a volcano, constructed or destroyed. What these volcanoes do during the eruptive phase is much more interesting than any descriptions of type or style so we'll focus on the action and the result, not the definition.

Types of Volcanoes

We already know that the definition of a volcano is simply an opening in the surface of the earth (the crust) through which hot molten rock and gas emerge eventually creating a distinctive landform. The opening is called a vent. Vents may be simple fissures in the ground or a conduit within a bowl-shaped crater on the summit of a volcano. Vents can break through continental or oceanic crust. Volcanoes do form in oceans as well as on land. The resulting landform of a volcano can be anything from a small hill to a steep mountain. The Hawaiian Islands are volcanoes that started their activity at the bottom of the Pacific Ocean. Mount St. Helens is an example of a steep, continental volcano.

Cinder cones are one type of volcano or volcanic landform. Often associated with subsurface contact with water which adds to their volatility, the magma in the top of the chamber is loaded with gas. The gas adds to the explosiveness of the eruptions while the magma in the bottom of the chamber has less gas and will often flow through a break in the cone. When frothy blobs of lava of basaltic composition, charged with gas (steam), are thrown in the air during eruptions, the lava shatters and hardens to small cinders and ash that pile up around the vent. Some blobs of lava remain intact after ejection from the vent. They wobble and spin through the air, at times good distances from the vent, then harden to bombs before they land. The black to red cinders and bombs will pile up around the vent, thus constructing the cone. The top of the cone has a bowl shape summit surrounding the vent. At times, lava flows may break out along the flanks of a cone and travel long distances. It looks like an inverted ice cream cone with much of the ice cream melted out one side. Cinder cones are usually steep but not large, rarely reaching a thousand feet. The typical behavior of a cinder cone is an eruption from a vent in the earth, accumulation of cinders to form the cone, followed by a possible break in the base of the cone from which lava will flow. Cinder cones are scattered throughout the west. As we've mentioned, one interesting collection of cones is along Interstate 40 east of Flagstaff, Arizona. North of the highway are scattered red to black hills excavated to the point that you can see the insides of the cinder cones. Sunset Crater near Flagstaff is a beautiful example of a cinder cone. The cinder is used for construction and spread by snowplows in winter to improve driving on snow-packed or icy roads. Our first hike is at Capulin Volcano National Monument in northeastern New Mexico. Capulin is a high cinder cone by any standard. It dominates the landscape at about 1,400 feet.

A small town named Folsom sits just east of Capulin. It was at this site in the mid-1920s where artifacts were found of prehistoric man, Folsom Man, along with bison bones—proof of what prehistoric man killed and ate. The findings at Folsom, and Clovis to the south, helped confirm the presence of humans in North America, in association with bison, at the end of the last Ice Age. The bison remains were often found with spear points located in the favorite target of Folsom Man—somewhere between the head and stomach, hopefully the heart, where the animals were most vulnerable. It was a lush, swampy environment at the time. Bison could be counted on to find water and so Folsom Man followed the bison to their watering holes where they dispatched the animals for food and clothing, even using their sharpened bones as tools. It is not known whether these early inhabitants had any experiences with volcanic activity. There is no written record, just the ability to date rocks and align the dates contemporaneously with remains of prehistoric man. Modern man has had many documented experiences with volcanoes, including cinder cones. In Mexico, a large cinder cone developed in the 1940s in a farming village named Paricutin. Thanks to Paricutin and its behavior, geologists were able to study and refine their definition of the activity of cinder cone volcanoes. The scenic hike up Capulin Mountain is a great lesson in cinder cone development.

Capulin Mountain, a Cinder Cone.

Shield volcanoes are another type volcanic structure but are much broader than cinder cones, generally covering large areas. And they are often times higher. Flowing lava is the standard behavior. They do not produce cinders, ash and rock bombs like the cinder cone volcanoes nor are they as explosive and destructive as the composite volcanoes. However, because their lava flows can cover large areas, they are dangerous to anyone or anything in the path of the flow. And there are usually multiple flows. While one flow is hardening, another flow may begin and run right over the top of the one before it. In this manner, the volcano builds outward into a broad slope, again, like a warrior's shield lying flat, as most geologists like to describe it. Its structure is high and wide, often covering many miles. The slope is more gradual than that of the composite or cinder cone volcano. The lava may flow from one or many vents. The only similarity with cinder cones is the basalt lava composition. Not far from the cinder cone of Capulin Volcano stands a beautiful and broad shield volcano, Sierra Grande. Some refer to it as a composite volcano while others insist it's a shield volcano. The structure is truly that of a shield. However, since the rock type is andesite, and andesite doesn't flow with the fluidity of basalt, there's a good argument for calling it a composite volcano. Let's just say that it has the shield structure and andesite and basalt are not that far apart in composition or appearance. For our purposes, we'll call it a shield volcano. Some of the largest volcanoes in the world are in Hawaii and they are certified shield volcanoes.

Remember the hot spot that lies under the Hawaiian Islands? We know that the tectonic plate that carries the oceanic crust, with the islands on top, moves in a northwest direction. Vents in the oceanic crust allow basaltic magma to pour out onto the ocean basin, eventually creating a volcanic island that stands above the water's surface. For instance, Mauna Loa appears above the water's surface and extends to more than 13,000 feet above sea level. However, there's more to it. Its origin is in a deep ocean basin. Below sea level it extends 15,000 feet down for a total elevation of more than 28,000 feet. Mauna Loa and its sister Kilauea are two of the largest active volcanoes in the world and they are both shield volcanoes. As the tectonic plate carrying that part of the Pacific Ocean crust moves north, the active island volcanoes will pass the hot spot and will cease activity. And over millions more years they will be eroded and disappear below the ocean much like many other volcanoes north of their location. The plate moves over the hot spot, builds a volcano, moves it northwest along with the oceanic crust. And while the elements erode the older volcanoes, younger ones will appear to the southeast as the plate moves over the hot spot. This movement, growth and erosion of volcanoes in the central Pacific allow geologists to not only study the process of volcano creation but also track the movement of the Pacific plate and the location of the hot spot, which is actually stationary. In the same manner, the North American plate continues to move west taking Yellowstone Park with it. And as it slides west, the hot spot under Yellowstone will some day affect another area of the continent to the east, eventually rendering Yellowstone's activity extinct. Old Faithful needs that hot spot to heat the rocks, which heat the water to produce the steam for its hourly show. Maybe someday millions of years from now, a shallow sea will cover South Dakota as it once did. And that part of the continent will have positioned itself over the former Yellowstone hot spot. We may end up with our own Hawaiian Islands right in the middle of the continent.

Sierra Grande, a Shield Volcano, viewed from the summit of Capulin.

Composite volcanoes, also known as stratovolcanoes, are the third type. These are the monsters; their mean disposition masks their beauty as they tower above the landscape. As magma moves to the surface from its source miles below the crust, the magma may change in composition. As we've seen, there are different types of magma which are associated with different types of volcanoes. Basaltic magma, which comes from deep within the mantle, may have undergone little chemical change during the ascent to the surface. It is quite fluid which allows it to release its gas safely. The resulting landforms are cinder cones and shield volcanoes. In composite volcanoes, magma's chemical composition may change to a more viscous type. The chemical composition will eventually be responsible for the creation of volcanic rock much different from basalt. The three most common rock types found in composite volcanoes, with many variations in their definition and composition, are rhyolite, dacite and andesite. Andesite is closer to basalt in composition but is still high in silica. Rhyolite is identical in composition to its parent that solidifies underground, granite. Dacite is in the middle in terms of composition. But they all serve a purpose in composite eruptions because they tell geologists the source of the magma and often times the phase of the eruption.

As magma moves through the crust toward the surface, it may accumulate in a reservoir a mile or so below ground. This magma chamber is very unstable because of the gas content. As the magma chamber expands and the magma surges, existing rock that surrounds the chamber will break causing earthquakes. There were hundreds of earthquakes just before Mount St. Helens erupted. The surging magma continues to break through crust or bedrock, causing fractures to develop around and above the chamber. As the quakes increase, one or more of the fractures will eventually punch through the surface forming a vent. This conduit will act as a pathway for the magma and gas. The first eruption is usually of pressure-released gas and ash. Steam and other gases continue to drive the magma up through the conduit to the surface fracture, the vent. With the release of pressure at the surface, the gas expands like a shaken bottle of soda. Magma and rock in the conduit are sent upward where the force of the gas-powered eruption throws shattered blobs of magma into the air, eventually solidifying to pieces of pumice and ash. Ash may be carried thousands of feet above the crater in a gas-powered cloud. Or it may settle along the flanks of the volcano. More eruptions continue, often times sending pyroclastic flows down the flanks, some approaching the speed of sound. This activity is what creates the grand structures of composite volcanoes and destroys them.

During my first trip to Mount St. Helens, I sat in the devastated area below the volcano and looked north toward Spirit Lake. The blast that took out the north side of the mountain drove downhill at hundreds of miles per hour, ripping up all trees in its path and carrying them into the lake. It then drove some of the water out of the lake and up a ridge on the other side. When the force of the flow dissipated, the water and many of the trees poured back into the lake. On the northwest corner of the lake you can see the gouged channel the avalanche carved when it slid back down the hill. As you sit there and try to imagine the force that could remove every tree between you and the lake and drive the lake water up the ridge, you eventually begin to see the reality in the lake. In certain sections, there's a brown color covering what is a beautiful blue for most of the lake. The brown is actually the clumps of trees floating along the shoreline. Mount St. Helens is a true composite volcano with a Plinian disposition. They are called composite or stratovolcanoes because they are large and composed of anything that can come out of the chamber through the vent. The flanks or cone of a composite volcano can therefore be composed of thick layers of ash from the initial eruptions along with chunks of existing rock brought up from the throat, the conduit, and hurled in the air. Other layers are solid ash-flow tuff and less solid ash-fall tuff. Some very hot pyroclastic flows that drove straight down the flanks also settled in layers and solidified into a tight rock formation called welded tuff. Along with this pyroclastic debris, lava flows may have broken through the side of the volcano or poured from the vent. The flows cover the previous material in thick sequences. So composite volcanoes are not just the material of cinder cones, or the lava flows of shield volcanoes. They are composed of everything a volcano can eject from the vent and that material piles up to form the steeply sloping cone of the volcano.

San Francisco Mountain (Peaks), the remains of a Composite Volcano.

Other Volcanic Structures

In the Four Corners area of the southwest, specifically northwest New Mexico, a huge craggy mountain towers above that corner of the Colorado Plateau. Named Shiprock, and sacred to the Native Peoples, it was once the throat, the conduit, of a large volcano. It's called a volcanic neck. Radiating from Shiprock are long wall-like structures. They are called dikes, or feeder dikes, because they fed lava to the volcano. Fractures in the crust that allowed magma to surge to the main conduit eventually clog with lava and harden. As the earth around the hardened lava erodes away, long walls or sheets of rock (dikes) extend across the countryside. Composite volcanoes, long after erosion, are often recognized by necks and dikes. After volcanic activity ceases, the outside flanks of the volcano are eroded over millions of years. The erosion process breaks down the rock of the volcano's flanks, or cone, and transports the debris elsewhere. The hardened plug (volcanic neck) of lava inside the conduit, being more erosion resistant, is still standing, while the outside walls are gone. Dikes seem to radiate across the countryside from necks. Another example of a volcanic neck stands within the Superstition Mountains, east of Phoenix. Known as Weavers Needle, one legend has it that once a year, depending on the angle of the sun, the Needle's shadow points to a cave where gold was buried but never found. Many people see the Needle and think gold. Others think volcanic neck, the internal plumbing of a huge volcano. Dikes and necks are typical features of old, eroded, composite volcanoes.

Weavers Needle viewed from a ridge south of the structure.

Recall that many stratovolcanoes have lava domes in their crater. Lava domes tend to plug the vent of the volcano after eruption. The lava piles up, solidifies, more lava may be forced up breaking through the already hardened surface which tumbles down the side of the dome. As more lava comes up, the structure increases in size. The lava's composition is often that of dacite. A lava dome may be considered another type of volcano itself because it can act like a volcano and is often times left standing after the volcanic flanks have eroded away. Mount St. Helens has a beautiful, still seething lava dome smoking in its crater. Mt. Lassen, in northern California, is a hardened lava dome, also known as a plug dome. At around 10,000 feet it is one of the largest plug domes in the world.

Many of our hikes are to and around composite volcanoes because of their structural variety and majesty. Traveling west from our starting point in eastern New Mexico, we'll see Valles Caldera, the remains of a big one, and Mt. Taylor, beautifully displayed from Interstate 40 north of Grants. Then on to San Francisco Peaks on Interstate 40 north of Flagstaff, Arizona. There are more along the way, ending in the Cascade Range where most of the volcanic peaks are stratovolcanoes, some still active like Mount St. Helens.

Rock Types and Formations

Rocks come in three varieties: sedimentary, metamorphic and igneous. Sedimentary rocks are just that, rocks that were compacted and cemented from pieces (sediments) of existing rock. An example is sandstone, which is composed of material eroded from other rock. Sedimentary rocks can also be composed of minerals precipitated out of liquid, like gypsum. Or in the case of most limestone, they are composed of the skeletal remains of animals, usually fish. Metamorphism changes existing rock through heat, pressure or hot fluids. Limestone is a sedimentary rock but when enough heat and pressure are applied, it changes to a metamorphic rock called marble. When magma comes in contact with a layer of limestone, the magmatic heat bakes the country rock (limestone), alters the minerals and marble is the result. And, as rock layers pile up, pressure from the top can alter the rocks and their internal minerals lower in the pile. Mountain building events also alter existing rock formations through pressure and heat. Many of the mountain ranges of the west are composed of metamorphic rock that was altered from another rock type because of the pressures caused during mountain building. The third rock type is igneous. Igneous rocks start as molten rock deep below the earth's crust and either hardened (crystallized) underground or made it to the earth surface during eruptions, then hardened to rock.

Magma from the mantle may crystallize deep below the crust. If it maintains its chemical composition from the mantle, it will harden to an igneous intrusive (plutonic) rock called gabbro. Gabbro is not an easy rock to find since it usually develops deep within oceanic crust. The ocean would have had to dry up. Then, through erosion of the crust or faulting, which brings the gabbro formation up from below, it may then be exposed at the surface for rockhounds. Gabbro has large, equal-sized crystals because it cooled slowly at depth, allowing large crystals to form. A relative of gabbro, diabase, makes up the famous New Jersey Palisades that face New York City across the Hudson River. Magma of gabbro composition migrated up through the crust and oozed between two layers of rock not far from the surface, which at the time was a lakebed. This horizontal layer eventually crystallized underground but not far from the surface under the lake. Not unlike today's New Jersey, it was swampy. But unlike today, it was probably surrounded by dinosaurs when New Jersey sat next to northwest Africa. Over millions of years, the dinosaurs died, the lake dried up, overlying rocks were eroded and the palisades of diabase rock appeared. The final act came when the Hudson River cut a path south to the ocean, right at the base of the palisades sill.

A sheet-like intrusion of magma that inserts itself between horizontal layers of existing rock is called a sill. It is considered concordant because it flowed and hardened between existing layers of rock. A sheet-like intrusion of magma that cuts across layers of existing rock is called a dike. It is a discordant intrusion because it cuts across existing layers. The diabase cliff that is now the palisades wall of the Hudson River is concordant and one long beautiful sill. Another feature of this type of rock is a columnar structure. As the rock layer is exposed at the surface, erosion cuts vertical joints in the rock. As these formations erode along the joints, huge columns form looking like a corrugated wall. Basalt, which is igneous extrusive and is of the same composition of gabbro, flows onto the surface, hardens and erodes in the same manner. The Columbia River Valley is composed of basalt flows that sit on top of each other and also display a columnar structure because of erosion. Columnar basalt is common throughout the west. Basalt flows often top-off plateaus because basalt is more erosion resistant than much of the surrounding rock, usually sedimentary. It protects the rock under it from erosion so what's left standing is a column of hard dark basalt on top of plateaus and mesas throughout the west. Vesicles are one last common characteristic of basalt. Vesicles are holes in the rock. As basaltic lava flows, gas bubbles percolate up through the flow and will remain as the lava hardens to basaltic rock. The holes or vesicles are quite common in basaltic rock.

Magma of basaltic composition may also undergo chemical change during its journey from the mantle. We know that as it migrates up through the crust, the metallic minerals may crystallize early and drop out of the mix. Also, as it passes through country rock it will absorb some of the chemical composition of that rock. Since much country rock below the earth's surface is granitic, the magma loses its basaltic content and takes on more silicate content. Granite is rich in silica minerals. It is loaded with quartz, which is pure silica and one of the hardest minerals on earth, being number seven on the hardness scale. Diamond is the hardest at ten. Once magma takes on more silica, it slows the movement and may stop its journey underground where it crystallizes to granite or diorite, or their intermediary granodiorite. If magma of granite composition makes it to the surface before it crystallizes it will create rhyolite rock formations. If it's granodiorite composition underground but crystallizes at the surface, dacite will result. If it's diorite composition, the resulting rock formation will be andesite at the surface. The plutonic rocks that crystallize underground will all show fairly even-sized and large crystals. The extrusive varieties of the same rocks that harden at the surface usually show minimal crystal growth and are fairly dense. However, in some cases, crystals may have formed much earlier in otherwise dense rock—the result is a porphyritic rock. Andesite will often take on a porphyritic texture with dark rod-like crystals of hornblende within a dense background. If there are no visible crystals, andesite can easily be confused with basalt. Dacite can also present a porphyritic texture. Dacite is generally gray but as it erodes it becomes darker, almost black. And it often contains white feldspar crystals, which can be seen without a hand lens. The color and porphyritic texture make it easier to identify dacite. As far as rhyolite is concerned, small pieces of pumice or quartz may be seen in the rock but rhyolite is usually dense with few visible crystals and rarely porphyritic. However, rhyolite does have a telltale characteristic call flow-banding. Many tuff formations, and some lava flows, are composed of rhyolite. The flow-banding occurs when the rock is still hot and weight from above, along with movement of the mass, tend to squeeze and flatten pumice crystals in the rock. Light colored, elongated crystals line-up within the rock creating the flow-banded texture.

Rhyolite and dacite often appear with certain types of volcanic activity. Rhyolite is mostly associated with violent eruptions that create ash, the resulting tuff formations, and pumice. Dacite is a somewhat darker form of rhyolite and is also associated with violent eruptions. Both are highly viscous so their ability to flow is restricted. They often are found in lava domes and may plug a volcanic vent. Many lava domes appear as rounded hills or mountains, such as Mount Lassen, and they often form along ring fractures of a volcanic field or caldera. If the lava cannot fight its way to the surface, it may dome up the earth from below. The result is a resurgent dome within a caldera, like Redondo Peak at Valles Caldera. Rhyolite and dacite are typically found in volcanic domes. Andesite can appear in the same environments but is a signature rock type found in volcanic arc environments. Arcs of volcanoes occur at the meeting point of tectonic plates where one subducts under the other. They are called volcanic arcs because they tend to form around the subduction margins of plates. Some occur along a continent's coast and are called volcanic arcs. Others form in the ocean where two oceanic plate converge and are known as island arcs. One such volcanic arc, the Ring of Fire, runs along the Pacific coast from South America north to Alaska, then over the Pacific to the Asian coast and down past Japan. It surrounds most of the Pacific Ocean. Seventy percent of the active volcanoes of the world are located in this arc. Many of the volcanoes are composed of andesite.

Basalt may flow great distances, resulting in large landforms, like shield volcanoes, which can also be found near volcanic arcs. However, shield volcanoes are often found around areas of thinned crust, like oceanic crust, or crustal rifts. Some composite volcanoes are formed on top of basalt formations. The basalt flowed first setting the base for the volcano, then the volcanic vent took a rest and later brought up lava with different characteristics and composition such as rhyolite, dacite and andesite. Many Cascade volcanoes have a basaltic base. Some landforms of rhyolite or dacite composition may have been created by ash flows and ash falls, such as in the Chiricahua National Monument and the Superstition Mountains in Arizona. The structures at these sites are the result of rhyolitic to dacitic magma that erupted from the vent and shattered into volcanic ash. As it settles, it collects, compacts and hardens to tuff. Most of the hardened ash (tuff) at Chiricahua is of a rhyolite composition and in the Superstitions it is both dacite and rhyolite.

The formations we will see on our hikes are composed of the entire range of igneous rock, from plutonic (igneous intrusive) granite to (extrusive) basalt with all possible variations in between. The behavior of magma and its chemical composition control the rocks it forms. All these rocks, and the ones in between, will be discussed during the hikes, where their identification will aid in defining the types of volcanoes and volcanic behavior. Now, with that out of the way, let's take a hike!

Plutonic (Intrusive): Granite (1) Diorite (2).
Extrusive: Rhyolite (3) Obsidian (4) Dacite (5) Andesite (6) Basalt without vesicles (7) Basalt with vesicles (8).

5

Hiking New Mexico's Volcanoes

Hike: Capulin Volcano National Monument

Short hikes into and around a cinder cone volcano with lots of views, geology and archaeology.

Location: Northeast corner of New Mexico on US Routes 64 and 87 approximately 30 miles east of Raton, NM and Interstate 25. Check in at the visitor center then drive the 2-mile road to the top. Be careful driving, there are steep drop-offs.

Hike Type and Length: Two short day-hikes to choose from. One takes you down into the volcanic crater to the plugged vent, is short (.2 mile) and somewhat steep. The other is a self-guided path around the rim of the crater and about one mile in length. There is some climbing in the beginning to get to the top of the rim.

Elevation: The summit is 8182 feet, about 1300 feet above the plains. The hikes take you up and down a few hundred feet.

Precautions: The hike elevation changes are only a few hundred feet. Bring plenty of water in the summer and watch out for July and August monsoon thunderstorms. You don't want to be hiking the crater rim with lightning bolts flying.

Planning Information: Hiking around Capulin can be done easily in one day. For park information, contact the visitor center at 505-278-2201. The best way to plan is visit their web site at
      www.aqd.nps.gov/grd/parks/cavo/
or the USGS site at
      vulcan.wr.usgs.gov/Volcanoes/NewMexico/Capulin/

Geologic Setting: This first hike provides an opportunity to set the stage for the other hikes in New Mexico. We'll cover the evolution of New Mexico and its volcanic background.

    A few billion years ago, the young North American continent was much smaller. The east corner of New Mexico was on the edge of the landmass but spent its time mostly underwater. In ancient New Mexico, volcanoes erupted, showering ash over land and water. Mountains rose—some were volcanic while others were jammed up by early plate collisions. More than once the land was beveled by erosion to a flat plain, allowing seas to advance. Over and over this sequence was repeated. The Rockies rose and were leveled more than once. Huge mountains in central New Mexico have long been eroded away. But on the eastern side of the state, considered part of the southern Great Plains, the craton (the basement slab of the young continent) held its ground with very little upheaval. The continent was adding land to the west as plates collided along a coastline that grew progressively west and south. The landscape of the Capulin area is composed of layer upon layer of sediments accumulated beneath the seas of the Paleozoic Era. Inland seas, continental river and lake deposits added their sediments during Mesozoic time while the erosion of the Rockies fed material south and eastward in large rivers. West of the plains however was very active. Mountains continued to rise in the Cenozoic Era and volcanism was quite active. The Rio Grande basin started to tear apart along two faults that allowed the basin to drop while mountains rose on each side. The basin was once separated along old faults, breaks in the crust, that acted like the hinge on a trap door. The land west of the hinged seam flapped up and down allowing seas to advance from the west. While east of the hinge, the land was stable—the craton held its ground. Then around 10 million years ago, the boundary between the North American continental plate and the Pacific oceanic plate changed. Along the coastline, instead of sliding under the continent, the oceanic plate began moving in a northerly direction, while the westward movement of the continent turned a bit to the south. Friction and movement along the coast stretched the west's crust to the breaking point. As the crust stretched, it thinned. Upwelling of the mantle followed. It was this activity that finally brought northeastern New Mexico the volcanic activity it had dodged for millions of years. The eruptions and lava flows lasted from about 10 million years ago until the activity at Capulin, which signaled an eventual cease-fire.

The Raton-Clayton volcanic field is composed of more than a hundred basaltic cinder cones. Many lava flows are associated with the cones. Most activity occurred in the time of the Pleistocene (the Pleistocene Epoch)—the time of man, the great Ice Ages and extensive volcanism. It all ended during the Holocene Epoch (10,000 years ago to the present) but the Raton-Clayton field, like many in the southwest, is likely to heat up again.

Yellowstone is another example of this violent period and provides evidence for new considerations about volcanoes a great distance from plate boundaries. Tremendous eruptions at Yellowstone created thousands of times more volcanic material than the Mount St. Helens eruption. Yellowstone is almost 1,000 miles from the nearest plate boundary where most volcanic activity occurs. So what caused that eruption? We know—the answer is a huge hot spot still located under the park. San Francisco Peaks in Arizona erupted at about the same time beginning a long cycle of activity in northern Arizona. With no plate boundary in site. At the same time, Mount Taylor north of Grants, New Mexico blew out its northeast side. Huge plateaus extending to the northeast of the mountain tell the story of ash and lava flows, easily seen from Interstate 40 east of Grants. Around a million years ago, the Valles Caldera eruption occurred near present-day Los Alamos. Over a thousand feet of ash fell and flowed, creating the rock exposed in huge cliffs at Bandelier Park. Some of the ash landed in Iowa.

Then the volcanic activity changed in an area of the southwest, from the San Francisco Peaks volcanic field all the way to northeast New Mexico. The volcanism associated with large composite volcanoes and rock types from rhyolite to andesite were the norm to that point. Something below the crust changed the action to the less violent lava flows, which created huge plateaus along the Colorado line and shield volcanoes in northern New Mexico. Cinder cones formed from the area around Flagstaff, Arizona to Capulin. This zone of volcanism would represent the most youthful volcanoes of the area and the farthest east volcanoes would reach, stopped once again by the stable craton, right where the Great Plains begin. The McCartys lava flows near Grants are the youngest. They oozed from vents south of Interstate 40 and covered many miles with textbook lava flows. During this period, most of the volcanic rock changed to basalt from andesite, rhyolite and dacite. What happened?

We've already discussed the Rio Grande rift valley being torn apart by intra-plate fractures and movement. It's still active. Pull crust in opposite directions and it thins, sometimes breaks. The Jemez Lineament from Arizona to Capulin added to crustal thinning over faults that extend deep into the lithosphere. And all the time, the fever down below continues. Magma in the mantle is constantly under pressure. The pressure comes from denser surrounding rocks and gas, particularly steam attempting to relieve itself. The magma has only one way to go, along with the steam, and that's through the lower crust on its way to the surface. Because the crust has fractured and thinned, this magma, which is of a basaltic composition has little resistance and less distance to travel. And we already know that basalt moves readily through the crust versus other magma compositions. All these factors taken together are favorable conditions for magma finding the right fractures or vents to ooze lava over the land or eject gaseous lava into the air. When highly liquid lava flows, lava plateaus are formed. They surround the Capulin area, particularly on the border with Colorado to the north. When basaltic lava flows are interrupted and a magma chamber builds below ground, dissolved gas within the lava increases. The lava often comes in contact with subsurface water. The steam within the flow builds until eruption occurs. Cinder cones are the result, created by a constant process of eruptions of ash, cinders and large bombs, all falling around the vent eventually building a cinder cone. As the steam is vented in the upper part of the magma chamber, the lava will often times find or cause a break in the wall of the cone, along the flank of the newly created mountain. Lava flows will exit at the break, the boca (mouth) of the volcanic cone. These flows will cover the countryside extending out from the cone. In the case of Capulin, they cover 25 square miles.

Hike Guide (with some archaeological considerations): There are two hikes. One down into the crater, to the vent. As the park material says, this may be the only time in your life you can stand next to a volcanic vent and survive. The other hike, up and along the rim, is the more informative trail with self-guided markers and information posts along the way. There isn't much to discuss about the hikes because they're short and you'll find plenty of material in the visitor center including a brief movie about Paricutin in Mexico. The

Paricutin volcano, which was more recent than Capulin, will give you an excellent overview of the life of a cinder cone. Just remember to stop at the visitor center and pay the five dollar entrance fee. You'll receive the park brochure. Between the brochure and the exhibits in the visitor center, you'll be well armed with information to understand Capulin. We'll continue our overview of the evolution of New Mexico, particularly this corner of the state.

At Capulin, let's take a different approach to hiking, one you may want to use for future hikes. Here's that Zen thing again. Zen would want you to walk out to the edge of the parking lot overlooking the crater and start thinking or reading. You can see the vent at the bottom with the paved trail ending at its lip. All else around the parking lot came out of that vent. The vent started its volcanic life as a long northwest oriented rip in the earth. The fissure eventually plugged with lava and closed, leaving only the hole below you. Cinder cones, like Capulin, usually have a singular life; they erupt over a distinct and limited time frame. Whereas composite volcanoes generally have a long eruptive history. The conduit of a cinder cone, and its magma below the surface, will find another area, another fissure, to relieve its pressure, leaving the original cone extinct. So usually where you see one cinder cone, you'll see others. As you look into the crater, sense that the surrounding walls came up out of that vent and came out violently. Fiery debris and lava blobs were thrown high in the air. The lava shattered and hardened to cinders, small rocks and large bombs and landed around the vent. As the material built up, a crater was formed with steepening walls. Note the large blocky chunks of rock along the trail. They are eroded, basalt remnants of the cone, which are the walls that surround you. Basalt comes up, like a messenger, directly from the mantle. The message it brings is that basalt is a good sign the crust in this area is being pulled apart (thinned), extended beyond its limits. With the stressed crust and molten rock looking for an escape from the mantle, magma has its opportunity to move up and will travel great distances to get to the surface. The dike that brought this magma up could extend all the way over toward the Rio Grande River valley. Dikes travel up through country rock but cover long distances as the lava finds other fractures vertically or laterally.

From where you're standing in the parking lot the mantle is about 30 miles straight down, give or take 10 miles. And that's only to the outer zone of the mantle where the rocks are heated to magma for the journey up. If you were to drive through the mantle, it would be the interstate distance from the parking lot to the east coast, maybe 2,000 miles. And the source of the heat that cooks the rocks in the mantle is the core, the oven, the center of the earth, about the size of the moon. Composed of nickel and iron, the degree of heat in the core approaches that of the surface of the sun. It was in fact, spun off from the same material that created our sun during the Big Bang 15 billion years ago. The core of the earth is a remnant of that event. While it sends heat to the mantle, rocks cannot melt because of severe pressure from surrounding rock. However, at the outer edge of the mantle, the pressure of surrounding rock is reduced, allowing rock to melt to magma and so it starts its journey toward the vent below you. The currents coming up from deep within the mantle, along with massive amounts of basalt, arrive daily in the Atlantic Ocean. In the mid-Atlantic, at its spreading center (the break in the Atlantic oceanic plate), basalt is oozing out of long fissures onto the deep ocean basin. Heated currents from the mantle are moving a section of the ocean floor, connected to the North American continental plate, to the west. You can't feel it. Or maybe you can. But your position is processing westward at a few centimeters a year. If you could spend a few million years in the parking lot, you may end up where Nevada is now. In another million years, you and the continental plate will grind by the Pacific plate in a southerly direction as that plate moves north. The stress of plate grinding by plate will cause earthquakes up and down the coast, as it does now. The rock that surrounds you and the currents stirring below bring an interesting message direct from the mantle. Now may be a good time to walk down to the vent.

Capulin's vent and vent trail (lower right) surrounded by the crater walls.

The rim hike offers even more. After the initial uphill climb, find a comfortable spot, some have benches, and take a seat. Look south toward the shield volcano, Sierra Grande. In its case, lava poured out of a vent, like the one in Capulin's crater, without the explosiveness. Gas-rich and very fluid, it just flowed. And when the flow quieted and the lava hardened, more came out of the vent and flowed right over the top of the earlier hardened lava, forming bench upon bench of lava flows that extend outward for miles. The eye can see and the mind can conceptualize this type of lava flow creating huge lava plateaus like those covering eastern Oregon and Washington. Or building shield volcanoes the size of Mauna Loa in Hawaii. We know that Mauna Loa stands more than 13,000 feet above the ocean. But it started its growth underwater, at a vent approximately 15,000 feet below the surface. At 28,000 feet from the ocean's bottom to the summit, it is one of the highest mountains on earth. And it continues to grow. The ocean floor is only about 4 miles thick above the mantle, allowing basaltic magma an easy exit. And as lava adds to Mauna Loa, the oceanic plate continues to move, taking Hawaii along for the ride.

Sierra Grande with ridges of Capulin's lava flows marked by dark lines running across the valley.

As you approach the east side of the rim, the Great Plains dominate the horizon. The plains are positioned at the southwestern edge of the North American craton. The craton extends all the way into Canada. The continent was born in what is now Canada. Called the Canadian Shield it has the oldest exposed rock in the world—almost 4 billion year old outcrops have been found in the Northwest Territories. Geologic time started around 4.5 billion years ago. The shield extends out from Canada and is part of the craton that runs right up to your position. The rock of the craton, North America's footings, is hard, unbendable and magma can't penetrate it.

The mind wanders back about 300 million years, the Paleozoic Era (the Age of Fishes). You're at this location looking south and east. Approaching from the south is a huge continent called Gondwanaland and it's carrying South America and parts of Africa. Like a tug boat behind a barge, it's pushing small microcontinents ahead of it. You'd probably feel the shock waves as it collides with the area that is now Texas and Oklahoma. It would be impossible to comprehend the mountains that came up from that continent-on-continent collision. And because of the compression from the impact—the jamming of the earth all the way through Colorado—the Rockies would rise behind you like someone just unzipped the earth. Then over millions of years they would erode to a flat plain, then rise again like a submarine surfacing for air, the result of another collision. The beautiful snow-capped mountains to the west are part of the Cordillera (meaning chain of mountains). All the way to the coast, there are mountain ranges that run north-south. If you were to look at a geologic map, it has the appearance of an accordion, mountains that were driven up by plate collisions and volcanic upheaval. And there's more to come. Capulin is a minor event!

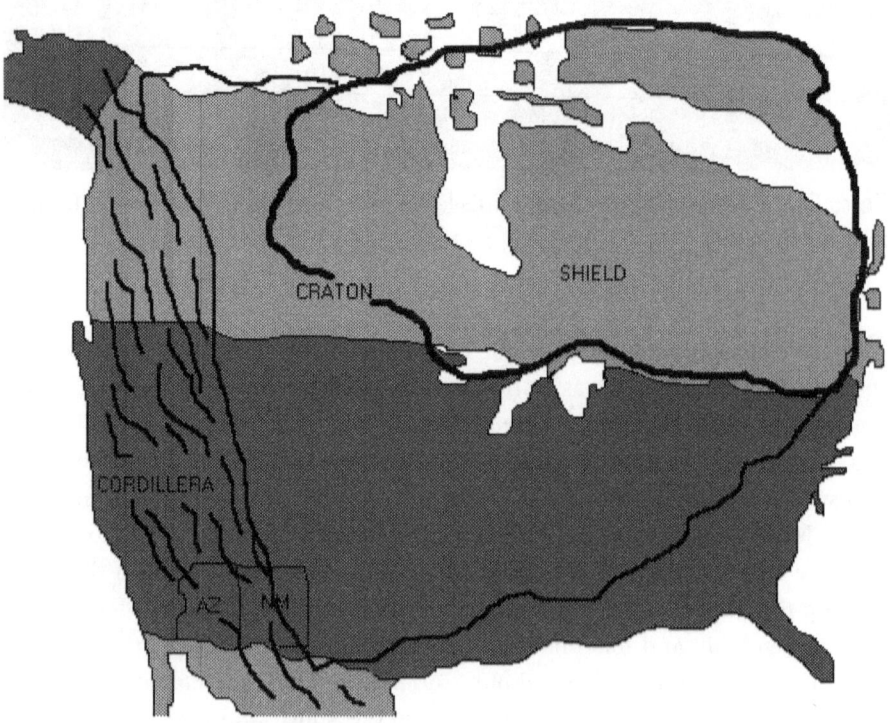

Major geologic regions of North America: the shield, craton and cordillera.

Still looking east, let's assume we're nearing the end of the Age of Reptiles (the Mesozoic Era). The largest dinosaurs are roaming the swampy plains below. The North American plate was still overriding the Pacific plate and mountain building was active. As the early Sierra Nevada and Rockies are rising in the west, a great basin is sinking to the east. A huge sea, the Western Interior Seaway, invades the continent and splits it in half. The seaway extends from the Arctic Ocean to the Gulf of Mexico. Water levels around the world at that time were higher than usual. As the mountains rise to the west, the uplift pushes the shoreline to your current location. It's a balmy, swampy beach loaded with reptiles. Eventually the sea will disappear as the environment dries. There would be no more inland seas in North America. The great dinosaurs of the Jurassic and Cretaceous roam below but are uncomfortably close to their extinction, caused by an asteroid, maybe even a swarm of asteroids, that would strike the earth around 70 million years ago. Perhaps, in conjunction with the asteroid strikes, great lava flows may have played a role. Geologists believe that a hot spot in the mantle may have caused flood basalts, massive lava flows, in Russia and India that affected the climate. The flows could have been so massive that the spin of the earth on its axis was affected. It probably wobbled. No matter the cause, to the southeast of Capulin, at Clayton Lake State Park, hundreds of dinosaur tracks in sandstone report their existence and eventual extinction. Dakota Sandstone covers much of this area. The sandstone was deposited around the seaway as it migrated east and eventually disappeared along with the great reptiles. Much of the sandstone and other sea and lake deposits have since been covered by the lava flows of the Raton-Clayton volcanic field.

The Clovis people had a connection to the Dakota Sandstone, which is also a conglomerate—it contains pieces of other rock, aside from sand. These chunks of rock accumulated over time in rivers and beachfronts along the seaway. The small to large pieces of rock found in the Dakota came from the erosion of the high mountains to the west of Raton. Rivers carried this debris eastward toward the inland sea. Geologists know that these sediments came from the high mountains because of their rock types. Within the sediments, quartzite makes up a good percentage. Quartzite rock is very hard and often associated with the compressional forces found in high mountains. Compress and heat up sand, with a high quartz content, and you get quartzite. During the sovereignty of the reptiles, the material of the Dakota was carried by streams and deposited in many areas of New Mexico, including the Raton-Clayton area. Around 11,000 years ago the Clovis people, searching for stone pieces they could sharpen and attach to a stick, found these rocks in the Dakota, particularly the quartzite. Pick up a piece of the sparkling quartzite from the Dakota conglomerate and you could favorably compare its makeup and age to sharpened pieces of the same rock found stuck in the thoracic cavities of bison killed during Clovis and Folsom time. In geology and archaeology, it's all connected in some manner.

The rim hike is more than just a hike. You'll read the information guides along the trail about the lava flows from the mouth of Capulin, the thundering cinder cone eruptions and the entrance of Clovis and Folsom man into this area at the end of the Ice Ages. What you won't read, but should try to comprehend, are the geologic events that brought you to this point in time and this location on the mountain.

Other Points of Interest: After the hike, I'd recommend the Raton area (or Las Vegas to the south) for food, shelter, camping and much history. There are some campgrounds in the Raton-Clayton area but mostly on private land. Sugarite Canyon State Park northeast of Raton has camping. Or take US 64 west to Cimarron Canyon State Park which has some nice campsites and hiking trails. The old Santa Fe Trail cuts between Raton and Las Vegas to the south. There are hundred year old wagon ruts that parallel parts of US 64. The Colorado Rockies are not far north and the southern extension of the Rockies, the Sangre de Cristo Mountains, are directly west on US 64. And finally, there's great food and fun to be had in Taos, or in many other places along the road on US 64 moving west.

On the Road to the Next Hike

There are a number of ways to get to Valles Caldera National Preserve from Capulin. The high speed approach is to take Interest 25 south through Las Vegas to Santa Fe, then up US Route 84 / 285 toward Espanola. Take State Route 502 west to Los Alamos. The preserve is located just outside of town on State Route 4. The most scenic itinerary is west, following US Route 64 to Taos. This road cuts through the Sange de Cristo Mountains. It winds through the range and slows you down but what beautiful views! In Taos, take State Route 68 south to Espanola then over to Los Alamos. An interesting feature south of Taos is the Embudo Fault. State Route 68 follows the Rio Grande River southwest. As the road approaches the town of Embudo, the perceptive driver will notice a change in direction to the right, west. There is an obvious turn right before the road turns south again. That jog right follows the Embudo

Fault. A fault is a break in the earth which affects crust in the area of the fracture. This particular fracture is a transform fault, like the San Andreas. The rift valley of the Rio Grande runs south but the fault literally cuts the valley in half forcing the section south of the fault to the west, while north of the fault shifted east. The entire valley south of the break was shifted to the west to accommodate the movement along the fault. That fracture in the earth extends all the way to Los Alamos, our destination. Faults tend to bring up magma from the mantle. Another reason this area of New Mexico has been active in recent time and will continue to be so millions of years from now.

If the Embudo Fault worries you, there is one other route to take to Los Alamos. Stay on US 64 west of Taos, over the Rio Grande bridge where you'll get some amazing views of the Rio Grande gorge. We've discussed how the earth is spreading in the Rio Grande basin. The gorge was actually sculpted by the river. The basin is more of a plateau, through which the gorge snakes. The basin is what's spreading. Most of the rock on the plateau is basalt, a good indication you are in a rift valley, or spreading center. As you look east and west, mountains flank the basin. These mountains are part of that movement. As the basin dropped, the mountains rose. As the earth spreads, the east side of the basin is stable. The west side is what's on the move. Perhaps out to sea someday. An Atlantic-size ocean could fill the void left by the parting crust. Continuing on US 64 west, near Tres Piedras, take US 285 south to Espanola then over to Los Alamos. The third approach is what I call the Road to Pegmatite.

Pegmatite is one of my favorite rocks. Composed of many beautiful and large mineral crystals, it sparkles and winks in the sun. Pegmatite is formed deep underground when magma of granitic composition begins to cool. As it cools, residual fluids rich in silica and other elements separate from the magma. Granitic magma has an attitude. Only the proper minerals are allowed to form early. The remaining elements that would be part of the rock are sent packing along with gas and fluids strained from the magma. These element-rich fluids can travel long distances or they can line the outer walls of the magma chamber, the pluton, as it cools. As the fluid travels, it enters existing fractures in the earth forming geologic structures called dikes. These intrusions, whether in dikes or in the walls that surround granitic rock bodies, are wonderful locations for the rockhound. Minerals such as beryl—emerald being a green variety of beryl—are found in pegmatite. There are two pegmatite locations well worth your consideration.

The Harding Mine, south of Taos, presents a wall of rock exposed in the middle of a excavated hill. Pegmatite is centered in the wall and is loaded with large mineral crystals, some beryl. You must contact the University of New Mexico, Department of Earth and Planetary Sciences (web site: http://epswww.unm.edu/) to get permission to enter the mine location. They provide a very informative leaflet on the mine and the pegmatite. You won't actually walk into the mine. The pegmatite is exposed on the north wall of the hill and mine shafts were dug into the wall. In terms of a learning experience, you'll get a full day of it at the Harding Mine. You may also find some interesting minerals in the mine dump. Another pegmatite location to consider is in the Petaca Pegmatite District and it's a more casual approach since the pegmatite dike is exposed in a roadcut. From Espanola, take route 285 north to Ojo Caliente or take 285 south from US 64 near Tres Piedras. Near Ojo Caliente, take state route 554 to route 111 to La Madera. In La Madera take a right onto 519 toward Petaca. After a few miles the road climbs a hill. At the top, a steep brown wall (roadcut) will be on your right with a guardrail on the left. The wall of the roadcut is mostly Precambrian metamorphic rock, it's over a billion years old. The pegmatite dike appears as a vertical, light colored vein, at the very beginning of the roadcut. The vein runs up the wall surrounded by the brown metamorphic rock. Once the metamorphic rock formed a billion years ago, the rich fluids from a granitic magma source in the area intruded the rock forming the large vertical dike. It then hardened, crystallized, to pegmatite. The fact that this area has massive underlying intrusions of granite, with the pegmatite, indicates that tectonic plate activity occurred here. While the southwest was coming together piece by piece, the mantle was sending up magma that intruded the chunks of new crust at the continent's edge cementing them together and to the larger continent. The brown metamorphic rock in the roadcut was originally beach sand. At the time, New Mexico, on the edge of the craton, was often underwater. The sand accumulated, hardened to rock, then was intruded by the pegmatite fluids. Park the car safely off the shoulder to the left and walk the cut. The vein sparkles from the various minerals in the rock, particularly the muscovite mica that appears as small silvery slices grouped together like pages of a book. Although the pegmatite is mostly granitic, the minerals are much larger and more obvious than in any granite you've ever seen. This is one roadcut you'll want to walk and put your nose to the wall.

Hike: Valles Caldera National Preserve

Hiking around and through a beautiful meadow, once the innards of a huge volcano.

Location: The Valles Caldera preserve is close to Bandelier National Monument, an archaeological site and a hiker's paradise. Wilderness areas and trails surround the park. Take US Route 84/285 northwest from Santa Fe, New Mexico toward Espanola. Turn west on State Route 502 to Los Alamos. Follow the signs for Bandelier and State Route 4 west, which will eventually enter the southeastern edge of Valles Caldera National Preserve.
Note: Driving distances for the hikes will be given from the intersection of Route 4 and Route 501. Route 4 passes Bandelier National Monument. Route 501, to Los Alamos, cuts off Route 4 (right turn) after the monument. At that intersection, set the odometer to zero and continue on Route 4.

Hike Type and Length: There are two ways to approach hiking around Valles Caldera. One is outside the preserve in Santa Fe National Forest (the Jemez Mountains), which surrounds Valles Caldera. You can hike anywhere in the National Forest. There are some established trails which can be found by purchasing a forest service map. Our national forest hikes will be fairly short, depending on how far you want to go, with some uphill. These hikes outside the preserve allow wonderful views of the caldera and a chance to look at the effects of the eruption from above the caldera floor. The second type of hike is within the preserve. For all but one hike in the preserve, you must make a reservation. A fee, that is more a donation, helps the preserve staff continue the great work they are doing to improve the trails and make more areas available to hikers. When you see the preserve, you'll appreciate their work.

Elevation: Elevations range from 7,000 to 8,000 feet and higher around the meadow to over 11,000 feet at Redondo Peak, a resurgent dome close to the center of the caldera.

Precautions: Heavy snows in the winter restrict travel at times. The fall and spring are best. Fall is recommended because of the yellow splashes of color on the aspen trees at the higher elevations. Summer is cool at night but warm during the day. Bring bug repellant and plenty of water in the summer and watch out for July and August monsoon thunderstorms.

Planning Information: Capulin National Monument hiking could be done easily in one day. Valles Caldera is entirely different. You could spend weeks in the Jemez Mountains and never see the same area twice. The best approach is to decide if your priority is hiking (day-hikes or backpacks), or if you want to camp and how long you plan to stay. Some trails are outside the preserve, in the Santa Fe National Forest, which surrounds the caldera. If you want to learn more about the preserve, visit their web site and register for a hike. You need to specify a day and trail when you register. The preserve hikes take you into the heart of the caldera. The trails in the national forest offer great overviews of the caldera. One we'll discuss skirts the southwest wall (rim) of the caldera and has some great camping areas. They are not established campgrounds. If you want an established campground, they're located along Route 4. As long as there are no restrictions, such as fire, you can hike anywhere in the forest outside the preserve and camp anywhere. Please be careful with fire at campsites, particularly when there are heavy winds, like in the Spring. And remember to completely kill all fires—no live ashes or coals.

    Begin your planning by logging on to the preserve web site at:
        www.vallescaldera.gov/
    Also, check out the Santa Fe National Forest site at:
        www.fs.fed.us/r3/sfe/

You can call the preserve and national forest phone numbers listed on both sites for current conditions. Most of the forest that surrounds the caldera is in the Jemez district of the Santa Fe NF. The forest service has nothing to do with the preserve. If you call the forest service, be sure to tell them you're interested in the national forest outside the preserve. Otherwise, they'll automatically assume you want the preserve headquarters.

Other interesting resources:

New Mexico Geologic Society web site:
   http://www.geoinfo.nmt.edu/nmgs/home.html

New Mexico Tech (Geology and Mineral Resources) web site:
   http://www.geoinfo.nmt.edu/

Both have some excellent guidebooks and field excursion bulletins. Two in particular (see below) are great references for Valles Caldera. They are a bit technical, not for the casual reader. You need some geology background to comprehend much of the material. But if you're comfortable with terms like "ignimbrites", then go for it. Here they are:

Field Excursions to the Jemez Mountains, Bulletin 134 (1996) is highly technical but a good road reference.

Jemez Mountains Region (Sept 1996) is less technical and a comprehensive review of the entire area.

Geologic Setting: There's good reason for the volcanic existence of the Jemez (HAY-Mess) Mountains, which surround Valles Caldera. The area is nowhere near a tectonic plate boundary; it's more an intra-plate structure. In the Precambrian Era, as the southwest was coming together, plates collided and added land to the nascent continent. The boundaries where these plates met and were cemented appeared later in geologic time as fractures in the crust, called faults. Some of the geologic structures responsible for the Jemez volcanic activity are bound by these faults.

We've discussed the geologic evolution of New Mexico during the Capulin (previous) hike. And noted that this area of New Mexico has a long history of volcanism. The Jemez Mountains sit at the junction of the Jemez Lineament, the Rio Grande rift and the Embudo Fault. Throw in the fault-bound Nacimiento Mountains that border the west side and you have a site ripe for all forms of volcanic activity. The Jemez Lineament, which may in fact trace one or many Precambrian initiated faults, is a crustal line of volcanic fields that run from east-central Arizona to the northeast corner of New Mexico. The Jemez volcanic field sits astride a large fault that traces the lineament along and eventually through the western boundary of the Rio Grande rift. The Rio Grande valley is spreading along the rift, thereby providing magma a shorter journey through the thinned crust. Studies show the crust to be 20 miles thick in this area. Given that continental crust ranges in thickness from 20 to 40 miles and the fact that the hot mantle is below the crust, this area has been and will continue to be a candidate for volcanic activity. Add to those structural features the Embudo Fault, which runs across the valley right up to the Jemez Mountains. The transform fault has shifted the valley south of the fracture to the west. Faults, particularly one this size, are passageways for magma surging from the mantle. The west and south boundary of the Jemez Mountains is marked by the heavily faulted Nacimiento Mountains which were lifted during the Laramide Orogeny and tilted more than 10,000 feet up and to the east. The basement of New Mexico, billion year old rock, is exposed in the Nacimiento range. The Jemez formed many millions of years later. It's not hard to imagine that the many deep faults of the Nacimiento played a part in the Jemez volcanic field growth. The Nacimiento formed over an ancient range that stood much higher in the Paleozoic Era but was eventually eroded to a nub. Then the Rio Grande Rift superimposed itself on the area, followed by the Jemez volcanic field, which superimposed itself on the rift and the Nacimiento range.

In the Miocene Epoch (Cenozoic Era), volcanic activity was initiated along the Rio Grande rift faults. Beginning around 17 million years ago, it slowly spread toward the Jemez Mountain region. Basalt was the first to come out of the ground and flowed many miles in all directions. These flows probably formed shield volcanoes similar to the Sierra Grande south of Capulin. They're now buried under the accumulated debris of the most recent eruptions. Driving through the Rio Grande valley and up to Los Alamos, the view is of huge river terraces, buttes and mesas. They were formed by the ancestral Rio Grande River carrying massive amounts of debris from the Rockies to the north and the Sangre de Cristos range to the east. The load transported by the ancient river easily competes with the carrying-power of the Mississippi River. The scenery in the Rio Grande basin seems to step up toward the Jemez Mountains with the highway cutting through step-upon-step of sediment. Most of what you see surrounding the valley is the Santa Fe formation; in its sediment are the decapitated remains of the Rockies and Sangre de Cristos. What sits on top of the Santa Fe strata are the initial basalt flows of the rift. Basalt is a hard rock. When it flowed out from the many vents in the area, it covered the land with its protective coating. Many mesas and plateaus of the west are basalt capped. They sit above the topography thanks to their resistance to erosion. The basalt is dark gray and sits on top of the very colorful Santa Fe formation.

As the highway approaches Los Alamos, the scenery changes to steep cliffs of a light brown to gray color. After the basaltic flows of the early volcanic period of the rift, the activity turned violent. There's plenty of evidence in the brown cliffs. The mountains provide a text book lesson in the full cycle of volcanic activity in Plinian eruptions. The Jemez Mountains, as well as containing an archetypal resurgent caldera, are classic Plinian as are many of the volcanoes we'll visit heading west. So we'll spend some time here setting the Plinian scene. A Plinian event usually experiences four, sometimes only three, stages. An eruption column of gas and ash arise from the volcanic vent. Ash is carried by the winds and falls on the landscape in a not-so-destructive manner—phase one. Phase two turns destructive. The ash and gas-charged column high above the volcano is overburdened and collapses, sending pyroclastic flows streaming down the volcano's flanks. A sort of climax comes in phase three when the magma chamber, vacated of its magma and gas supply, collapses inward. New vents are cracked open around the outer edge of the volcano's crumbled structure—called ring fractures. From these fractures, new pyroclastic flows are sent boiling down the mountain. In the final phase, eruptions of the remaining gas, usually steam, sends ash into the air. The cloud isn't supported so it will immediately fall into the caldera, partially filling it. There are many variations to this Plinian theme but these are the classic events.

The light brown cliffs that rim the highway near Los Alamos are defined as Bandelier Tuff. The formation represents one of the final phases of volcanic activity in the Jemez and marks the eventual collapse of a huge volcano, or an entire volcanic field, thus forming the Valles Caldera. Tuff is a fine-grained igneous rock composed of volcanic ash and dust, with a rough feel to it. Ash and shattered debris are the pyroclastic (fragmental) remains of rock and lava erupted from the vent. A caldera is a large depression in the earth caused by the collapse of a volcano which was built by accumulation of all of the above over many years, sometimes millions. As the magma chamber within the volcano sends up lava, gas and rocks through the conduit to the vent, the vacated chamber weakens. Ring fractures develop around the crater because of the weight from above and gas below trying to escape, which it will do through these fractures. The entire crater becomes very unstable as the chamber sends up much of its gas, lava and pulverized rock. As it empties, the entire structure weakens until, in most cases, the volcano collapses inward like bursting a bubble. The result is a depression, which may continue to receive ash and lava from the ring fractures for many thousands of years. Lava domes appear along the ring fractures as highly viscous lava oozes through the cracks, creating piles the size of hills or even mountains. Thousands or millions of years later, the activity may continue, perhaps building a new volcano. There were at least two volcanoes in the Jemez Mountains.

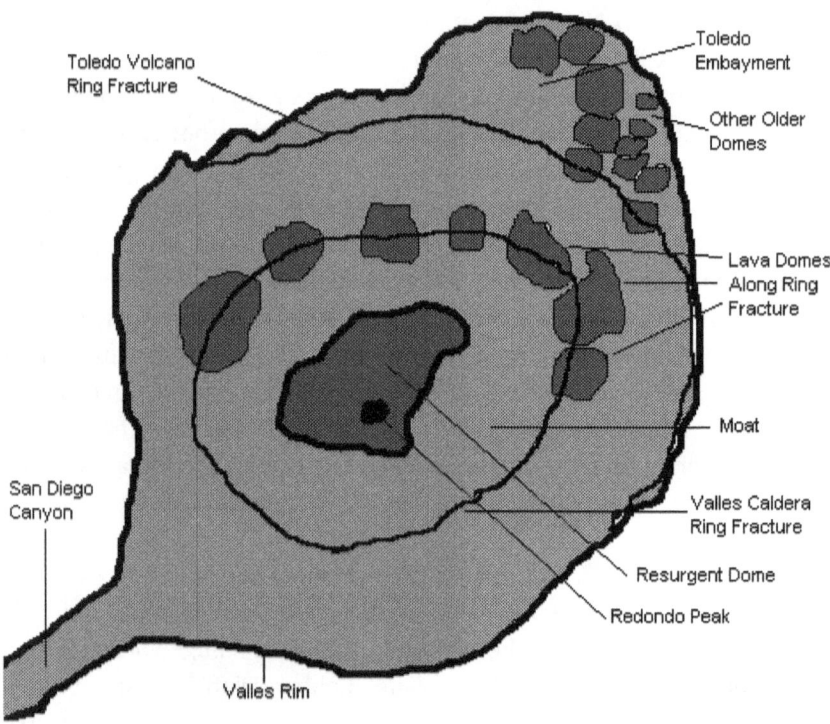

Valles Caldera structure: resurgent dome, moat, ring fractures, lava domes and Valles rim.

The sequence from the very beginning of volcanic activity is typical. The rift derived basaltic composition of the magma began to change to andesite nearer the Jemez, marking alteration of the magma below the surface. By 10 million years ago, the Jemez were beginning to build from accumulations of pyroclastic flows and lava flows. From many vents everything from the high silica content rhyolite, to dacite and andesite poured out and erupted as ash, rock and gas. With the change to these more viscous gas-rich lavas, the eruptions became more violent. Gas tends to migrate (bubble up) to the top of the magma chamber providing the explosiveness of the initial eruptions. As the gas is spent, the lava in the lower part of the chamber can flow out, with less gas-charged results. Something like half of the Jemez volcanic debris was erupted in a 3 million year period ending around 7 million years ago. It was about this time that the basaltic flows had totally ended but would revive a few million years later. There would be a lull in activity around 7 million years ago but would reinitiate a million years later. The mountains of volcanic debris at that time grew considerably and must have been impressive sights. Through the lull, magma chambers were again building at the intersection of the structural lines of weakness, the deep fractures. Geologists estimate the magma chamber may have been 4 to 5 miles down and 10 miles in diameter. The chamber sat within the old Precambrian basement rock. Then in the early Pleistocene, the most explosive events occurred. Some of the material erupted can be found in many parts of Texas and the Great Plains.

The Valles Caldera was formed when one volcano erupted and collapsed, followed by another, with a similar result. These two circular calderas overlap each other. For our purposes, we'll refer to pre-caldera and post-caldera activity. The first significant eruption around 1.6 million years ago led to the creation of the Toledo Caldera, the initial caldera forming event. The pre-caldera and post-caldera activity is evidenced all around the Valles Caldera in debris sheets that flowed and covered land in all directions. Pyroclastic flows, ash falls and ash flows, lava flows all combined to create the scenery along Route 4 and outside the preserve. Much of the rock composition is rhyolite; being the most viscous, it adds to the violence. Plinian eruptions are so powerful that large boulders, or bombs, weighing tens of tons have been thrown miles from the vent. The Valles Caldera activity was no exception.

Perhaps what is more interesting, at least to geologists, is the post-caldera activity. First the Toledo Caldera was formed, then a million years ago another volcano collapsed, leaving the Valles Caldera. The volume of material (mostly ash) erupted, which eventually formed the Bandelier Tuff, is said to be more than 70 times that of the Mount St. Helens eruption. Within the caldera existing layers of Bandelier Tuff were pushed up to form a resurgent dome. Redondo Peak, at 11,254 feet, sits on the edge of the dome, which gives the valid impression that the entire dome is huge. Lava was pushing the tuff layers up from below creating the dome. As the bulge increased, ring fractures along the periphery of the caldera sent more ash and debris into the air, along with lava flows. Around the domed-up earth, a moat formed. The term Valle Grande is often used to refer to the Valles Caldera. Actually, the Valle Grande (big valley) is the moat; seen from Route 4 it appears as a huge meadow. The moat was controlled by the resurgent dome in the middle and the outer walls of the caldera. In time during the Pleistocene, which included the Ice Ages, lakes formed within the moat. Lava domes grew along the ring fractures that encircle the moat. As highly viscous lava releases its gas after the major eruptive phase, it seeps out of vents but can't flow far because of its honey-like consistency. Lava domes capped vents (ring fractures) all around the caldera. Many of these domes separated lakes within the caldera. Eventually breaks in the caldera wall allowed the lakes to drain. The largest drainage is down San Diego Canyon on the southwest edge of the caldera wall. The streams that drained out of the lake followed the earlier pyroclastic flows and lava flows down an ancient valley. Before the lakes, during the eruptions, this earlier valley filled with volcanic debris that solidified to hard welded rock. As erosion took over, everything except the hardened debris was eroded and removed, eventually leaving the welded rock standing above the topography as ridges and hills. What surrounds San Diego Canyon is an example—the drainage from the Pleistocene lakes cut the canyon through the hard volcanic topography. One of our hikes will begin in San Diego Canyon, a location of pre-caldera and post-caldera volcanic rock. We'll also look at some of the youngest flow units of the El Cajete formation at Battleship Rock and the beautiful Banco Bonito obsidian flows, the last eruption from the caldera. These date to about 60,000 years ago, recent in geologic terms. The obsidian is a beautiful black glass the Native Peoples used to manufacture arrowheads, now scattered all over the Jemez Mountains, particularly at Bandelier Monument. Finally, mother nature wants us to know it's not over. There are hot springs and fumaroles (holes that emit steam and gas) in the caldera. Soda Dam, near our first hike and composed of travertine, is one such carbonate-rich remnant of mineral laden hot springs. The intersections of the Jemez Lineament, the Rio Grande Rift and the Embudo Fault will continue to allow water to percolate through hot rock. Geologists know that magma is not far from the surface.

Hike Guide: There are two approaches to hiking in the Valles Caldera Preserve and Jemez Mountains:

1) Register (online or phone) for one of the trails in the Valles Caldera National Preserve. Hikes are only allowed on certain days. As of this writing there were five hikes, four are fee-based. Rabbit Ridge and Coyote Call, along the southeast edge of the caldera, allow the hiker good overviews of the caldera, moat, resurgent dome and lava domes. The Cerro del Abrigo and El Cajete hikes get you right into the geology of lava flows, Bandelier Tuff and other deposits. Abrigo's trail circles one of the lava domes while El Cajete skirts Redondo Peak and the dome along the East Fork River.

2) Purchase a Santa Fe National Forest Service map and find a trail, or hike anywhere (cross-country). Cross-country is recommended only for experienced hikers who know how to use a compass. It's very easy to get lost when you're surrounded by trees. Our first hike was chosen using the forest service map and one of the guidebooks recommended in the planning section (Field Excursions to the Jemez Mountains). We'll call it the Rim Hike. It follows the Valles Caldera rim (the outer wall of the caldera) and offers excellent views of parts of the caldera moat, outlying lava domes along the ring fractures and the main resurgent dome including Redondo Peak. Above all, it offers solitude. The second hike, also in the national forest, will be on an established trail (Trail 137) off Route 4. The forest service calls it a recreational trail, which means more people. This hike follows a stream (Jemez River) cut into some of the youngest volcanic rock in the caldera as well as exposures of very old Paleozoic limestone and shale. These ancient limestones and shales still contain small fossils—the skeletal remains of creatures that once inhabited a 300 million year old sea.

Finally, hiking inside the preserve is up to you. A trip to Valles Caldera should include at least one foray in or around the preserve where the wide-open spaces of the moat (meadow) intermingle with the forested slopes of the resurgent dome. Make your own choice, contact the preserve headquarters and reserve your spot. Material is available from the preserve headquarters to explain the hikes. Directions to the trailheads are available through their web site. For the Abrigo hike, a courtesy bus takes hikers to the trailhead. You're on your own; choose your hike and enjoy the beautiful caldera.

Now, for the drive to our hikes and some sight seeing along the way, set the car odometer to zero at the intersection of Route 4 and Route 501 (to Los Alamos). Route 4 (west) initially climbs a hill, the caldera wall, toward the preserve. At about 6 miles, note Forest Service Road 289, left turn off Route 4. FS 289 leads to some of the best hikes in this area of Santa Fe National Forest. It provides access to the Dome Wilderness trails and some of Bandelier National Monument trails—good hikes for backpackers. Also, around mile 6, Route 4 arches over the southeastern wall of the caldera, exits the forest and there it is—the meadow (part of the moat) of Valles Caldera. Redondo Peak, the resurgent dome, towers to the northwest with many hills and mountains (lava domes) to the north. At about 16.3 miles look for realtor signs and mail boxes on the left. For the Rim Hike, this is where you take a left onto Forest Service Road 10. For the Trail 137 hike, continue on Route 4 for another 10 miles to the Battleship Rock trailhead parking area on the left. Just beyond are the Battleship Rock picnic grounds where you can also park but may have to pay a fee. Or, continue on Route 4 for another 4 miles to the Soda Dam. We'll discuss these stops in the Other Points of Interest section after the hikes.

Rim Hike:

A low-clearance vehicle may not make it all the way to the (Rim Hike) hiking area, almost 4-1/2 miles of dirt road. Most of the road is fairly smooth, while the last half mile bumps over ruts and mounds. Most cars should have no problems. A low-rider won't survive this road. You can always stop, park the car and walk the rest of the way. Stay off the road during or after heavy rains or snows; one of the locals says it's like driving on goose droppings—he didn't use the word "droppings". Camp anywhere in the national forest, as long as there are no restrictions. Call the forest service office first.

After exiting from Route 4 to FS 10, continue on FS 10 for about 2.3 miles. Just after crossing over a cattle guard, take a right on FS 135 (note a small sign for 135 just down this road). Continue on FS 135 for 2 miles and pull over just before the road makes a sharp left uphill. If you start driving up a steep hill, you've gone too far. There's a clearing on the right with a small road (actually more like two tire tracks than a road). Park anywhere on the small road off FS 135. This is the Rim Hike location where we'll review the geology of this area first. Then, you're on your own. Which means, you can go anywhere. I'd recommend hiking up FS 135 as far as you want. There are many interesting overlooks and lots of areas to explore. This is also a designated wildlife area. Sightings of elk are common. You'll notice others have camped at this location.

First let's take a look at the geologic features. Follow the small (two track) road where you parked, only a few hundred feet, to the end—to a cliff and beautiful views of the caldera. This location sits atop the southwest wall of the Valles Caldera, part of the volcanic rim. Caldera walls (rims) are excellent sites for understanding a volcano's history. The walls of any volcano or volcanic field are composed of the material erupted overtime and accumulated in piles. The walls are a layer-upon-layer history of eruptive behavior. At this location, you're standing on the remains of the earliest Bandelier Tuff; it marks the beginning of the two caldera forming events. The rock formation is referred to as the Lower Bandelier Tuff (LBT) and was deposited at the time that the Toledo Caldera (the first caldera) was created around 1.6 million years ago.

Cliff of exposed Lower Bandelier Tuff.

If you look down to the left, at the cliff facing your location, what you're seeing is the history of the first eruptions of Bandelier Tuff. The layers, represented by different colors and textures in the rock, mark different episodes of volcanic activity. The lower part, with the interesting pointed teepee-like formations, are the result of burning, pyroclastic flows of ash and pumice. Once the hot material settles and hardens, erosion takes over. The teepee-like appearance is the result of erosion. Harder rock prevents erosion from above. As the surrounding rock erodes, the harder rock sitting on top keeps the rock below from eroding, to the point that they look like teepees or tents. These formations are referred to as hoodoos or tent rocks. There are beautiful tent rock formations farther down Route 4 (see Other Points of Interest at the end of this section).

Pumice is a rock similar in composition to rhyolite, which itself has the same composition as granite. Pumice comes from the frothy mush found at the top of magma chambers. As the magmatic gas bubbles to the top of the magma chamber (like shaking a soda bottle), great pressure builds within the chamber. When a fracture or fractures are created in the rock above the chamber, the eruption begins. The frothy mixture at the top, loaded with gas, is sent upward through the vent(s). Shattered to mostly ash from the eruption, it may drive directly down the mountain like a burning cloud or rise high into the air. As the weight of this airborne material increases and the volume of gas supporting it decreases, it falls back around the crater creating massive burning flows of pyroclastic ash, rock and gas. Farther up the cliff, you may notice a rock layer that doesn't appear as solid as the lower half. Made of small rocks and boulders, it is called breccia. Breccia is another sign of violent eruptions. Breccia is basically the broken fragments of hardened lava and rock the magma picked up from the conduit as it moved up toward the vent. The rock in this breccia is composed of older volcanic rock dating to some of the earliest volcanic activity in the Jemez, about 13 million years ago. Also found in the breccia are chunks of Paleozoic rock, maybe 300 million years old and pieces of basement rock (Precambrian Era), over a billion years old. When magma moves up from the mantle it picks up everything it can and incorporates it in the mix. When the magma chamber is formed, it breaks of country rock surrounding the chamber as it bloats from gas and added magma. And as it rises to the surface, it breaks off even more rock. So the breccia resulted from magma that assimilated everything from the old basement rock, to the rock formed during the Age of Fishes (Paleozoic) to chunks of hardened lava flows of the early phases of Jemez volcanic activity. Along with the debris that came up with magma, rock is also shattered during violent eruptions. All this material, called clasts, cement together with the lava, as it flies through the air or flows, to form volcanic breccia. Geologists believe this particular layer indicates we're fairly close to the vent from which the material was ejected—maybe one of the ring fractures created as the volcano collapsed. The top of the cliff to the left matches our mesa top location (Cat Mesa) in terms of rock. The rocks along the trail and at our overlook represent late phases of the Lower Bandelier Tuff event. The Toledo complex had collapsed, creating the Toledo Caldera and with the collapse more ash and lava were ejected from ring fractures. Take a walk along the mesa, pick up some rock and notice the different minerals or chunks of rock in the mix. The more fragments of other rock in the samples, the more violent the event that created them. Now, let's take a minute and discuss the beautiful scenery to the north.

Banco Bonito lava flows (center) and caldera wall or rim (far right).

The view from our southwest caldera wall overlook reports the results of a classic Plinian event. To the northwest, a prominent mesa extends toward the north and then sweeps down to a saddle. Beyond the saddle, the ridge on the horizon is the northwest section of the caldera wall. One can barely conceptualize the eruptive power, given the distance to that part of the caldera wall. Down below the saddle and closer to our location, dark flows of Banco Bonito lava can be seen. We'll see this rock along Route 4. Directly in front of our location, the high rounded peak is Redondo, which makes up part of the resurgent dome within the caldera. The hills and mountains to the right are mostly lava domes that oozed out of the ground as sticky lava, piled up around the various vents along the ring fractures and hardened to the hills in view. These hills follow the ring fractures between the moat and the caldera walls. So, from the center of the caldera outward, we have the resurgent dome, surrounded by the moat (meadows to the lower right), then the ring fractures—all enclosed within the outer caldera walls on which we're perched. As you hike along the rim, or up FS 135, different angles of view will give you different perspectives of the makeup of the caldera. Hopefully, you'll come away with a more complete picture of all the elements of a resurgent caldera—resurgent dome, moat, ring fractures capped by lava domes and the caldera wall.

View north of resurgent dome with Redondo Peak, lava dome hills to far right and forested moat below.

Trail 137:

This trail follows the Jemez River and Route 4. There are a number of trail access points along Route 4—we'll catch the trailhead at Battleship Rock. Unlike the Rim Hike, this one follows a streambed in San Diego Canyon, which cuts down on the views. It's also a popular trail. However, it is a pleasant stroll through some of the most recent pyroclastic flows that in some areas along the stream mix with limestone and shale outcrops from the Pennsylvanian Period of the Paleozoic Era. The limestone outcrops appear along the trail as white to dark gray shelves or ledges. Compared to the dark and hard volcanic rock in the area, most of which are eroded pieces of Battleship Rock, the limestone is lighter and can be scratched with a knife (a good test for limestone). Trail 137 passes Jemez Falls, after about 2 miles of hiking, and then crosses Route 4 at the East Fork campground area, around 3 miles. For this hike, we'll focus on the limestone formations and the Battleship Rock ignimbrite (rock created from pyroclastic flows).

Battleship Rock at the trailhead parking lot.

The limestone formed as sea creatures died and their shells (and skeletal remains) piled up along an offshore shelf of a sea that covered this area. New Mexico, a few hundred million years ago, was partially submerged under a sea that advanced from the south. North America was part of the megacontinent Pangea. Gondwanaland, a large southern continent carrying South America, had collided with the southern edge of North America. The collision caused enough compression inland that the ancestral Rockies rose as well as the first round of Nacimiento Mountain uplift mentioned earlier. South America and Africa would collide again with the North American continent but farther to the east, mashing the Appalachians. The trail and Route 4 follow a fault that brought the old and deeply buried fossiliferous limestone and shale into view alongside the volcanic rocks of this area. You'll notice that many of the limestone ledges along the trail have been picked through by fossil-hounds. With some patience, fossils can still be seen within the rock. Some fossils are shell like, rounded and striated; others are cylindrical and stem-like. Fossil collection is generally not allowed in national forests.

As you start your hike, Battleship Rock looms above. The trail cuts to the south and around the formation before heading east. You're walking in Pleistocene time remnants, which lasted from 2 million years to 10,000 years ago. The Pleistocene was a grand epoch in terms of man's appearance and movement through North America as well as a violent volcanic time. The Cascades, Yellowstone, San Francisco Peaks, Mount Taylor, Valles Caldera and many more violent eruptions built volcanic structures throughout the western cordillera during the Pleistocene. It was also the time of the Great Ice Age. Ice sheets advanced and retreated across the world. In this area of the west, the ice moved from the north down to northern New Mexico and Arizona. So much water was sucked up from the seas to create the sheets that a land bridge appeared between Siberia and present day Alaska. At the end of the Pleistocene, the first North American man walked across the bridge, following mammoths and bison. It was this first NA man that used obsidian and other rock, such as quartzite and chert, for spears and arrowheads to bring down large mammoths for food and clothing. Directly north of the Jemez Mountains is a narrow, flat-top mountain named Cerro Pedernal. Chert found on that mountain was used by Paleo-Indians about 10,000 years ago to make tools and weapons. Their artifacts are found throughout many states east of New Mexico. They made their weapons and moved on, following their food source.

Route 4 snakes through San Diego Canyon southwest from the caldera, as did a large overflowing lake during the time of eruptions. It's believed that the bulging of the earth from the resurgent dome in the middle pushed the lake over the southwest wall. The lakes drained along the ancient canyon that is now Route 4. Then, about 60,000 years ago, eruptions brought waves of hot, burning pumice and ash down the canyon, the resulting rock eventually dammed the breach in the caldera wall. On the trail, the boulders eroded from Battleship shine, like dark glass. The glassy appearance is the result of fast cooling. Rhyolite lava forms a glassy rock called obsidian when it cools rapidly. The Banco Bonito flows, which occurred soon after Battleship, are even purer obsidian and can be seen along Route 4. When the eruptions that formed Battleship sent burning clouds of debris down the ancient canyon, the debris filled valleys to the point that the land seemed to flatten—not a valley in sight. Then over thousands of years of erosion, the hard volcanic rock resisted erosion while the softer surrounding rock eroded and was transported downstream. Battleship is a great example of reversed topography—the flows that created it filled the valley and hardened. All else around eroded and was transported away leaving Battleship standing above the landscape. Some volcanic boulders along the trail show ash and lava movement. As volcanic rock cools it may still be moving or pressurized from above. The minerals and other hot, molten chunks within the rock stretch along the direction of movement. They are also squeezed and compressed by weight. One boulder in particular stands out, facing the trail in the early going. It displays this squeezed appearance, including a characteristic feature called fiamme. The fiamme flakes are mostly dark pumice crystals flattened by movement while the mass was still hot and compressed by overlying rock and ash. Some of the fiamme (stretch marks) extend a few inches through the rock and are very obvious. As you hike, imagine the eruptions of hot clouds blowing down the canyon, bringing ash, rock, chunks of lava and gas. They burn everything in sight, accumulate as more flows rush down the canyon, eventually creating structures like Battleship Rock. Ancient trees have been found in some of the volcanic debris around the caldera. A forest existed in this area much like the current surroundings. It could happen again!

Valles Caldera Preserve Hikes:

Again, you must make a reservation for all hikes within the preserve except for the one short hike at the southeastern corner of the moat. Abrigo and El Cajete are recommended hikes because they are located within the preserve where you can see the results of lava and pyroclastic flows and doming. Material will be available from the preserve staff to explain the sights along the trails. These hikes are a must for their beauty and the fact that this preserve needs the public's support. The staff does a wonderful job preserving this magnificent work of nature.

Other Points of Interest: As mentioned earlier, to get to the preserve, Route 4 passes Bandelier National Monument, within which a huge canyon shelters the remains of prehistoric Anasazi Indians who had moved from the Four Corners area around 1,000 AD. As resources became depleted in one area, they had to move on to find wood for structures and animals for food. Their culture at Bandelier peaked around 1500 AD. It is believed that at this time many of the cliff dwellings were built for defensive purposes. Their lifestyle was changing from nomadic hunter-gatherers, to one of longer-term sedentary existence. Eventually they moved down into the Rio Grande valley as ancestors to the current Pueblo Native Peoples. Bandelier and the outlying national forest have many trails and an established campsite on the mesa above the canyon. A fee is required to enter but it's well worth it. Some trails follow the mesa tops overlooking the canyon. Along the mesa, obsidian arrowheads are scattered in areas where the ancient ones must have set up manufacturing sites for their tools and weapons. Mesas and high ridges were preferred sites so they could overlook the canyon, watching for animals or enemies. More recently in this area of New Mexico in the 1800s, major battles between the US Army and the Native Americans marked their long history of trying to find a place to settle and live peacefully. Fortunately, many were able to maintain their pueblo lifestyles.

As you drive west on Route 4, near Battleship Rock and Soda Dam, look at the canyon walls just below the high mesa to the upper right (northwest). Like the Rim Trail, you'll see light colored formations that look like teepees or tents. They're called tent rocks and are formed by erosion. Again, volcanic debris may contain many different sized rocks—anywhere from ash to boulders. As the smaller sized grains erode away, the larger boulders remain eventually forming a pedestal that protects the smaller grains underneath. As all else erodes and is transported away by wind and water, the tent-like formations result, often balancing a large boulder on top. These formations are also called hoodoos. Soda Dam, below Battleship Rock, is another interesting site. Soda Dam is proof that mineral laden hot springs feed the streams in this area. The dam is composed of travertine that was deposited as the river flowed and precipitated minerals which eventually formed the large mass that blocks the river's course.

Now for one last close-up of the geology of volcanoes along the road. As you return east from Battleship Rock, Route 4 hits a junction with Route 126 at La Cueva. Set your odometer to zero at this junction and continue east on Route 4. At about 5.4 miles, the road passes Jemez Falls campground and another connection to Trail 137. At 5.6 miles you'll notice a roadcut on the left that exposes different layers of volcanic rock. Find a safe place to pull over and walk the cut. These layers represent the most recent (circa 60,000 years ago) activity in the caldera. The bottom layer at the very base of the cut, below the multicolored middle section, are lava flows associated with domes emplaced along ring fractures and are much older than the top two strata. The next layer, characterized by light colors with darker bands, are the El Cajete pumice, lava and ash flows with some surge deposits. Surge deposits represent violent outward blasts of very hot ash, rock and gas from vents along the ring fractures. If seen from the air, they would look like an atomic bomb blast where the ground-hugging cloud spreads out from the vent at high speed. In this area it buried a pine forest. Some tree trunks have been found in the strata. In some areas, the flows were hot enough to bake trees to coal. The eruptions that created Battleship Rock occurred during the El Cajete episode. Overlying the El Cajete are the Banco Bonito obsidian flows. They have been eroded to mostly large boulders. As you walk the cut, you'll notice dark, glass-like, shining rocks. This is the rhyolite magma and ash that flowed and cooled so fast it created a volcanic glass (obsidian), used by ancient Native Peoples to manufacture tools and weapons. It tends to chip to hard, sharp angular pieces, which makes the manufacturing process much less time consuming. The obsidian at this location doesn't have the truly pure obsidian appearance, which is black glass through and through. But as you hike the Jemez Mountains you'll eventually come across the pure obsidian the Native Peoples preferred. And there's a good chance it'll have the shape of an arrowhead. The obsidian at the roadcut contains mineral crystals, called phenocrysts. The white to gray minerals are feldspar, a rock forming mineral. They crystallized at a different rate than other minerals in the rock, allowing them to achieve sufficient size to be noticeable by the naked eye. Most of the other rock at the roadcut is light gray, to brown (with some red) welded ash and pumice. Rotate these rocks in the sun and notice the beautiful crystals that present bright flashes. The abundance of these crystals are evidence of a violent eruption. As magma is sent into the air during gas-charged eruptions, it is shattered into ash and small rocks, which accumulate on the ground and weld together. The debris that makes up the rock are fragments of frothy pumice and minerals crystals of quartz and feldspar. If you stand back, you can imagine the cloud of burning pyroclastic debris rolling in your direction. In fact, geologists believe the vent that created this flow is not far from the road and the burning cloud moved directly at your position. Geologists love roadcuts.

Roadcut of rhyolite formations, including the El Cajete and Banco Bonito obsidian flows.

After the roadcut stop, in less than a mile, Route 4 passes the preserve's El Cajete and East Fork trailheads. And finally, after passing Forest Service Road 10 (our cutoff for the Rim Trail) at about 8 miles pull over to the left at any of the parking areas with overviews of the caldera. From these stops the beautiful view is of the meadow (moat) in the foreground, the resurgent dome with Redondo Peak perched on top to the left (northwest) and to the north and east the hills representing the lava domes that erupted along ring fractures. You are looking at only one, very small, section of the caldera. A holistic view would present a huge dome, still active, bulging in the middle, surrounded by the moat, then the ring fractures around the moat near the caldera wall or rim, which is the outer boundary of the collapsed structure. This is a prime location for understanding a resurgent dome caldera and Plinian eruption behavior. Add to that the beauty of Valles Caldera and you realize one day here is not enough.

Redondo Peak on resurgent dome, with moat (meadow); note small dome middle left.

On the Road to the Next Hike

Aside from being the Land of Enchantment, New Mexico is also known as the Volcano State. So deciding where to visit next can be difficult. You could spend considerable time in the state given all the volcanic landforms and trails. You could also drive north to Colorado, specifically the San Juan Mountains. These mountains are the eroded remains of huge calderas, much larger than Valles Caldera and there are more than one within the range. However, because they are so eroded, their appearance is not as obvious as the Valles Caldera. The Gila Mountains in southwest New Mexico are the same story. Huge volcanic eruptions during the mid-Tertiary orogeny were responsible for large calderas in the Gila and surrounding ranges. In their case erosion also had an effect on the mountain's appearance, as did the Basin and Range Orogeny, which split the calderas into large landforms, some were uplifted as mountains, others were dropped into basins. Picture the Valles Caldera being split in half, with one side lifted up thousands of feet, while the other half drops into an adjoining basin. It would be hard to recognize a volcano, or caldera, so torn apart. Most of the scenery in southern New Mexico and Arizona, along with most of Nevada and western Utah all the way to Idaho was created by this schizophrenic lifting and dropping. The faults along the west coast that are sliding by each other, such as the San Andreas, continue to stretch the crust of the west. Pull crust apart and the hydraulic effect forces large blocks to split off and drop while mountains on either side rise. Most people who drive through Nevada don't understand that the basin the road follows and the ranges that surround the basin are still active. If you were to drive off the road and head straight to one of the mountains you'd notice a surprisingly limited amount of debris from the rising mountains. That's because they are still young and haven't shed their summits yet. And, they're still moving up as the basin continues to sink. You may also notice many mining towns in Nevada. As these ranges are driven up, the rich ore veins buried deep underground come up with them. Your mountain view may be the next big strike for some lucky miner. Or another dead-end mining claim near a dried-up ghost town. Nevada's loaded with them.

We'll continue to follow the Jemez Lineament and visit one more site in New Mexico. The lineament terminates in east-central Arizona at the Datil-Mogollon volcanic field, another site of multiple caldera events. Our destination is the El Malpais (badlands) National Monument and Mt. Taylor. El Malpais is part of the Zuni-Bandera (McCartys) volcanic field, a great site to learn more about basalt lava flows and for short day-hikes. Mt. Taylor, on the other hand, is a beautiful composite volcano just north of Grants, with a wonderful hiking trail to the top. This volcano didn't collapse like Valles Caldera or Crater Lake. Its behavior was similar to that of Mount St. Helens and San Francisco Peaks—the entire northeast side was blown away giving geologists a view of the innards of the volcano, much like studying roadcuts on a grand scale.

To get to our next location we can travel south on Interstate 25 from Santa Fe to Interstate 40 west to Grants. Or, from Valles Caldera, travel northwest on route 44 to a small town named Cuba. From Cuba, take route 197 west to White Horse, then route 509 south to route 605 to Milan and Grants. Check a road map before taking this drive as it is very remote. But that's the beauty of this route—its remoteness, the beautiful plateau country of the San Juan Basin, driving along the Continental Divide and a backdoor approach to Mt. Taylor. From this direction you'll get a great view of the entirety of Mt. Taylor and the lava flows that run east from the mountain. Remember to gas up in Cuba and observe the speed limit. Most of the drive is through Indian reservation land. Sheep, horses, goats, cattle and other forms of wildlife roam the road. But what a beautiful trip!

On the other hand, if you choose the interstate there are possibilities. Driving south from Santa Fe on Interstate 25, the highway descends from the plateau upon which Santa Fe sits. Once it levels out, the Rio Grande River valley will appear on the right (west). Notice the heavy foliage from cottonwood trees. Along the river, there are old volcanic necks, the eroded innards of volcanoes. In this case, they appear to be cinder cones. However, as the highway approaches Albuquerque you should notice in the distance to the southwest, three volcanoes lined up in a north-south direction. These are also eroded volcanic necks and as you transfer onto Interstate 40 west to Grants, you'll get another view of the alignment. These volcanic necks follow a dike that fed much lava to this area not long ago. There is a highway sign for a street named Vulcan west of Albuquerque on I-40.

At the intersection of I-25 and I-40 there is a bit of a dilemma. You could proceed south toward Las Cruces. The volcanic roadmap to the south is no less spectacular than to the west, our direction. Just south of Albuquerque, the highway passes Socorro. There are only three active mid-crustal magma bodies in North America: one in California, the other at Yellowstone and the third under Socorro. Farther south and east, near Ruidoso (pronounced by the locals as ReeUuDoSo), sits Sierra Blanca, a large composite volcano with an elevation close to 12,000 feet. One of the most beautiful trails in New Mexico runs from the Ski Apache parking lot to the top of Sierra Blanca. In the spring and summer, the trail is surrounded by color from the wildflowers—like a carpet that runs all the way to the summit. At the top you have a 360 degree view of southeast New Mexico. Another area of interest is near Carrizozo, on the way to Ruidoso. Valley of Fires Recreation Area is another basaltic Malpais, much like our area of interest outside Grants. Farther south are the volcanic Organ Mountains outside Las Cruces and last, but by far not the least, is Kilbourne Hole, southwest of Las Cruces. If you don't mind driving a long rough dirt road and dodging rattlesnakes, the hole is quite unique. It looks like a meteor impact crater. It is, however, volcanic. Kilbourne lies within a huge volcanic field that covers part of southern New Mexico. It resulted when hot, gas charged magma, encountered water in rock strata below the surface. We know that magma carries its own gas but when it came in contact with water the pressurized steam it created underground blew everything above it for miles in many directions. The result is a hole, more like a bomb crater and termed a maar by geologists. There are many maars in New Mexico, one is now a lake and is part of the Zuni-Bandera (El Malpais) field we'll visit during our stop in Grants. So Grants, here we come!

Hike: El Malpais National Monument and Mt. Taylor

Two beautiful and educational hikes—one an easy walk, the other strenuous but well worth the effort.

Location: Interstate 40 skirts the south end of the town of Grants, New Mexico. For El Malpais (the badlands) National Monument, take NM State Route 53 (Exit 81) south from I-40 for about 23 miles to the El Malpais Visitor Center. There is no fee, only donations. But a stop is worth it. Pick up the El Calderon Area trail guide. The El Calderon trailhead is back up Route 53 a few miles. There are some other interesting hikes in this area. The Continental Divide Scenic Trail, which runs from Mexico to Canada, cuts right through El Malpais. A trail guide is available at the center. The Divide Trail connects with the Zuni-Acoma Trail that runs to the east side of the monument. As for Mt. Taylor, there are a couple of trails. We're going to take a cross-country ski trail. From I-40 and NM State Route 53 (Exit 81) follow the signs to Grants, north of I-40 and east. Look for New Mexico State Route 547 north (left turn at stoplight). Or coming from the east on I-40, take exit 85 to Grants and look for the same route 547 north. Route 547 turns into Lobo Canyon Road. Just before the left turn onto Lobo Canyon Road note the El Malpais National Monument office near the cemetery on the right. After turning left onto Lobo Canyon Road, look for the Mt. Taylor (Cibola) Ranger Station on the left as you proceed out of town. Stop there for maps and trail information. Continue on 547 to the Coalmine Campground. At the campground, set the mileage odometer to zero and proceed on 547. At 2.3 miles the road passes Forest Service (FS) road 193. This road to the right takes you to the Gooseberry Spring Trailhead, another beautiful hike to the top of Mt. Taylor. Continue on 547, which changes to FS 239, a well maintained gravel road. At about 5.6 miles turn right at the La Mosca (the fly) Lookout sign, FS 453. Take FS 453 for another 2 miles. Look for a shelter on the left and the parking area for the cross-country ski trail on the right. Park there and start the hike on the ski trail. Note the ski trail, degree of difficulty, descriptive sign on a tree farther up the trail.

Hike Type and Length: The El Calderon Trail, at El Malpais, is 3 miles roundtrip. The trail is fairly flat, except for a short climb to the cinder cone's summit. Remember to stop at the visitor center for the El Calderon Area Trail Guide. The Mt. Taylor hike is strenuous, uphill all the way, and about 7 miles roundtrip.

Elevation: This area of New Mexico straddles the Continental Divide so expect hiking in high elevations. El Malpais ranges from 7,000 to 8,000 feet. Mt. Taylor, on the other hand, is the highest structure in New Mexico on the divide. Our hike starts around 9,500 feet and climbs to just below 11,000 feet. If you want to mount the summit of Taylor, you'll top out at 11,301 feet.

Precautions: At El Malpais, the hiking offers no special challenges. Bring plenty of water in warm months and wear sturdy hiking shoes. Also, read the El Calderon Trail Guide before the hike for any precautions. For instance, if you plan on exploring Junction Cave, they recommend 3 flashlights, candles or lighters and a hard hat. Remember to read the brochure first and ask the rangers at the visitor center for hiking tips. I'm not a fan of caves or bats so Junction Cave and Bat Cave aren't on the itinerary. Mt. Taylor is another story. This is backpacking country. Prepare for this hike the way you would for any strenuously long day-hike. Water, medical kit, some food, proper clothing, rain gear are a few articles you should consider. Check at the ranger station on Lobo Canyon Road for road conditions, trail conditions and any restrictions. During the last hike we encountered a day-hiker who climbs Mt. Taylor three times a week. He tells us it's not uncommon to see black bear and has seen mountain lions more than once. Also, cattle are allowed to graze in the national forest. You'll definitely pass a few. Just keep walking and mind your own business. Make some noise so they know you're approaching. Most cattle will stand their ground and watch you with curiosity. It also helps to make noise in bear country as you round trail turns or are hiking in areas where sight is restricted by trees. It always helps to broadcast your approach in bear country. You can also expect to see deer and elk. And if you're into birding, you're in the right place.

Planning Information: There isn't much material available for Mt. Taylor. The Cibola National Forest, Mt. Taylor Ranger District forest service map is helpful and recommended. They also have a brief guide for the Gooseberry Spring Trail if you want to take that to the top. You can purchase forest service maps at the ranger station. Or logon to the national forest service web site and lookup the Cibola NF at:
> www.fs.fed.us/

As for El Malpais National Monument, check out their web site at:
> http://volcano.und.nodak.edu/vwdocs/Parks/el_malpais/el_malpais.html

As for more geologic information on the Zuni-Bandera volcanic field and McCartys lava flow, check this site:
> http://volcano.und.nodak.edu/vwdocs/volc_images/north_america/mccartys_flow.html

At the visitor center, pick up the El Calderon Area Trail Guide and the El Malpais Official Map and Guide.

Geologic Setting: Two volcanic fields, sitting astride the Jemez Lineament, dominate northwestern New Mexico: the Zuni-Bandera (basaltic) field and the field that contains Mt. Taylor, a composite volcano. Zuni-Bandera has more than 100 vents from which basaltic lava flowed and erupted as cinders and bombs. The Mt. Taylor field has hundreds of vents, which produced everything from rhyolite to basalt. In both cases, the younger eruptions and flows are in the northeast corner of the fields. In most of the Zuni basaltic flows, Hawaiian-type flow characteristics are evident, such as: aa (blocky) or pahoehoe (ropy). Mt. Taylor presents many characteristics of more violent eruption types, most centered around and on the mountain. They include lava flows, ash-fall and ash-flow. Both fields sit in what geologists call a transition zone. They are wedged between the thick crust of the Colorado Plateau to the northwest and the thin crust of the Basin and Range Province to the south and the Rio Grande Rift to the east. Along with the Jemez Lineament, a line of crustal weakness known for volcanic activity, this area is still ripe for eruptions. The last volcanic eruptions and flows were less than a thousand years ago—a few seconds ago in geologic time.

Along the road, as it enters the national forest, State Route 547 reports the eruptive power of Mt. Taylor. The view in the beginning is of volcanic cliffs of mostly rhyolite ash and lava flows. The light brown to buff colored cliffs will give you an idea of the volume of activity. Pull over and walk some of the roadcuts. Pick up a rock and note the small crystals that formed as the lava surged from the magma chamber to the vent. Mineral crystals form as the magma cools while other fragments represent the violent shattering of rock and blobs of lava during eruptions. Near the top of some rhyolite flows, vesicles (holes) form as gas is released. The holes are often filled with silica-rich fluids, which crystallize late in the cooling process. Beautiful specimens of jasper and opal have been found in the rhyolite formations along the road. Farther up the road, the rock color turns darker. The initial eruptions spewed out gas and frothy lava from the top of the magma chamber. Then, various cycles of eruptions over a million years drew from deeper within the chamber to bring up magma of different composition. The darker rock is andesite and basalt. Andesite is typical of volcanoes that form along plate boundaries at subduction zones. But this magma formed nowhere near a plate boundary. Once again, it was the influence of the Jemez Lineament but other factors were at work. The geologic record of this area of New Mexico tells of crust being tortured, compressed, squeezed and generally abused by tectonic forces out of control.

Hold a stack of paper between your hands. Pull it tight, then push the stack together, thus representing the compressive forces that squeezed the west during the violent Laramide Orogeny beginning 80 million years ago. The Pacific plate was riding under the continent and as it dove it also compressed the continental crust inland all the way to New Mexico, warping the landscape. Mess with the land that way and magma, looking for an exit from the mantle, will exploit any weakness it can find. Mt. Taylor eruptions began around 3 million years ago while Zuni-Bandera started a million years before that. The stack of paper represents various rock layers, mostly sandstone and shale, accumulated over millions of years at the end of the Age of Fishes and throughout the Age of Reptiles. Most of the layers represent sedimentary rock that accumulated during the time of the great reptiles, the dinosaurs. The sedimentary beds are loaded with dinosaur fossils, making it easier for geologists and paleontologists to date the strata. Dinosaurs were dying, their bones were accumulating while sand and mud sealed the tomb. For the earth's crust and the stack of papers, compression from the sides has the same effect—the layers may bulge up in the middle. The up-warped strata are called an anticline by geologists. If they slump down in the middle, that's a syncline. If they warp toward one side and lay flat at the other, that's a monocline. Whatever the case, this area was tortured for a long time before the Mt. Taylor and Zuni eruptions. The warped crust would play a role in the eventual volcanic arousal throughout northwest New Mexico.

The Zuni-Bandera volcanic field, composed mostly of basalt and a victim of the Jemez Lineament, commenced volcanic activity around 4 million years ago. While the volcanism at Mt. Taylor started at 3 million and ended about 1.5 million years ago, Zuni-Bandera lasted until about 1,000 years ago when the McCartys lava flows put the finishing touches on the El Malpais landscape. The McCartys flows started from a small cinder cone vent that sat on top of a huge shield volcano. The flows moved to the south, then followed existing drainage patterns to the north, eventually reaching the present location of Interstate 40, about 40 miles from the vent. From the highway the view north is of Mt. Taylor surrounded by mesas of sedimentary, dinosaur encapsulated, rock capped by volcanic flows. And as the highway proceeds east, a huge, thick finger points toward Albuquerque. From the air it becomes more obvious as a large (lava flow) mesa that extends from Mt. Taylor halfway to Albuquerque. The Mt. Taylor flows and ash deposits were one event north of the highway. The McCartys flows that surround the highway were another event coming from volcanic centers many miles to the south. Their behaviors are controlled by the Jemez Lineament and their unfortunate position—jammed between the Colorado Plateau and the rifting Rio Grande valley.

Mt. Taylor from the northwest.

The Defiance uplift, the Defiance and Nutria monocline, the Zuni anticline, the Gallup sag—all quite descriptive of the compressive torture this area of New Mexico experienced before volcanism reigned. At the end of the Mesozoic, when the dinosaurs had reached their maximum height and length, the entire area was down-warped allowing floodplains and a large seaway to bring in loads of sediment. The Morrison and Dakota formations accumulated sand and mud in thick layers that now sit under El Malpais and Mt. Taylor. A great syncline, where the layers warp down in a U-shape, sits under Mt. Taylor. Perhaps this syncline brought the hot mantle closer to the upper crust allowing magma a shorter route to the surface. Mt. Taylor sits between two old uranium districts where the Morrison formation, aside from being the great burial ground of the largest dinosaurs, contained sufficient uranium within its strata to get the attention of the Atomic Energy Commission in the 1950s and 1960s. Holes have been punched all around Mt. Taylor as the search for uranium heated up and our nuclear arsenal expanded. Mt. Taylor was studied by US Army geographers back in the middle 1800s and was eventually named for President Zachary Taylor. After hundreds of years of study, and as a testament to the warping of the crust, it was decided that the initial eruptions followed the development of the syncline and that the main vent sat right above the deepest crustal penetration of the syncline, nearer the mantle.

The Mt. Taylor volcano was assembled during a two million year period by eruptions of lava and ash (tuff) that lasted from 3.4 to 1.5 million years ago. Many of the mesas around the volcano were constructed of the material erupted and eroded as the volcano grew in size, was decapitated and then reconstructed itself, before going through the same drill again. After the eruptions of high silica content rhyolite to andesite, basalt flows topped off the mesas. The entire structure, Mt. Taylor and the larger volcanic field in which it sits, extends to the north and east. When the main vent plugged, other vents took over. Geologists have counted more than 200 vents scattered throughout the field, which over a few million years created maars (steam-exploded crater), cinder cones and lava domes atop the many mesas. From Interstate 40 traveling east, or better yet, at Mt. Taylor's backdoor driving down routes 509 and 605 from the north, huge volcanic necks can be seen scattered throughout the field. These necks, monoliths that project high above the mesas that make up the volcanic field, are the inner remains of volcanic vents. Cabezon Peak, to the east, is a huge one and can be seen for many miles from the highways north of the mountain. It's a driver's guide, like a lighthouse for trade routes. The Native Peoples regard many of these mountains as sacred. At the summit of Mt. Taylor, which probably stood a few thousand feet higher than it is now, the crater has been eroded to form an amphitheater spilling out to the east. The last major eruption tore off the northeast side of the cone and erosion added to the removal of most of the east flank. Creeks now flow from the crater through the gap, which is a few thousand feet below the rim. Almost the entire history of lava flows and ash deposits are recorded in the walls within the crater. And geologists have mapped large dikes that tend to point inward toward the vent. The dikes fed magma from the central chamber to the volcano. On our hike, we'll see one such dike within the crater running up the hill toward what may have been the central vent.

South of Interstate 40, the Zuni-Bandera volcanic field, about 50 miles long by 10 miles wide, had a different life and duration than Mt. Taylor. Eruptions occurred in two phases: one about 4 million years ago and the most recent from 1.7 million years to 1,000 years ago. El Malpais, composed mostly of basalt, sits on the north corner of the field. Our El Calderon hike takes us by some of the oldest exposed flows in this area (over 100,000 years old). The McCartys flow is one of the youngest. These flows present features that were originally studied and named in Hawaii. Later studies of the Zuni-Bandera area enhanced geologist's knowledge of Hawaiian-style volcanoes. Lava formations called aa and pahoehoe are common throughout El Malpais. And large lava bombs are as prevalent here as they are on the slopes of the Hawaiian volcano Kilauea.

Hike Guide: There are two hikes: one at the El Calderon area in El Malpais, the other up to the rim of the crater at Mt. Taylor. Other hiking trails are available at both locations. Check with the El Malpais Visitor Center and the Cibola Ranger Station in Grants for maps and trail guides.

El Calderon:

As you drive from Grants to the El Malpais Visitor Center on New Mexico State Route 53, you'll pass a road to the trailhead for El Calderon a few miles before reaching the visitor center. Remember to check in at the visitor center for the El Calderon Area Trail Guide and other information, including the El Malpais Official Map and Guide. For this hike, use the El Calderon Area Trail Guide. Some of the hike highlights are presented below but the guide is your best bet along the trail. Also at the visitor center, note the display of the different rock types—aa to pahoehoe lava flows, cinders and bombs. Basalt bombs have a distinctive appearance. They're easy to spot along the trail. During eruption, most of the lava was shattered into small pieces that solidified in the air and landed as small pea-size rocks (cinders). At times, large blobs of lava flew from the vent and solidified during flight into elongated, almost football-like, rocks that have a smooth appearance. Some bombs hit trees and wrapped around the trunk before falling to the ground. Bombs are interesting given their size and the force needed to toss them great distances from the vent.

At the El Calderon parking area, start the hike to the left (clockwise) toward Junction Cave, Double Sinks and Bat Cave. The three mile walk follows a gravel path, then a dirt trail and finally a dirt road as it loops back to the parking area. Along the way the trail is surrounded by chunks of basalt. The landforms and rock types are first rate examples of Hawaiian-style volcanism. When basaltic lava flows, it begins to harden at the front and top of the moving mass. As the flow continues, the hard frontal lobe breaks into large angular chunks that are pushed forward by the more liquid flow from behind—this is called block lava or an aa flow pattern. These aa rock types are often referred to as clinkery. They sound metallic when struck with another rock. Other flows string out like rope—this is the ropy pahoehoe flow pattern. The area is covered with cinder and spatter cones, pressure ridges, lava tubes, gas cavities and a beautiful example of a lava trench that extends to the east from the El Calderon cinder cone. El Calderon erupted about 115,000 years ago, a more recent event given the Zuni-Bandera field had already been active for a few million years. The Calderon eruptions came from many fractures in the earth, actually from a line of vents. Lava was thrown into the air giving the appearance of fire fountains. This type of volcanic activity is termed Strombolian. Eventually one vent dominated as the fissures plugged from the hardened lava. Small cinders and bombs, up to a few feet in diameter, flew hundreds of feet in the air. And like many cinder cones, lava flowed from a fracture at the base of the cone. These flows probably lasted a year or so and covered 10, 20, 30 miles and more. As the top of the flows cooled and hardened, lava tubes were formed below—the still hot and liquid flow continued beneath the crusted top, like forcing jelly into a donut. These lava tubes extend for miles from the various cinder cones. As the trail approaches the El Calderon cone, you'll get a text book look at a lava trench between you and the cone. The trench, a former lava tube, hardened but the roof collapsed leaving a trench filled with blocks of eroded basalt. With this background in place, here's a suggestion on taking the hike. With the El Calderon Area Trail Guide in hand, have a seat and drink some water at the trailhead and read the guide. Note those areas along the trail you find interesting. Then start your hike. As you walk, try to sense the Jemez Lineament under El Malpais and consider the amount of volcanic activity it has created all the way from east-central Arizona to the northeast corner of New Mexico. This hike covers a very small section of El Malpais, which itself covers a small northern corner of the Zuni-Bandera field, obviously a very large volcanic field.

El Calderon cinder cone in background with lava trench.

Mt. Taylor:

This hike is strenuous; uphill for most of the 4 miles one way. It helps to have a pedometer to verify your distances. At the parking area, you can decide which route to the top you prefer. There are three:

1) Follow FS 453 all the way. I'd recommend saving the forest service road for the return trip.
2) Take the more difficult (strenuous) ski trail. Note the ski trail sign for the degree of difficulty.
3) Take the less difficult (less strenuous) ski trail. This is the recommended (blue) approach.

The less strenuous trail actually provides the best views. It is still strenuous though. Notice in the beginning of the hike the dense gray boulders along the trail. They are mostly andesite, with some basalt. If you remember, driving along route 547, then Forest Service Road 239, the rock was lighter. There were roadcuts in softer slopes and others through ledges of harder rock. Those rocks were mostly rhyolite. The typical rhyolitic eruptions eject gas rich ash and blobs of lava, frothy pumice loaded with gas and pyroclastic flows that stream down the mountain. On the road you drove through lava flows and welded and semi-welded tuff (ash). When eruptions occur, the shattering of rock and lava into ash causes great clouds to form over the crater, some rising high into the jet stream. As gas is spent from the initial eruptions, the pressure supporting the cloud dissipates allowing the ash to fall. Some falls lightly to the ground (ash-fall). Most of the ash however flows downward (ash-flow) in one huge hot cloud around the crater, then drives down the flanks burning everything in its way. Also, some lateral eruptions of hot, glowing ash and gas stream down the mountain at hundreds of miles an hour. The ash-falls tend to solidify into loose tuff that erodes to slopes. The super-hot ash driven down the mountain welds together like cement and does not easily erode. This is called welded tuff. Both are evident along the forest service road. There are also signs of surge deposits (beds) that blew out like an atomic bomb (lateral) cloud hugging the ground, traveling outward from the vent. These roadside examples represent a very violent episode in the eruption cycles. As you start on the trail, the darker andesite and basalt represent mostly lava flows, a bit less gas-charged, hence a bit less violent.

At about .8 miles, the trail exits the forest for the first time as it climbs a flank of the mountain. This is the reason for choosing the less difficult trail up—it's more scenic. Mt. Taylor is directly ahead though its grandeur is not evident until you reach the crater rim. Then back into the forest until about 1.3 miles where the trail opens again to First Meadow. The more difficult trail joins your trail from the left. You'll see the sign for First Meadow on a tree facing down the hill of that trail. At this point you may have noticed the rock along the trail has changed character. Once again, like the transition from rhyolite to andesite and basalt, the rock at this location appears to be andesite porphyry and quartz latite. Break a piece and you'll notice the beautiful mineral crystals within the more dense, darker mass of the rock. The larger crystals give it the porphyritic character, hence the name andesite porphyry. For andesite, the larger crystals are feldspar, a common rock forming mineral. The crystals within the denser ground mass formed at a different rate than the rest of the rock, allowing the crystals to grow larger than other minerals in the rock. Don't get too hung-up on the rock types or names. But take a close look at the beautiful mineral crystals within them. If you had a hand lens, geologists use what's called a Hastings Triplet, you'd take a seat and spend some time gazing at the colors, angles of the crystals and the luster they produce when turned in the sun. This is a good point to have a seat and take a break. The views to the south are magnificent. Grants is to the left of the valley, with Interstate 40 traversing the plateau country across the Continental Divide and off in the distance the mountains responsible for the many lava flows south of the interstate.

The trail reenters the forest, on the left, the north side of the meadow. By the way, if you haven't run across any cattle by this time, particularly in the summer, you may be on the wrong mountain. As you reenter the forest, note the Quad 20 sign. Every year Grants sponsors a race from the downtown convention center. Starting off as a foot race, the participants change to bikes, then to skis and finally snowshoes to the top of Mt. Taylor. Soon the trail exits the forest out to another meadow and another change in rock types. At this point, you may have lost interest in rock types because you've seen the sign for Heartbreak Hill and the trail going straight up to a ridge at the end of the meadow. This is a strenuous climb. The best approach is to lower your head, stare at the rocks, bend into the hill and move forward. It's an intense climb but well worth it. At 2 miles from the trailhead, the trail tops out at a ridge, close to the crater's rim. There are more beautiful views at this point. La Mosca Peak Lookout is to the northeast (left). And looking farther to the left, in the valley, you'll notice at least one large slab of rock standing at attention and above all else. It's a volcanic neck and what a beauty, an excellent example of the many volcanic structures that dot the Mt. Taylor volcanic field. Now the trail flattens.

At this point you can go left toward La Mosca Peak or right along the road back into the forest. Go right toward Mt. Taylor and follow this road as it winds around eventually heading back east, then back toward La Mosca. At about 3.3 miles the road comes out of the forest to a small clearing on the left. Hikers have obviously camped at this location. About 10 yards up the road, the Gooseberry Trail (no trial signs) comes down from Mt. Taylor on the right, crosses the road and then moves downhill to a beautiful east-facing view. Take the Gooseberry Trail to the left from the road. In just a few hundred feet, you'll be experiencing scenery that only certain mountains of the west can provide. Looking east you can see the blown-out and eroded remains of the crater—a great opening to the world below. The view also includes hills that appear to be domes, bulging from restless lava below the mountain. Far out to the northeast, toward the horizon, is the Mt. Taylor volcanic field. Soon the trail crosses through a fence and as you hike, directly ahead on the nearest hill you can see large sheets (walls) of dark rock outcrops protruding from the top of the hill. This is one of the many dikes that fed magma from the magma chamber to the vent. Geologists have mapped many of them and most seem to point right to where the vent is located, somewhat northeast of your location. There are also some beautifully crystallized rocks along this trail. And in some of the rocks you can see flow-banding. When certain lavas, or even ash, are hardening, the mass may continue to move as lava pushes from behind or compressive weight from above squeezes the mass below. The mineral crystals, flakes of pumice and gas holes, tend to align along the direction of movement or pressure.

Dike exposed as dark rocks sticking out from near hill, looking northeast from Gooseberry Trail.

Continue on the Gooseberry Trail until it intersects with a road, almost 4 miles from the trailhead. At this junction, you can take the road to the left back to the ski trail and down the same way you came up. Or, take the road to the right to the next junction, FS 453. FS 453 is the road up from the trailhead to La Mosca Lookout. This road offers an easy 3 mile hike back down to the trailhead. Before hiking down, this is a great place to take a break and take in the views. It may be difficult to picture the rim of the crater given the amount of erosion. La Mosca Peak, with the lookout and electronic towers, is north. Behind you, to the southwest is the summit of Mt. Taylor. Imagine the rim of the crater running from the Mt. Taylor summit north to La Mosca Peak, then east and around to the south, connecting again with the Mt. Taylor summit. Both the Mt. Taylor and La Mosca peaks are on the crater rim. The rest of the crater and rim are gone, destroyed by the eruption, eroded and transported down the hill. If you look east at the rock outcrop on top of the near hill, you'll see the dark gray dike pointing in your direction. Actually, you can only see the front of the dike, as the rest of it traces downhill. At this location, you're probably pretty close to the main vent. The small hills you see to the east and south appear to be lava domes that probably grew after the eruption that removed the northeast flank of the volcano.

Mt. Taylor summit, with Gooseberry Trail climbing the hillside.

For backpackers, this would be a great place to set up camp. There must be beautiful displays of stars at night, along with the bellowing of elk and, during the day, an opportunity for some day-hikes. Another trail leads down the hill to the east, probably to the creek that drains the crater. And a hike to the lookout tower would offer great views to the northeast and the full extent of the volcanic field, including the many volcanic necks within the field. Mt. Taylor is not a busy place. There are few hikers, an occasional vehicle headed to the La Mosca Lookout and maybe more bear and elk than people. The company you'll keep at the top will be mostly noisy ravens that seem to follow you along the rim. But above all, the quiet and peace at the top, and the beautiful scenery, contrasts with what must have been a grand display of violence just a few million years ago. There's tremendous energy at the summit and you'll sense it as you relax and feel the earth.

Other Points of Interest (including archaeological): Aside from the geology, this area of New Mexico is well known for its historic and prehistoric significance. Archaeologists know that the original Native Americans, the Paleo-Indians, arrived in this area of the New World around 11,000 years ago. Some of the oldest known humans in North America populated the Great Plains, swampy at the time, and migrated to other areas as resources were depleted— first the Clovis people appeared about 11,000 years ago and then the Folsom people about 10,000 years ago. It is believed they took one of two routes to get to North America. First of all, the general consensus is that they were following the woolly mammoths and bison, their main source of food and clothing. The Clovis people are associated with mammoths and the Folsom people with bison. Some have postulated that they took advantage of land and ice bridges from western Europe, using primitive boats of skin. Geologists do know that the Appalachian Mountains once extended from North America to Greenland and then over to the British Isles. Maybe there was enough land and ice to accomplish such a journey. To add to their theory, some scientists associate paleolithic man in North America with a similar branch of early man in Europe. The most probable route however was the Bering Strait land bridge from Asia to Alaska and down into the center of the continent. Although Clovis and Folsom artifacts have been found scattered all over the lower 48 states, it was in the then swampy Great Plains, specifically eastern New Mexico, where they were associated with the mammoths and bison, allowing archaeologists to piece together their means of survival. Through spear points found in mammoths and bison, the presence of prehistoric man in the New World was established at the end of the Ice Age. When the ice sheets melted, the land bridge probably submerged cutting off the flow of humans. But by then they were here and would in time collide with the Europeans coming from Spain.

Eventually migrating from the northern plains, the early native cultures, predominately the Anasazi, populated the Four Corners area. Mesa Verde National Park is one of the most comprehensive sites in the southwest and reports the early history of the Anasazi before they abandoned the Four Corners.

As natural resources were depleted, they moved south, through Chaco Canyon, then into Bandelier. Finally they settled along the Rio Grande River valley where resources were plentiful. Their migratory habits changed to a more sedentary life style, just in time to witness Spain's exploration of the New World. In the mid-1500s, first Coronado then other Conquistadors moved north from Central America to find resources—one in particular, gold, being important in the Old World. They encountered this area of northwest New Mexico and named it El Malpais (the badlands). Horses and wagons didn't do well on the irregular surface of basalt flows. The Zuni-Acoma trail is one ancient route known to both Native Peoples and the Spaniards. West of El Malpais, on Route 53, El Morro National Monument presents a short hike to a wall of rock, actually a huge cliff with a pool of water at the base. It's pretty obvious the early Spaniards stopped here for water. Their names and dates are inscribed all over the wall. If you're into history, stop at the Northwest New Mexico Visitor Center, just off Interstate 40, exit 85. Our purposes though are volcanic and Arizona is the next stop.

On the Road to the Next Hike

There are a number of ways to enter Arizona from New Mexico. US 64 through Farmington in the northwest corner of New Mexico presents Shiprock Mountain, a volcanic neck with lava feeder dikes radiating outward like the spokes of a wheel. A sacred mountain to the Native Peoples and a source of study for geologists, it's a textbook example of the innards of a large eroded volcano. US 64 enters Arizona near the center of the Colorado Plateau, at the Four Corners—the only point in the United States common to the corners of four states. At the base of the Colorado Plateau, which in places is up to 25 miles thick, lies old twisted rock that can best be seen at the bottom of the Grand Canyon. This rock represents the remains of micro-continents and volcanic islands that slammed into the southwest corner of the young North American tectonic plate about 2 billion years ago. As the pieces of land sailed into North America, they were crushed and mangled against the young plate. Magma from the mantle welled up during these collisions and filled in fractures and crevices, in time cementing everything together. In this manner, the southwest grew outward. Also evident in the Colorado Plateau strata, above the ancient basement, are fossil and rock remains that tell geologists this section of the growing North American plate was located near the equator and as the continental plate drifted northward it covered a few thousand miles twisting into its current position. About the same time the entire Colorado Plateau area dropped one to two miles into a deep basin. Eroded rocks from the original Mogollon (aka Central) Highlands to the south were carried by streams to parts of the plateau. Then, about 70 million years ago, the plateau started to rise and finished its two-mile uplift recently in geologic time. The Colorado River then cut into the plateau only within the last few million years. The Colorado Plateau is so well preserved because of weather, or should we say the lack of it. Precipitation that brings erosion is limited to the higher elevations on the plateau. Water from the Pacific Ocean is cut off by the Sierra Nevada Range—it's called the Rain Shadow. The plateau country only gets precipitation during the winter from storms that can bypass the Sierra to the northwest and in the summer, monsoon rains come up from the Gulf of Mexico. The lack of rain helps to preserve the rock but when it does rain plateaus are carved, then smoothed by the constant winds.

Another route, Interstate 40, enters Arizona at the southeastern edge of the Colorado Plateau. Painted Desert and Petrified Forest national monuments tell wonderful stories of the Mesozoic time on the plateau, where streams, lakes and swamps collected the bones of dinosaurs for almost 200 million years. As the interstate approaches Holbrook, dinosaurs surround the road—one next to a school bus and another smiling with someone's leg hanging out like a loose cigar. Interstate 40 can get boring at times but this section is a laugh a mile. Another entry point is via US 60 to Springerville, the southeastern terminus of the Jemez Lineament. The highway travels through the former Mogollon Highlands that once towered over the Colorado Plateau and sent stream-laden sediments north to New Mexico, Colorado and Utah. The sediments piled high, were buried by other sediments, and are now known as the Morrison Formation—loaded with uranium and the largest of dinosaur bones from the Jurassic and Cretaceous Periods. Farther to the south you can enter Arizona on Interstate 10. This area of the southwest is called the Basin and Range Province and there's quite a story to be told. Read John McPhee's *Basin and Range* and you'll want to take the interstate all the way to California.

Arizona is composed of three geologic provinces. To the north lies the Colorado Plateau that covers almost 1/3 of the state. Most of the southern part of the state is the Basin and Range Province. In the middle lies the Transition Zone, also called the Mogollon or Central Highlands, which at one time in the geologic past were so high they dominated the landscape of Arizona and parts of New Mexico. Now they're a series of eroded plateaus, mountains and intermediary basins that mark the transition from the great plateau to the north to the basins and ranges of the south. Basin and Range mountain building had much to do with shaping Arizona and bringing up the copper, silver and gold deposits that created riches and wonderful ghost towns like Tombstone.

My favorite approach into Arizona from New Mexico is on US 180, which skirts the western edge of the Gila National Forest, within which is the most remote spot in New Mexico. It is also the site of many large calderas. The town of Glenwood is a great place to stay or camp north of Glenwood. The Catwalk Recreation Site provides a beautiful trail into the Gila Wilderness and plenty of mining history, some of it located in the town of Mogollon. I'd recommend bringing a gold pan. Above all else, it is one of the most beautiful (and least known to tourists) hiking locations in New Mexico. One can spend months there and never see the same trail twice. But you might see a wolf.

6

Hiking Arizona's Volcanoes and the Yellowstone Caldera

Hike: Chiricahua National Monument

Great trails, bizarre volcanic rock formations and an entirely different look at a violent eruption.

Location: Southeast Arizona—Interstate 10 to Wilcox, south on Route 186 to Route 181 to the monument entrance. Other approaches are from Portal, AZ off Route 80 on Pinery Canyon Road, a long winding dirt road. The monument is located at the north corner of the Chiricahua Mountains and Coronado National Forest. Camping is allowed anywhere in the national forest. There is one campground within the monument available all year on a first-come, first-served fee basis. The first two hikes are within the monument. To reach the third hike trailhead—before entering the monument on Route 181, take forest service road FR 42 on Pinery Canyon Road for about 12 miles to FR 42D to the Rustler Park Campground. The trailhead is on the west side of the campground. The forest service roads may not be passable in the winter. Contact the Douglas Ranger District office at 520-364-3468 for road conditions.

Hike Type and Length: Take your choice from three recommended hikes. The first is to Sugarloaf Mountain and is the shortest but by far the most informative in terms of geology. The second hike, to Heart of Rocks, is much longer and strenuous but takes you to the heart of the weirdest volcanic formations in the park or anywhere else for that matter. The third hike is outside the park, at the higher elevations of the Chiricahua Mountains and can be as long or short as you like.

    1) Sugarloaf Mountain is two miles roundtrip uphill going, downhill returning. Take this hike if you want to learn more about the geology of this area of the southwest and the effects of violent Plinian eruptions. The summit presents great views and an exhibit that graphically displays the actual location of the volcano and caldera.

    2) Heart of Rocks can be approached via a few different trails. Consult the Chiricahua Official Map and Guide, which you'll receive upon entering the park. My favorite approach is from Massai Point, past Inspiration Point, at a little over 8 miles roundtrip. The trail has some ups and downs but the effort is in the length versus elevation changes. Bring your camera. This route is more scenic than educational, with the many weird rock formations.

    3) Crest Trail #270 is a Coronado National Forest trail, with a number of interesting spur trails that follow the central spine of the range. This trail is ideal for backpacking or camp at the Rustler Park Campground and take day-hikes. The trail begins in the national forest and eventually enters the Chiricahua Wilderness. Take this trail if you want peace and quite, freedom to go anywhere and are into birding. The east side of the Chiricahuas is a prime birding location as many species fly north from the Sierra Madres in Mexico during the warmer months.

    One interesting location on the drive in is the Faraway Ranch site, just after entering the monument grounds. It is both an historic and geologic site. During early eruptions before the main event, lava flows covered this area. A number of vents oozed highly viscous rhyolite lava. As you look at the ledges on the north side of and above the level of the parking lot, a geologic feature called flow ramps stand out like cliffs. Magma oozed up through the vent, spilled out onto the land and began to harden. As more oozed out, it flowed over the top of the previous batch forming flow ramps—like stairs stepping down the mountain, one flow on top of another. On the hill north of the parking lot they appear as light brown rounded (eroded) outcrops.

Elevation: At the hike locations in the monument the trails are generally around 7,000 feet give or take a few hundred feet. Although the Heart of

Rocks hike has a significant elevation change (not quite 1,000 feet), depending on which trail you take to get there. The Crest Trail follows the highest ridge that forms the backbone of the Chiricahuas where elevations are anywhere from 8,000 to over 9,000 feet.

Precautions: Sugarloaf Mountain is an easy stroll. Bring water and prepare for summer monsoon storms during July and August. The walk to Heart of Rocks is a long 8 miles roundtrip. Expect to spend most of the day on the hike. Prepare appropriately for such a long and strenuous hike. As for the Crest Trail, it's in national forest and wilderness. The last two times I was at the trailhead in Rustler Park there was no one in the campground. It is remote. This hike has elevation changes of a thousand feet or more depending on where you go. Also, note the Beware of Bear signs at the campground. Remember to stow your trash. And make noise as you're hiking to warn bears of your approach. For all hikes, check the Visitor Center or National Forest Service office for maps and trail conditions.

Planning Information: The Douglas Ranger District of Coronado National Forest can be reached at 520-364-3468. Contact the district, if you're hiking anywhere in the national forest, for conditions (fire, water, roads, etc.). Check out the monument on the web at:
    http://www.nps.gov/chir/
Or, call the Chiricahua National Monument Visitor Center at 520-824-3560. Or, check out Arizona's Volcanic past at:
    http://vulcan.wr.usgs.gov/LivingWith/VolcanicPast/Places/volcanic_past_arizona.html

Geologic Setting: Arizona's geologic beginnings have some similarities to New Mexico's given that they both underwent the same tectonic construction process while volcanism marched across both states as though it was staged. Arizona's formative years however are a bit more interesting and bizarre. To put it bluntly, Arizona was like a parked car that couldn't get out of a tight parking space. And as it banged back and forth to force it's way out, pieces of the other cars attached to Arizona's bumpers until it grew in size to its current shape and location. The future state of Arizona just couldn't get out of its own way!

About 2.5 billion years ago the first large continents of the globe began to appear, surrounded by mostly shallow seas. Then around 2 billion years ago a chunk of the young and much smaller North American continent broke off from what is now Wyoming and started traveling south into open ocean. It changed course and sailed back piling up the sea floor like a snowplow. Salt Lake City was probably part of the muck. A subduction zone was created in this deep ocean environment spawning volcanoes that were responsible for much of Arizona's early crust, which was still deep underwater. An island arc of volcanoes was formed at a distance from the shores of Wyoming. Geologists know about this activity from rock found in the Bradshaw Mountains around Prescott, Arizona. The earlier subduction zone was swallowed under an oceanic plate and another was created pointing in the other direction. Young Arizona was headed back out to sea. As it traveled it scooped up crust from the ocean's floor and volcanoes piled lava on top. Deep under the oceanic crust large plutons of magma formed and were eventually exposed as granite in north and central Arizona. Enough lava came out of the ocean's crust that land eventually appeared above the water line. The behavior and appearance was similar to today's Japan, which is situated along a huge arc of subduction. Over millions of years, Arizona's basement footings were formed—the oldest rock being in the northwest part of the state with progressively younger rock to the south. After a half-billion years of sailing back and forth, Arizona attached itself to the southwestern edge of the continent, along with parts of Utah, Colorado and New Mexico. By about 1.5 billion years ago, Arizona and New Mexico were a part of the North American continent which, a few million years later, lay within a huge continental mass—geologists call it Pangea 1 (the first Pangea). This was the first major event that affected Arizona, the results of which are graphically displayed at the bottom of the Grand Canyon and on the flanks of Dos Cabezas (two heads) Mountain north of Chiricahua National Monument.

    The Age of Fishes (Paleozoic Era) came and went, piling thousands of feet of marine sediment and fossils on Arizona—also well displayed at the Grand Canyon. The Age of Reptiles (Mesozoic Era) arrived; the results are reported on the Colorado Plateau in Utah, northeast Arizona and northwest New Mexico. The next major event to affect Arizona was the Laramide Orogeny. As the dinosaurs of the Jurassic and Cretaceous Periods grew larger, and the North American plate sailed west, a great collision occurred with the Pacific Ocean plate, which dove under the continent. Volcanoes erupted along the young coastline and inland the crust was compressed by the plate battle. Originally dipping deeply under the continental crust into the mantle, the oceanic slab flattened, rose up from its steep angle and headed inland. As it progressed in an easterly direction it penetrated the mantle farther into the interior, under Arizona then New Mexico. And as the oceanic plate rose to an almost horizontal position under the continent, the crust of Arizona and New Mexico was compressed by the grinding battle of the two plates. Mountains rose. The Western Cordillera, of which the Rockies are a part, were squeezed up like someone pushing a rug against a wall. Around 50 million years ago, soon after the extinction of the dinosaurs, the mountain building ended and a long period of erosion occurred. Estimates point to something more than 20,000 feet of rock was deroofed from the Rockies. With no volcanoes to report in the middle of the Eocene Epoch, the brief lull was termed the Eocene Magma Gap. The stillness must have been eerie, as the only sound may have been rocks tumbling off mountains, streams carrying the sediment to deep basins and mammals flourishing. The stage was set for the Mid-Tertiary Orogeny and the volcanic chaos that created the Chiricahua National Monument. It is said there were no volcanic eruptions recorded by man that even come close to what happened after the earth quieted and the mantle had an opportunity to get back into the action during the Mid-Tertiary Orogeny.

Geologists believe that the oceanic plate once again started to dip steeply into the mantle. As the angle increased, volcanism was reinitiated but this time it progressed to the west. As the plate left its horizontal position under Arizona and New Mexico and punctured the mantle westward, great volumes of magma rose to the surface. About 35 million years ago all hell broke loose, starting first in New Mexico. Then as the oceanic plate dipped deeper into the mantle its focus of heat moved under Arizona. It is possible that the movement of the plate also caused the crust to thin, bringing the mantle closer to the surface. Geologists know that Rio Grande rifting began at this time so extension of the crust started in New Mexico and may have proceeded west along with the dipping plate. They also believe the crust may have been stretched fifty to a hundred percent. If you were to drive west on Interstate 10 from Las Cruces, New Mexico across the Arizona line you'd be following the heat source miles down in the mantle where the now ancient oceanic crust was still being consumed in the furnace. Great volumes of magma were forming a few miles underground. One such magma chamber grew just south of where the Chiricahua Monument is today. Imagine yourself there. It's 27 million years ago, a great blast was about to make the eruptions at Mount St. Helens look like a firecracker.

Just a few miles below the surface, gas-charged magma loaded with water vapor and carbon dioxide stressed the earth above to its crustal limits. Finally the roof of the chamber fractured the hard rock crust above. Over a hundred cubic miles of magma blew through the ground sending gas, ash, pumice and rock fragments thousands of feet into the air. What remained within the eruption cloud when it fell back to earth covered everything like a burning blanket—a big blanket that smothered over a thousand square miles. Mount St. Helens volcanic production was less than a tenth of that. The magma chamber, having ejected such a large volume of magma and gas, collapsed inward to create a caldera (the Turkey Creek Caldera) about the size of Valles Caldera in New Mexico. The hole in the earth was over a mile deep and continued to eject gas and ash from ring fractures.

With most Plinian eruptions that produce a caldera, the lower part of the magma chamber remains active with magma not yet vented after the collapse. Pyroclastic flows where blown down the mountain at hundreds of miles an hour. As the ash and pumice settled and fused, a hard welded volcanic tuff formed. Geologists believe that the monument area was once a valley that filled to a depth of 1,600 feet of hardened ash and pumice. The rock composition, high in silica, is mostly rhyolite and the name of the entire formation that filled the valley is Rhyolite Canyon Tuff. Ring fractures around the caldera produced lava domes while in the caldera itself a resurgent dome formed, surrounded by a moat. At Valles Caldera in New Mexico these features can be seen from the main road. At Chiricahua they aren't that obvious unless you take the Sugarloaf Mountain hike. One of the last events occurred after the magma chamber took a rest. The bottom of the chamber still contained magma composed of dacite. With much less gas and a bit more fluid than rhyolite magma, lava flows began. These flows filled the caldera and flowed out around the countryside covering some of the ash that had already hardened to tuff. As it flowed to the north it filled a valley of solid tuff. When the tuff eroded away over millions of years, the harder dacite lava flows remained. As we've seen at Valles Caldera, what was once a valley is now standing above all else as the old lava flows. At the Chiricahuas, the former valley and now a mountain is the location for our first hike, Sugarloaf Mountain.

The Turkey Creek volcano and caldera must have appeared similar to the Valles Caldera in New Mexico. However, 15 million years ago the Basin and Range Orogeny changed things. The oceanic slab and the spreading center that pushed the slab under the continent had been swallowed in the deep trench that marked the subduction zone. The oceanic slab under North America was consumed but the Pacific plate was still active. With the subducted slab broken off, the plate was now free to change direction, which it did as it began its move northward along the coast. This movement north allowed the North American plate to change direction southward along the coast. Now the two plates were sliding by each other. The result was earthquakes along the coast, along the San Andreas and other faults. And as the plates slide in opposite directions, tension at the plate boundary stretched the crust inland to accommodate the movement. The stretching crust facilitated the block faulting of the Basin and Range Province from southern New Mexico all the way to Nevada north to Idaho. Stretch the earth and large crustal blocks fall, while blocks on each side of the new basin rise to form mountains. This is what happened to the Turkey Creek Caldera. As you hike in the monument at higher elevations, you'll notice that the entire mountain range has a large valley (basin) on each side. Down in those basins are parts of the volcano. The block faulting tore the mountain apart—split it into parts that went in different directions. One section of the volcano entered the basin, the other rose above it all. Driving through southern Arizona, you'll notice mountains that stand out by themselves alone with basins on each side. The Native People called the mountains "sky islands". To geologists it's basin, range, basin, range, on and on. The Valles Caldera was not affected by this block faulting event because the caldera was created long after the Basin and Range Orogeny. The crustal stretching has diminished in most areas of Arizona and New Mexico. But in Nevada, it continues. Las Vegas may some day be the helm of a large crustal ship heading out into the Pacific Ocean. For gamblers, a perfect ocean-going cruise! At the top of Sugarloaf Mountain, our first hike, the view south is textbook tectonics. Basin and Range mountain building preserved Sugarloaf as a window into the behavior of the Turkey Creek Volcano.

Strange rock formations of the Chiricahuas.

Hike Guide: Again, there are three hikes. Sugarloaf Mountain is the most informative in terms of geology, with great views. Heart of Rocks is the most photographic and a wonderful walk. The Crest Trail takes the hiker along the former rim of the volcano but it won't be noticeable. What the hiker will notice are the beautiful meadows, pine forests and alpine features of the higher elevations of the Chiricahua Range. And more so, the serenity of these sky islands above all else that have no likeness in that human world below.

Sugarloaf Mountain:

The trailhead is almost 5 miles from the monument campground. Follow the signs for the Echo Canyon and Sugarloaf Mountain parking area to the right as you approach Massai Point. The two mile roundtrip starts at almost 7,000 feet and climbs to the forest service lookout tower at about 7,300 feet. Elevation change is almost 400 feet.

As you start hiking, notice the Rhyolite Canyon Tuff rock formations on the left. The trail loops around the mountain and provides a good look at the many layers of ash, pumice and other volcanic bits that piled up and solidified to tuff. Geologists see evidence of three distinctive episodes of eruption—one right after the other. The different cycles are separated by horizontal lines you may see along the trail. The lines mark a cessation of eruption, followed by some fusing and hardening of the tuff, then another episode. Geologists also mark the different episodes by light colored (almost white) beds separating the darker (light brown to gray) beds of Rhyolite Canyon Tuff. The lighter beds, seen in certain areas along the base of the trail, are pyroclastic base surge deposits or surge beds which are lateral gas-filled blasts of pumice and ash driven down the volcano's flanks in a ground-hugging cloud. These beds are looser than the tightly welded tuff and mark boundaries between the three eruptions that produced the 1,600 feet of Rhyolite Canyon Tuff.

During the hike, look for these lighter colored beds along the trail on the left at the base of tuff ledges. And in the tuff, look for elongated streaks of pumice. The rhyolite tuff here is composed of various minerals, such as quartz and feldspar, along with volcanic glass and pumice flakes that stretch or are squeezed as the ash settles and is pressured from above. These white streaks are called fiamme. We've seen fiamme on the creek trail at Valles Caldera although there they were dark pumice flakes. We've also seen that pumice is the result of rhyolitic magma that fills with gas at the top of the magma chamber. This froth is charged with so much gas that initial eruptions are explosive. As it is thrown in the air during eruption, the froth is still loaded with gas bubbles. When it lands, the hardened rock is so packed with holes it floats. In the tuff formations along the trail, the pumice never had the chance to form floating rocks. The eruptions shattered everything to small flakes and crystals.

We know that rhyolite is rock of the same chemical and mineral composition of granite. Granite solidifies deep underground where the slow cooling allows large crystals to grow in the rock. When granitic magma makes it to the surface and flows as lava, it solidifies faster preventing large minerals from forming. When the frothy mixture begins to solidify in flight during eruptions, which is very fast, pumice rocks are the result. Or rhyolitic lava may cool quickly at the front or base of lava flows. Black volcanic glass called obsidian is the result. Same mineral composition but the speed of cooling affects its appearance. Here, nothing in the magma had a chance because it was violently shattered by the eruption. As you hike the trail, take a break and picture the eruption that sent great ash and gas clouds high in the air. The weight of the clouds eventually overcame the gas pressure that suspended them, causing these glowing clouds (also known as Nuee Ardente, a French term) to fall along the flanks of the volcano and rush downhill like a burning avalanche at hundreds of miles an hour. If the mountain had trees they were either uprooted or burned and as the super-hot ash piled up it was fused by the heat to the tuff cliffs surrounding the trail. As the ash accumulated, steam and gas still suspended in the ash escaped creating tubes or vents in the pile. Called fossil fumaroles, they are evident along the trail as hollowed out pipes or wavy holes in the beds of tuff.

As you approach the summit you'll be able to see the large columnar, jointed tuff formations surrounding the mountain. After the eruptions, the cooled tuff contracted (compressed) creating joints or fractures that run vertically and horizontally across the beds. Over time, particularly during the Ice Ages, water seeped into the cracks and as it froze, then thawed, it pried the cracks open. Then in more recent time, rain, snow, freezing and melting added to the fractures while wind born sand and dust smoothed the surfaces of the beds. Eventually the crisscross pattern of joints eroded further into sculpted blocks that are now part of the strange formations throughout the monument.

At the summit, look around for the dark gray dacite rocks. Some have holes, vesicles, that are filled with minerals. The dacite lava flow solidified, gas escaped creating holes, then mineral laden fluids filled the holes creating some beautiful crystals. Some dacite on the mountain contains a glassy mineral called chalcedony. Again, the dacite lava flows occurred after the Plinian violence died down. There were some minor flows and eruptive activity after the caldera filled with lava and ash. We've seen similar action at Valles Caldera. The eruption begins, the magma chamber collapses, ring fractures around the rim allow more magma and ash to vent creating lava domes and piling more lava and ash inside the crater, filling the moat. In the middle of it all, the magma swelling in the chamber below is doming the earth, forming a resurgent dome. These Plinian, caldera-forming events are classic and almost predictable. If you can call such activity predictable. You're standing on a mountain that was once a valley filled with lava. And the mountain is just a small, eroded reminder of what a volcano can do to the landscape.

Finally, on the south side of Sugarloaf you'll find a graphic display board that outlines the actual caldera in the Chiricahuas. The original caldera was torn apart by Basin and Range block faulting. But if you look hard enough, you can picture the outline of what it must have looked like. The higher elevations of the Chiricahua Mountains to the south of the monument mark sections of the original crater. The tallest peaks sit on the rim the way the peaks of Mt. Taylor dotted its crater. If you take the Crest Trail hike, you'll be there on the ancient rim.

Heart of Rocks:

This hike will consume the good part of a day because of its length and the time you'll spend staring at the strange rock formations. Some of the formations have names: Punch & Judy, Duck on a Rock, Big Balanced Rock and many more. Just think of Duck on a Rock—it really is Duck on a Rock! The recommended approach is to park at Massai Point, the end of the road at 6,870 feet. Start hiking through the Nature Trail and pick up the trail to Inspiration Point, which is a little over two miles away. At Inspiration Point, you can walk out to the point, about a half-mile, or continue on the trail toward the Heart of Rocks Loop, a little over a mile. The loop itself is about a mile long. One way the total hike is a bit over 4 miles. Heart of Rocks is at about 7,000 feet but there are ups and downs along the trail so the elevation change varies quite a bit during the hike. Many of the rock features you've seen at Sugarloaf Mountain are evident along this trail but not as obvious as at Sugarloaf. Again, this trail is a hiker's trail, fairly long but well worth the effort for its great views and rock formations. There are other approaches to Heart of Rocks. One is directly from the Visitor Center and about the same length. And from Massai Point, spur trails like Hailstone and Echo Canyon eventually hook up with the Sarah Deming Canyon trail to Heart of Rocks. Pick up a map at the visitor center and take your choice. All in all, the Massai Point approach has the most to offer. Bring plenty of water, lunch or a snack and at least one roll of film.

Balanced Rock.

Crest Trail # 270:
First of all, be sure to check with the Forest Service in Douglas for road and trail conditions. Forest Service Road 42 (dirt and gravel) is just outside the entrance to the national monument. The road takes you over some winding switch-backs through Pinery Canyon for about 12 miles. Then a spur road, #42D (right) takes you 2 miles to the Rustler Park Campground. I'd definitely recommend camping or backpacking because there are many day-hike opportunities on the Crest Trail. If you want to camp, you have the established campground, with tables, cooking grates and bathrooms. Or, camping is allowed anywhere in the national forest unless there are restrictions. Many people

camp at Rustler Park in the summer when school's out. I prefer spring or fall. Fall is best for color when the deciduous trees are changing, particularly along stream beds or the quaking aspen at the highest elevations. On the other hand, if you're a birder spring is a good time because the birds are migrating north from Mexico and the sky islands are their preferred roadside rests. You may even see the Elegant Trogon, a parrot like bird that sounds like a porpoise.

The Crest Trail is more than just a trail. There are many connecting trails that come up from the valleys on each side of the ridge the trail follows. You'll be hiking along the spine of the Chiricahuas with many opportunities for side trails; most are in the Chiricahua Wilderness. The Forest Service has trail maps and guides. You can expect to hike through beautiful meadows and, depending on the time of year and the winter snows, the display of wildflowers is magnificent.

As for the geology of the area, it is more diverse at the top. First of all, the highest peaks sit on the rim of the ancient caldera. As you start hiking south, Ida Peak is behind you and in front are Flys Peak, Chiricahua Peak and Monte Vista Peak, all mark the east side of the caldera. This side of the mountain was faulted up during the Basin and Range Orogeny. At Monte Vista Peak, the circular caldera turns west and runs all the way into the valley west of the mountains (Sulphur Springs Valley). That part of the split caldera dropped into the basin. It then loops back north and east by Fife Peak and back to Ida. It's hard to believe the massive block faulting that broke this huge volcano in half but it happened in the Chiricahuas and all across the west to Nevada, where it's still active. Also, because of the block faulting that raised this section of the volcano the trail follows, many interesting rocks have been brought up along faults that expose not only the recent volcanic rocks of the monument but also some of the earlier lava flows and deposits that occurred long before the caldera activity. The volcanic episodes go back about 35 million years. Long before volcanism reigned in this area of the southwest, a half-billion years of deposits from the Mesozoic and Paleozoic Eras were piled in layers, now sitting below the volcanic debris. Some of it has been brought up by the faults. Certain areas of the Chiricahuas have limestone, with ancient sea creature fossils, exposed along faults. When you hike these mountains outside the monument, expect to find anything and everything. This was also the home of the Apache. So there's much history buried in the range. It helps to get off the trail at times. You never know what you'll find.

Other Points of Interest: For starters, Rockhound State Park is just across the border near Deming, New Mexico. It's the only park I know where they encourage hikers to pick up rock and mineral samples. The mountains in that location were born in the volcanic frenzy that created the Chiricahuas. There are some interesting mineral crystals located in the volcanic outcrops. You can hike on-trail or off-trail, cross-country, up washes, anywhere erosion might have exposed some interesting crystals.

In Arizona, Route 186 down from Wilcox and Interstate 10 has some interesting history and geology. Wilcox Playa can be seen from the interstate and Route 186 cuts through the east corner of the former lake. In Basin and Range country, lakes have no outlet to the sea, which in this area is mostly to the Gulf of Mexico or Gulf of California. In these block faulted flats, water coming off the mountains accumulates in the lakes and then dries up, leaving many evaporite minerals, like halite (salt). In this manner, the Great Salt Lake in Utah formed, with no outlet to the sea. During the Ice Ages, the playa, then a lake (Lake Cochise), was surrounded by vegetation and tall trees. It was a lush, swampy, watering hole where horses, even camels roamed. Camel fossils have been found in and around the former lake. Continue down Route 186 and there's a cutoff for historic Fort Bowie. Continuing on 186 the road cuts through the town of Dos Cabezas, an old mining community. This is rockhound country; you can see it in some of the house structures along the road.

Southeast of Dos Cabezas, between highway mileposts 346 and 347, there's an interesting geologic feature. If you watch both sides of the road, beyond the wire fence that parallels the road, you should notice large blocks of rock that sit at strange angles as though someone broke them off a mountain and dropped them like rolling dice. These blocks tell an interesting story. When Arizona was forming, about 1.5 billion years ago, it finally attached itself to the southwest edge of the young North American continent. Because of the convergence of young Arizona with the larger North American continent, volumes of magma were generated deep underground, mostly under the sea. This magma circulated into the mess of rocks and muck from the collision of the plates. It solidified to granite and stitched the smaller plate to the larger continent. Arizona was then hard-attached to North America. The problem for geologists in this location, as in the bottom of the Grand Canyon, is that there is no rock exposed to present what happened over the next half-billion years (or more) after the stitching of the plates. There is evidence along the road of Paleozoic Era rock dating to a little over 500 million years of age. Pull over along the road and search for these large blocks thrown like dice on both sides. If you look closely, you'll see part of the angular boulders are composed of conglomerate, a mixture of large to small rocks cemented together. The conglomerate part of the boulders is a fusion of mostly rounded rocks of all sizes. These rocks accumulated with sand and mud at the beginning of the Age of Fishes along rivers and beaches. Then, the conglomerate pile was cemented together in layers on top of what was below, which is the other part of the roadside angular boulders—the smooth gray rock that, on closer inspection, displays the large mineral crystals common in granite. This is the granite that stitched the continent together. It laid deep underground for almost a billion years until it was exposed by erosion and the Paleozoic Era stream and beach deposits accumulated on top. Then over many millions of years it lay there, hardened together in mountains and recently broken up and tossed alongside the road. The imaginary dividing line between the 1.4 billion year old granite and the 500 million year old conglomerate is called an Unconformity by geologists. It marks a time of no geologic record, either a time of great erosion, or no deposition, or both. The mind may have a hard time grasping all this but the road has proof the geologist can't ignore. This is one beauty of an Unconformity!

There are many more places to visit in southern Arizona. I would recommend a trip to Sierra Vista, which is due west of the Chiricahuas. If you go through Douglas on the border with Mexico, then through Bisbee, you'll have a chance to see one of the largest, deepest open pit mines in the world. It produced mostly copper. Where there's copper there's other mineral deposits and so gold and silver have been found in this area which is dotted with ghost towns. South of Sierra Vista, the Nature Conservancy's Ramsey Canyon Preserve sits hidden in a large cut in the Huachuca Mountains. This is probably the best birding spot in the southwest. People come from around the world, in the spring, to see what flies up from the Sierra Madre in Mexico. Coronado National Monument is just south and between Coronado and Ramsey Canyon are some of the most beautiful hiking trails in the southwest. Trails connect both the monument and the conservancy through the once volcanic Huachuca Mountains—another caldera that was broken up by Basin and Range. During my last hike in Ramsey Canyon, on a ridge rightfully named Bear Saddle, my wife and I walked past one of the largest bears I had ever seen in the wild or in a zoo. I'm 6'2" and about 200 pounds. The bear was easily twice my weight and I'm glad to say I didn't have an opportunity to measure its height. Maybe it was the proximity, about 15 feet away from us in a creek bed, that made it look so big. It was honey brown and faced away from the trail. Once I saw it I made noise but figured it was too late, I'd probably startled it into attack mode. This monster turned its head, looked at us for a few seconds that actually felt like years and then turned back to his digging for roots in the stream bed. He basically ignored us, too insignificant, not enough meat on both of us or just not hungry enough to bother. We gratefully and quietly moved down the trail and all I remember, more so than fear, was the absolute feeling of awe for such an animal with so little concern for the two of us. I continue to be grateful for that poor attitude!

On the Road to the Next Hike

Arizona was most affected by two orogenies or mountain building events. First, the Laramide Orogeny (80 to 50 million years ago) brought volcanism and compression of the crust to most of the North American west. The Pacific plate's movement back and forth under the continent and into the mantle brought up magma and squeezed the crust inland. Volcanoes fired up and mountains rose. Then the Basin and Range Orogeny began with the rifting of the Rio Grande River Valley in New Mexico about 25 million years ago and continued in Arizona from 15 to 8 million years ago and is still stretching the crust in Nevada. Even New Mexico may some day split in half along its famous river valley. In the Basin and Range Province, the crust was and is spreading, a result of the action of the transform plate boundary along the coast. As portions of the Pacific plate move north and the still westward moving North American plate slides in a southerly direction at the plate contact along the west coast beaches, crustal stretching continues. These two events affected Arizona the most through recent geologic time.

If you have time, drive through southern Arizona and notice the sky islands, the mountains that seem to line up in a north-south direction. Separating them are the basins that capture debris shed from the mountains along with water that runs off during heavy rains. The drive through Bisbee to Sierra Vista and then north to Tucson presents Arizona's Basin and Range configuration at its best. As Interstate 10 approaches Phoenix, the Superstition Mountains appear to the east. Then within the Phoenix city limits, South Mountain, North Mountain, Squaw Peak, Camelback Mountain and others surround the valley, the basin. The eroded mountains are what remains of the former large blocks of crust of the Basin and Range Orogeny. One block once covered most of north Phoenix. What remains of that block are Squaw Peak and North Mountain, now eroded to separate structures. These two mountains present in their uplifted structures the early Precambrian Era basement of the valley. If you hike the trails through the Phoenix Mountain Preserve and climb to the summits, old twisted rock surrounds the trails. These billion year old rocks tell stories of the building of this area of Arizona—of island volcanoes, submarine vents that spewed mineralized water and basaltic lava onto the sea floor that was early Arizona. It all came together, hardened, changed from pressure and heat to metamorphic rock, now on the flanks of Squaw Peak and North Mountain. These mountains wouldn't be in full view if Basin and Range hadn't happened. One great block of crust came out of the ground like Rodan came out of the ocean. Erosion altered the scenery long before Interstate 10 and 17 were cut through Phoenix.

One possible hiking side-trip you may want to consider is to the Superstition Mountains, east of Phoenix. In my last book, I cover hiking in the Phoenix Mountain Preserve, the Superstitions and the Mazatzal Mountains north of the Superstitions. So for the sake of not repeating myself, I'll just mention that the Superstitions are well worth the visit. As part of the Mid-Tertiary Orogeny, large volcanoes created the rock of the Superstitions over of period 10 million years starting around 25 million years ago. Prior to the eruptions, the area of the Superstitions was one highly eroded flat surface. No Paleozoic or Mesozoic rock exists between the Precambrian basement under the range and the lava and ash flows of the volcanic event. In some creek beds in the Superstitions you'll find pieces of volcanic (mostly dacite) rock along with billion year old Pinal Schist, the same rock that forms the flanks of Dos Cabezas south of Wilcox. Geologists have mapped many calderas, craters and a large dome within the Superstition range. There are two very scenic hikes in the mountains to a huge volcanic neck, called Weavers Needle. You can take the trail through Peralta Canyon from the south or take the Dutchman's Trail from the north at the First Water Trailhead southeast toward the Needle. What makes the Superstitions attractive to the hiker also makes it attractive to the historian and the prospector. Weavers Needle has been implicated in the Lost Dutchman gold mine saga. There really isn't a mine. Gold was said to be transported there either by the Dutchman, a shadowy miner, in the 1800s or by Indians after killing off the Spaniards who enslaved them as workers digging for gold to be sent back to Spain. Some people still believe there's a cave, maybe close to Weavers Needle, that contains the cache of gold just waiting for someone to stumble up a remote wash, jump over a rattler and land in the gold-filled hole.

As Interstate 17 climbs out of the Phoenix valley into the Central Highlands, the geology changes. To the west of the highway are the Bradshaw Mountains, one of the best producers of gold, silver and copper. The hard metamorphic innards of these mountains were formed during the Precambrian Era. The ore deposits were injected as hot mineral-laden fluids, a byproduct of the magma that surged up from the mantle during the Laramide Orogeny. Basin and Range mountain building brought the veins into view for the ore rushes of the 1800s. Hike in the Bradshaws and you're libel to come across a miner panning for gold in one of the many creeks. After heavy rains, the washes fill with runoff and sediment that are carried into the larger tributary streams. That's where the prospectors like to concentrate their efforts. Back to the interstate, off to the east and another product of the Laramide Orogeny, are the Mazatzal Mountains (with great hiking trails). Soon, the highway completes its climb through the Transition Zone, the Central Highlands, and follows a gigantic fault down into the Verde Valley. The valley dropped during Basin and Range mountain building, cutting off large streams that fed debris from the Mogollon (Central) Highlands north to the Colorado Plateau, which itself was a basin. Then also during Basin and Range, the Colorado Plateau rose, cutting off the streams and started turning clockwise to accommodate the plate movement on the west coast. At the same time, the beautiful Sierra Nevada (snow mountains) came up out of the ground while the basin that marks its eastern limit dropped to offset the large block to its west. Even the Rocky Mountains, that had been buried up to their necks in volcanic debris from giant composite volcanoes in Oregon, Idaho and Nevada, jumped above the volcanic plain and shed enough material to expose their great peaks to the sky.

So when we discuss the volcanic activity and mountain building that occurred during the time the Chiricahuas and the Superstitions were formed, we aren't just woofing in the desert. The entire west poured out lava and ash while the mountain chains of the Cordillera came out of the ground like one great tectonic contest.

We're on Interstate 17 driving north and have just reached the southern edge of the Colorado Plateau south of Flagstaff, Arizona. Suddenly the road opens to a beautiful view of San Francisco Peaks, most of the time snow covered around its 12,000-foot peaks. The former stratovolcano is a recent event. When the Colorado Plateau was rising during the Basin and Range, this volcanic field was nowhere in site. But thanks to it being near our old friend the Jemez Lineament, this young volcano offers a challenging but wonderful hike to its summit.

Hike: San Francisco Mountain and Volcanic Field (including, Sunset Crater)

Another large and young volcanic field with a beautiful trail to the summit of the highest mountain in Arizona.

Location: The entire volcanic field is in northern Arizona. San Francisco Mountain, often referred to as San Francisco Peaks, sits northwest of Flagstaff. Follow US Route 180 northwest from Flagstaff toward the Grand Canyon (South Rim). On the way out of town, visit the Northern Arizona Museum for cultural and geological information about this area of the Colorado Plateau. About nine miles out of town US 180 comes out of the forest to a large meadow. Look for the road to the Arizona Snow Bowl (winter skiing area) on the right. Follow that paved road for about 6-1/2 miles to the first parking lot on the left at the main gate. The lower trailhead is at the other end of the parking lot where the trail crosses the large meadow and then enters the forest at the end of the meadow. If you want to save some hike time and elevation, and if the gate is open, continue through the gate to a gravel road, which ends at the upper lodge. Park on the left of the lot where the trail is located. Most people park on the right near the lodge. Follow the service road up through the woods where it will intersect a trail that crosses the meadow to the left and enters the woods. From the upper parking lot, through the meadow and into the forest, the trail covers about 1/2 mile before you reach the Kachina Peaks Wilderness sign, where you register before hiking. Whichever approach you take, you will eventually be hiking on the Humphreys Peak trail to the top.

Hike Type and Length: This is a very strenuous day-hike of about nine miles roundtrip. You can climb to the summit of Humphreys Peak at 12,633 or just go as far as a saddle (ridge) below the peaks at about 12,000 feet. You can see all you need at the saddle but if you want to peak-out, the climb to the summit adds about a mile to the roundtrip.

Elevation: The parking lot is at 9,000 feet plus. The saddle is at about 12,000 feet. So you'll climb 3,000 feet and cover about 9 to 10 miles. This is a very strenuous hike. It is not for the casual hiker. You have to be in shape and be able to deal with hiking at high altitudes. You could hike as far as your physical condition allows. There are periods where the hike is in deep alpine forest and other sections in meadows with beautiful views.

Precautions: Elevation change, distance and altitude are the major concerns. Also, the season is critical. July and August are monsoon season so you're almost guaranteed a thunderstorm before the end of the hike, usually noon to late afternoon. These storms are severe at this location. The best season is spring after the snow melt or fall, when the fall foliage along the trail, particularly the yellow quaking aspen, add gold to the mostly green flank of the mountain. Winter is out unless you're into skiing.

Planning Information: First of all, camping is allowed in most national forests. However, the Coconino National Forest Service requests that, at this location, you camp only on Forest Service Road 522 (Freidlein Prairie) about 2 miles up the main Snow Bowl road, on the right. There are designated camping areas along this road. Also, Flagstaff is a college town with many fine hotels and restaurants. There isn't much material available regarding San Francisco Mountain in terms of geology perhaps because geologists are still debating the source of magma that produced the volcano and whether the crater was blown out during an eruption or collapsed. There's some debate on the source of magma for the entire field. We know it came up from the mantle but why and how many magma chambers did it take? Regardless, here are the best sites for planning a trip to the area of San Francisco Mountain and Sunset Crater: Sunset Crater National Monument site:

http://www.nps.gov/sucr/
Coconino National Forest Ranger District site:
http://www.fs.fed.us/r3/coconino/
Other informational sites include Volcano World:
http://volcano.und.nodak.edu/vwdocs/Hopson/hopson2.html
Arizona Geologic Society - Arizona Volcanoes and Volcanics:
http://vulcan.wr.usgs.gov/Volcanoes/Arizona/framework.html

View of the peaks from the meadow with chair lift.

Geologic (and Archaeological) Setting: Humphreys Peak within San Francisco Mountain reaches 12,633 feet. It is the highest point in Arizona and stands on and above the Colorado Plateau as the summit of Arizona's signature composite volcano. The series of peaks that make up San Francisco Mountain once stood almost 16,000 feet above sea level. Volcanic activity in the San Francisco field began a few million years ago and climaxed only a few hundred thousand years ago when an eruption (and/or collapse) deroofed the mountain, removing almost 3,000 feet of the summit. Erosion took the rest. Considering that Mount St. Helens lost about 1,300 feet of its summit, the eruption that decapitated San Francisco Mountain was a big one. Geologists are still debating what affected the mountain the most: eruption, collapse or erosion? But there was obviously a catastrophic event. Strangely enough, whether eruption, collapse or both, the event took out the northeast flank of the mountain, in the same manner and direction that Mt. Taylor and Mount St. Helens erupted. There must be something about the northeast side of volcanoes in the west. After the eruption, glaciers stripped off some of the flank and created glacial landforms in the Inner Basin where the guts of the volcano are exposed. It was the time of the Pleistocene Epoch, the Great Ice Ages and eventually the appearance of man in North America. Although Native Peoples were too late to see the San Francisco Peaks eruption, they did experience the shower of cinders and burning lava flows from the Sunset Crater eruption, the last volcanic episode in Arizona. Geologists believe volcanism in the San Francisco Mountain volcanic field is far from over. They have counted over 400 cinder cones just around the base of San Francisco Mountain itself. Cinder cones rarely reawaken but volcanic fields, particularly young ones like this, still have magma sitting in chambers waiting for the next run to the surface.

The Pleistocene Epoch (of the Quaternary Period of the Cenozoic Era) marked an eventful age, highlighted by prehistoric-man's (and woman's) arrival in North America. Here are a few examples of what the Pleistocene Epoch brought us. There were some final episodes of uplift in Arizona and New Mexico, including the rise of the Colorado Plateau. Much erosion followed. Most of the volcanic activity involved basalt flows. The Colorado River had cut a deep canyon to the west eventually emptying into the Gulf of California. The process is called stream capture. Faulting along the coast created the gulf while erosion moved upstream toward where the Colorado River was cutting down and west, eventually meeting and capturing the great river, allowing it to run to the sea. The basalt lava flows continued all the time, damming the Colorado River more than once. Each time the river would cut through the hardened lava plateaus and dams in its longing to connect with the ocean. These basalt dams can be seen in parts of the western Grand Canyon, near Vulcans Throne. At the same time, sections of the Pacific Oceanic plate dove under Oregon and Washington, beginning the creation of the Cascade Range. Also in the Pleistocene, Italy's volcanic mountains, Vesuvius and Etna, rose up when parts of northern Africa dove under southern Europe. East of that, the southern edge of the Asian continent was battling with India at the time; the Himalayas rose at the convergent continental plate boundaries as crust was mashed between the two continents. The Himalayas are still rising as the northern edge of India slips under Tibet and India's bulk drives north pushing China out of its way. Geologists believe that since the beginning of the collision many millions of years ago, reaching a peak in the Pleistocene, India has shoved Tibet a thousand miles to the north and someday the Himalayas may double in size.

Two million years ago as the Great Ice Age began, water was sucked from the oceans to feed the advancing glaciers. So much water was removed that land bridges between continents rose above sea level. One such bridge connected Siberia with Alaska. There were four distinct periods of glaciation in the northern half of North America where most of the higher peaks were covered with snow and ice, including a few in northern Arizona and New Mexico. The glaciers melted and receded about 10,000 years ago and water once again covered the land bridges. But the migration across the bridges was well on its way by then. First woolly mammoths (mammuthus primigenius) appeared in North America, followed by the bison, camel and horse. All were being followed by the earliest men and women on the continent, the ancestors to today's Native Peoples—archaeologists know them as Paleo-Indians. The climate had warmed and glaciers released much water back into the oceans. The now dry Great Plains were swampy and a perfect place for the mammoths. We are still in an interglacial period although climate changes haven't favored the Great Plains. As it dried out, and animals moved, so did man. One branch of early man settled in the San Francisco Mountain area. In 1065 AD, Sunset Crater sent cinders over cornfields and lava flows buried living structures. The inhabitants gathered their belongings and left. But over a short period, moisture trapped in the cinders and under the lava flows, created a rich soil beneficial to plant growth. Where the first group moved is not known but other groups soon moved back. Not only had the crop-growing environment improved but more families of various native groups took advantage of the land, intermingling to form a rich culture. The sophistication and social advances of these cultures can be seen at Wupatki National Monument not far from Sunset Crater which is east of San Francisco Mountain. The Hopi and Navajo people of the Colorado Plateau consider the peaks of San Francisco Mountain sacred. The Hopi believe the home of the Kachinas is on the summit. Kachinas are religious figures, beings, whose existence represent a mixture of human and god-like attributes, a sort of go-between that helps them solve many of their daily concerns. That their home is on top of San Francisco Peaks is no surprise to those who, for their first time, have seen the mountain appear through a thicket of ponderosa pine trees like a great green, white haired god rising above the highway's center line.

The eruption of San Francisco Mountain may be called Plinian at least or Vulcanian at best, while the rest of the volcanic field was often Strombolian (a field of fire fountains). In the San Francisco volcanic field, there are two types of volcanoes: cinder cones, of which there are hundreds, and large volcanoes, now large mountains like San Francisco Mountain, Kendrick and Bill Williams. Although Kendrick and Bill Williams Mountains are actually lava domes, they can easily be mistaken for composite volcanoes. San Francisco Mountain is definitely a composite volcano. Along with the two types of volcanoes in the field, another landform is common—lava flows that helped build the large mountains and those that broke out from the base of the many cinder cones. Geologists know that magma is created in the mantle where heat and pressure help to break down minerals in hot rocks to ions which bond together into blobs of magma. These blobs eventually migrate and come together in magma bodies, chambers, miles underground. The mechanics that start the magma building process is plate interaction at either convergent plate boundaries or divergent plate boundaries. But like all volcanoes we visited from New Mexico to Arizona, only the Chiricahuas and the Superstitions can safely be regarded as subducted plate-influenced landforms. The others are intra-plate landforms, having formed inland, deep within a plate and nowhere near a boundary. Geologists are still trying to decide the culprit(s) that caused the volcanic fields in Arizona which run all the way to the gigantic field at Pinacate in northwestern Mexico. Either the crust is thin or faults along a line that runs southwest provide the conduits for the magma. Or, the chain of volcanic fields that starts in northeastern New Mexico and runs through Arizona (the Jemez Lineament) could be the reason. Geologists are careful not to use the words "hot spots" or "mantle plumes" but we know they're tempted. We know there's a hot spot under Yellowstone and an unnamed one may exist under northern New Mexico. But whatever it is, magma has found an easy route from the mantle to the surface. And there are probably many magma chambers below the surface feeding the various fields. Who knows what goes on down there?

A few million years ago the San Francisco volcanic field came alive. Lava with the composition of basalt started the action. Strombolian eruptions were common throughout the field, not unlike Hawaiian eruptions. Thick clots of basaltic lava are flung high in the air by trapped gas within the lava at the top of the magma chamber. The fire fountains appear as luminous arcs filling the sky in many directions above the various vents. Soon, as the gas is spent, lava streams slide down the slopes of the vent mixing with the fire fountain lava. In this manner, large shields of basalt rock were created throughout northern Arizona. The composite volcano that is San Francisco Mountain started construction about this time. Lava and ash piled up around the vent, eventually building a saucer shaped crater, which rose thousands of feet above the Colorado Plateau. The lava's composition was everything from basalt to the more silica-rich andesite, dacite and the highest in silica content, rhyolite. Once the overpressured magma chamber finds or creates a fracture in the rock above, the eruption of gas-rich high silica magma occurs. As the eruptions proceed, and as high silica lava such as rhyolite is expelled from the chamber, the remaining lava may differentiate. Differentiation is the geologic process where magma will change its chemical composition as it either passes through other rocks and assimilates some of its chemical character or the magma body loses some of its original composition (chemical makeup). In this case, the high silica rhyolite was ejected from the top of the magma chamber leaving lower silica composition magma below. In this way, composite volcanoes often show a wide range of composition in the ash and lava flows that build the mountain. In the case of San Francisco Mountain, this construction process lasted from about two million to a few hundred thousand years ago, building, then exploding, then building again until the final event. Geologists are still debating that event. Some maintain the last major eruption blew out the northeast side while others claim the northeast flank collapsed as the magma chamber was depleted. Glaciers of the last Ice Age and erosion took care of the rest. What remain are the higher peaks around the summit and the vacated, or exploded, remains of the northeast flank, known to those of Flagstaff as the Inner Basin. Also within the Inner Basin hardened dikes appear as dark walls (sheets) that run across the surface. These dikes fed the volcano its magma. Many trails within the Inner Basin give the hiker a great view into the insides of the original volcano. In the inner walls you can see the remains of volcanic tuff often sitting above or below a tongue of hardened lava flow. Composite volcanoes are assembled by alternating episodes of eruption of ash, rocks and debris that pile up and harden to tuff, followed by lava flows that pile up around the vent, then more pyroclastic debris, then more lava. This is how a composite volcano is constructed over thousands or millions of years. The final eruption at San Francisco Mountain removed the northeast wall to expose the history of this once great volcano. On the top of the mountain you hike the head, the summit, the location of the vent. In the Inner Basin, you hike the guts of the volcano displayed along the walls, a mixture of lava flows and debris deposits along with the veins that sent lava to the vent.

Hike Guide: Let's take a different approach to this hike—understanding the Colorado Plateau and the amazing countryside that surrounds the mountain. The volcanics of San Francisco Mountain are similar to Mt. Taylor in New Mexico so approaching this hike with a different perspective may add a little more to our journey. The best way to start is with a geologic map while sitting on the saddle, the summit of our hike. Or for that matter, any place along the trail that gives you great views north, south, east or west. One of the best maps is the Geologic Highway Map of Arizona published by the Arizona Geological Society and the Arizona Geologic Survey. If you're interested, the map can be purchased by calling the Geological Society at 520-770-3500. A geologic map is a graphic representation of rock types exposed at the earth's surface. It also displays geologic structures and features, such as faults, mountain ranges and area cross-sections that show surface and subsurface rock strata. What jumps out when you first open the map are the colors. Each color represents a specific unit of rock exposed at the surface along with letter abbreviations of the rock unit name and age. The story is in the colors and the rocks.

On the map you may notice that Flagstaff is surrounded by pink and designated as QTb and Tb. QTb encloses Flagstaff while Tb covers much of the south and west of this area of the Colorado Plateau and Central Highlands (Transition Zone). QTb is Quaternary Period (Pleistocene and Holocene) basalt rocks, specifically basaltic structures like lava flows, cinder cones and others associated with the San Francisco volcanic field. Looking at the area it covers, it becomes immediately obvious this is one large field. South and west, Tb represents Tertiary Period (the one before the Quaternary) basalt, specifically huge mesas constructed and covered by massive basaltic lava flows. These flows were mainly the result of the Basin and Range Orogeny, when the west's crust was being torn apart, allowing basalt an easy, direct route from the mantle. In Basin and Range country, basalt lava is common. Just north of Flagstaff on the map, there's a brown blob that matches two smaller blobs of brown to the northwest of the city. QTv is the designation for the brown spots, meaning Quaternary Period volcanics, specifically rhyolite to andesite lava flows and associated rocks (like tuff)—the same material that built San Francisco Mountain and the other volcanic mountains in the area. These brown areas represent our mountain of interest and other large mountains like Kendrick, a lava dome with a great trail to its summit.

There's a large area of blue on the map that drowns out the pink and brown. The blue runs all the way to Utah and almost all the way to the New Mexico border. This is classic Colorado Plateau color to geologists, specifically the color when they're thinking Grand Canyon. The letter abbreviation is a simple P for Permian Period sedimentary rocks of sandstone and limestone, left there when the Colorado Plateau was a basin and seas had advanced from the west one last time covering the land in shallow water loaded with sea dwellers. Their remains, fossils, are easily found in the Kaibab Limestone that serves as the sidewalk at the Grand Canyon. Interstate 40 follows the blue. It was constructed on the ancient sea limestone. As the highway approaches New Mexico, the geologic map is splashed with green—the color of the dinosaur period. Interstate 40 comes out of the sea and onto the beach. The Triassic sandstones and mudstones (Trm) were deposited along a coastal plain as the seas retreated and the climate dried. Then another green, farther east, representing the Triassic Chinle Formation (Trcs), the sandstone rock of the Painted Desert deposited by a huge river that meandered throughout the southwest. And finally, as you scan the geologic map to New Mexico and north to the Four Corners you note the colors and abbreviations are all representative of the remaining time of dinosaurs (Mesozoic Era), including the Jurassic and Cretaceous Periods.

Let's say you're driving along Interstate 40 east from Flagstaff. The highway starts out on the San Francisco volcanic field basalts, then cuts down into much older rock, the Paleozoic Era (the time of fishes), then up again in the time scale to the Age of Reptiles, the dinosaurs. Highway roadcuts often tell more than the trail. On the road, you refer to your geologic map. Looking for fish fossils? Go for the blue, the Grand Canyon. Looking for dinosaur fossils, look for the green, all over northeastern Arizona. The map colors tell a story of the construction of Arizona. First the strange purple and yellowish-green that lines the Colorado River, the two billion year old Precambrian rock of the collision of tectonic plates and the construction of Arizona's basement. Then the beautiful blues that surround the canyon over most of northern Arizona, the shallow seas and deep oceans of the Age of Fishes, the Paleozoic Era. Then the extinction of the fish where the blue line meets the green of the Age of Reptiles, the Mesozoic Era. And across the center of the Arizona map, from top-left to bottom-right (northwest to southeast) a mixture of colors representing the strange happenings in the Transition Zone, the Central

Highlands. And then south of that, a great splash of mostly lighter colors running from Las Vegas, Nevada down to the southeast border with New Mexico—Basin and Range country. And another great story to witness from the summit of San Francisco Mountain, where we're off the highway and back on the trail.

The Transition Zone, the Central (or Mogollon) Highlands, have their own story and an interesting one in terms of dinosaur bones and uranium. At the time of the appearance of the larger reptiles, the Jurassic Period, northern Arizona was fairly flat. There was no plateau. At that time, if a mountain existed in northern Arizona and you were standing on a trail looking south, the horizon would stop at a great mountain range looking like the Himalayas. These were the Mogollon Highlands. Sand was sweeping in from the west covering northern Arizona and then New Mexico in sand-duned deserts. Occasional swamps and lakes provided water for the dinosaurs. But as you look south from your trail, the mountains towered above all. Then the process of erosion took over. A sea meandered through the western mountains and flooded toward the plains. Along with this sea and large rivers, debris eroded from the Mogollon Highlands peaks was carried all the way to Montana. Shales (originally clay and mud), sandstone and conglomerates were transported and settled along seaside coastal flood plains, in swamps and lakes where the large dinosaurs found their water. The meat-eating dinosaurs favored the swamps, which were often surrounded by trees that fed the plant-eaters. Whether they died from old age, disease or competition for food and space, their large bodies ended up buried in the swamps and lakes. At times, great floods would carry hundreds of dinosaur bones to a central burial ground, usually another lake. From Arizona and New Mexico to Montana, the Morrison Formation was created mostly by the erosion and decapitation of the Mogollon Highlands. The debris was carried to the north by rivers. At Dinosaur National Monument, in northern Utah, an entire wall three stories high presents visitors with an overwhelming view of how floods transported these monsters to a central burial ground, now frozen in the shales of the Morrison Formation. I remember the first time I walked into the three story building that houses the wall, which is a cross-section of a former swamp. I passed a large tree trunk hanging out of the wall like a giant cigar. It turned out to be a dinosaur's leg bone. Honestly, it looked like the trunk of a ponderosa pine tree.

As we found out in our Mt. Taylor hike, the Morrison Formation was a favored location for uranium the Atomic Energy Commission needed to maintain the cold war. Somewhere along the Humphreys Peak trail, when you get a good view to the south, which will be most of the time when the trail exits the woods, stop and imagine the Mogollon Highlands. When the Basin and Range episode stretched the crust, the range dropped and broke apart to the smaller mountains and basins common throughout the Transition Zone, now the Central Highlands. Geologists believe that with continued stretching of the crust the highlands will someday become part of the Basin and Range province to the south while the Colorado Plateau may itself break apart without the protective barrier of the highlands.

As you struggle uphill over the last switchbacks on the trail, here's one thought to consider and maybe relieve the pain. With the change of elevation, the vegetation changes. In the desert country of southern Arizona, it is simply called the Sonoran Desert. In the Central Highlands, it's pinon (pronounced pinyon), juniper and ponderosa woodlands. But on the plateau, at the highest elevations of San Francisco Mountain you reach tundra. Hard to believe you'll find tundra in Arizona. The dictionary defines tundra as one of the vast nearly level, treeless, plains of the arctic regions of Europe, Asia and North America. At the trailhead, the path cuts through a beautiful meadow with great views to the south and west where lies the southern edge of the Colorado Plateau and the Mogollon Rim transition to the Central Highlands. The trail enters the woods known at this elevation as a conifer forest. The lower elevations are represented mostly by ponderosa pine. With an increase in elevation toward 8,000 feet, douglas fir dominate along with the beautiful quaking aspen, a deciduous tree that turns golden yellow in the fall, which at this elevation starts in September. With the sight of aspen, you know you are at some of the higher elevations in Arizona. Some of the trees are sprinkled at the lower elevations, in the meadows that surround the mountain, as the natural transport service of erosion and birds carry seeds downhill. Spruce trees take over at about 9,000 feet. As the trail approaches the ridge overlooking the other side of the mountain, the Inner Basin, you're at subalpine. Seen from the highway, if it's not covered with snow, it looks like gray barren rock and it mostly is. This is treeline, no more trees. Near the tundra at the top (note the tundra marker on the trail) you come across bizarrely twisted bristlecone pine. Travel the coast highway along the Pacific Ocean and you'll see the same twisted manner of the trees overlooking cliffs that drop into the ocean. These trees are twisted by the winds. Winds at the top of San Francisco Mountain can do strange things to trees. Imagine your fate in such winds during the winter when the temperature can dip 20, 30,40 below freezing, or more. Hence, the hardy bristlecone pines at treeline and the arctic-like tundra, both a rare find in Arizona.

Tundra sign just before reaching the rim.

At the top, whether you hike to Humphreys Peak or end the hike at the saddle just beyond the tundra sign, the view is spectacular, in all directions. The most impressive is of the Inner Basin where the truncated cross-section of the volcano's innards are on display. From the saddle, scan the cliffs to the left and right for signs of transition from one rock type to another, from lava flows to explosive ash-based tuff deposits. Each different layer represents another episode, maybe spanning thousands of years in the mountains volcanic growth.

At this point you can hike to Humphreys Peak to the left or hike the ridge to the right. Or, take a break, eat some lunch and enjoy the view. And consider how such beautiful landscape was born. It's almost impossible to imagine it as just a random act of nature. The Kachinas may have played a hand. Enjoy the hike down.

View from the crater rim (saddle) overlooking the north flank removed by eruption.

Other Points of Interest: Sunset Crater (Volcano) National Monument, a young and extinct cinder cone, and Wupatki National Monument, a Sinagua Indian historic site, have already been mentioned. Both are northeast of Flagstaff. Sunset Crater is similar to Capulin in New Mexico because both take the hiker to the innards of a cinder cone. We've already visited cinder cones and lava flows at Capulin and at El Malpais. However, Sunset Crater does have excellent examples of lava flow patterns like aa and pahoehoe in the Bonito lava flow field. The most interesting aspect of Sunset Crater and Wupatki is the fact that they are both tied geologically and culturally. The eruptions at Sunset Crater affected the lives of the Sinaguan people. They moved out of the burned area but were later followed back in by other groups. A one-day visit to both would be educational because it shows how the early Native Peoples adapted to some hostile environments and the unpredictable behavior of a volcano's vent, the youngest in Arizona.

The Colorado Plateau has so much to offer it's hard to even begin to recommend areas to visit. The huge plateau itself is composed of other plateaus and landforms. Painted Desert, Coconino Plateau, Zuni Uplift, Kaibab Plateau, Monument Uplift, Wasatch Plateau, Uncompahgre Uplift, Grand Mesa, Mesa Verde, San Juan Basin—on and on it goes, all surrounded by the Rocky Mountains, the Rio Grande Rift Valley and the Basin and Range Province. The Colorado Plateau sits in the middle of three very active geologic provinces that guarantee volcanism and crustal movement will continue for millions of years to come. That having been said, the Grand Canyon is close and worth the trip. A hike into the canyon on any trail will take you through rock that represents the initial construction of Arizona's basement two billion years ago and layer upon layer of Paleozoic Era rock that reports around 300 million years of seas advancing, receding and depositing thousands of feet of sediment now on display in the canyon's cliff-slope-cliff strata. The top of the canyon represents limestone left by the last advance of seas from the west. The bottom of the canyon represents the basement. After a billion years of erosion of the basement, the seas moved in and covered it. The steep brown sandstone cliff over the dark Inner Gorge represents the initial invasion of the first sea—the first beach. Then the shale slope above it presenting a graphic picture of how the seas moved inland and deepened over the southwest as it flapped up and down, allowing seas in, then washing them out. Each time a new deposit, new fossils and another record of the Age of Fishes right to the top of the canyon which itself represents the time when reptiles left the water and crawled onto the land. The top of the canyon lays witness to the eventual extinction of most of the fish of the Paleozoic Era and the emergence of reptiles on the land. These were the early dinosaurs. At the Grand Canyon, there is no Mesozoic (dinosaur time) rock. However, if you travel northwest to Zion National Monument in Utah, you'll be in dinosaur country. Zion is interesting because its main rock strata, the Navajo Formation, reports the cemented remains of a great Sahara-size desert that covered most of the southwest. Utah has a number of national parks that present this theme. And each park is a step on the Grand Staircase of the plateau country. Each rock formation tends to erode northward such that steps, actually separate plateaus, appear like a staircase starting at the bottom of the stairs, the Grand Canyon. Each step tells a different story. The top rock layer of the Grand Canyon is the bottom layer of Zion and the top layer of Zion is the bottom of the next plateau (step) and so it goes, step by step. Grand Staircase Escalante is a new monument in Utah that presents the stairs in beautifully colorful fashion. The stairs end as you approach northern

Utah where Dinosaur National Monument sits on the northeast border of Utah with Colorado. Drive in through Vernal, Utah and visit the building that houses the dinosaur remains frozen in the three story wall of the Morrison Formation. There are nice camping sites in the monument and some very interesting hiking trails.

If you decide to go to Dinosaur, you're on the border of Colorado and just south of Wyoming. Colorado is well known for the Rocky Mountains and Rocky Mountain National Park. The problem with these parks is that many tourists also know about them. So they can be as busy as the Grand Canyon in tourist season, mostly the summer. I've found that visiting the Grand Canyon in the winter is the best bet. The Rockies are the same except for snow at the higher elevations. So spring and fall may be the time to go. Summer time is family travel time so crowds are to be expected. We'll head into Wyoming and save Colorado for another book.

On the Road to the Next Hike

Why Wyoming? Simple—Yellowstone! Why Yellowstone? Simple—hot spots! Why hot spots? Not so simple to geologists but fascinating nonetheless. Yellowstone gives us an opportunity to discuss hot spots right where the big one caused the most destruction ever recorded in the west. Yellowstone, Long Valley in California and north-central New Mexico are the only places on the continent where we know active mid-crustal magma bodies exist. There are no plate boundaries within hundreds of miles so the mid-crustal action is inviting to geologists. The fact that the one under Yellowstone has been definitely acknowledged as a hot spot and has been tracked from other areas to its current location gives us a unique opportunity to do some investigating. All this before we move on to the Cascade Range and the effects of an oceanic plate still riding under the northwest. But hot spots are interesting so let's track this one. The trip to Yellowstone is intended mainly to discuss its geology and hot spots. It's less about hiking because there are so many trails and so much to do in the park. You'll find at Yellowstone that something specific will, at some point, stir your interest so we'll leave the visit wide open for your exploration. We'll focus on the geology and leave the rest up to you. At this point, I should say that from the time I first saw Yellowstone I was convinced it is the most beautiful, powerful and dynamic location in North America. The Grand Canyon, Yosemite and Rocky Mountain National Parks all have their unique attractions. Yellowstone has them all, in and around one great caldera.

Hike: Yellowstone National Park

Y ellowstone has more to offer than any other park in North America (my opinion).

Location: Yellowstone is located in the northwest corner of Wyoming, surrounded on the north by Montana and the west by Montana and Idaho. There are many entrances to the park. From the north on US 89 through Gardiner, the northeast through Cooke City and Silver Gate on Route 212, the east entrance on Routes 14, 16, 20 and the west entrance on Routes 191and 287 through West Yellowstone. If you do take Route 212 through Cooke City, keep an eye on highway roadcuts coming through the Beartooth Mountains as you cross the line between Montana and Wyoming, southwest of Red Lodge. These mountains display some of the oldest rock in the park area—pink granites are dated to 2.7 billion years old. I prefer the south entrance through Jackson Hole and the Grand Tetons, US Route 89 and Routes 191 and 287, along the Snake River. This is the most scenic route and offers many hiking possibilities well before entering the park. Once you see the Grand Teton Mountains on the parks southern edge you may not make it to Yellowstone. But it would be a shame to get sidetracked.

Hike Type and Length: We're going to focus on a geologic feature of Yellowstone called hot spots. A short hike of about three miles, Elephant Back Mountain Trail, will give us the view we need. The Elephant Back Mountain hike is moderate with some uphill. There are so many trails in Yellowstone we'll leave the selection up to you.

Elevation: Elevations vary considerably all over the park. The Elephant Back hike starts at not quite 8,000 feet and climbs about 800 feet to the back of the elephant, which is more like a plateau than a mountain.

Precautions: The usual precautions hold for this hike but in Yellowstone the key concern is bear, particularly the Grizzly. There are two living monsters in this world that I truly fear: the Great White Shark and Grizzly Bear. But given enough space and warning that you're in the Grizzly's neighborhood, there shouldn't be a problem. Any material you pick up in the park will eventually get to the subject of bears so I won't get into what I think you should do during an encounter. Suffice it to say that for every recommended approach to bear encounters I have read, not one comes even close to what I really would do!

Planning Information: The only way to plan is to gather as much information about the park as you can well in advance of the visit. And assume you won't cover the whole park, on roads or trails. Most information can be found online or you can call the park and ask for an information packet, which includes the Yellowstone Official Map and Guide. There are some day hike pamphlets, like the Day Hikes in the Fishing Bridge & Lake Areas. Start your planning at their web site and go from there. Note the Grizzly and sow on their home page:
    http://www.nps.gov/yell/
Here are a few others:
    http://www.yellowstone.net/
    http://www.americanparknetwork.com/parkinfo/ye/history/

Geologic Setting: In the introduction to this book, we discussed hot spots and the Hawaiian Islands. The islands are a hundred percent the result of volcanic eruptions. Wherever you walk, you're on basalt. Even the beaches are ground volcanic grains. Tectonic plates, like the one the islands sit on, cover the globe. The Pacific plate is a huge one, surrounded by subduction zones along an arc that runs from the west coast of South America, up through North America to Alaska and over to the western Pacific. Hawaii's location on the plate is almost dead center of the Pacific Ocean, maybe 2,000 miles from the nearest plate boundary. Yellowstone sits on continental plate about 800 miles from the nearest plate boundary. After tectonic plate theory was established in the 1960s, something or someone had to address a glaring contradiction. Both Hawaii and Yellowstone are part of an active volcanic field but nowhere near a convergent or divergent plate boundary. What happened?

Hawaiian lore has it that Pele, the Goddess of Volcanoes, had a run-in with a relative and was forced to flee from one island to the next in a southerly direction. Her last move was from Maui to the main island of Hawaii where she now lives at the summit of the Kilauea Volcano. As she moved, the island she left cooled—the volcano that fed it died. Each time she moved, a new volcano was created at that location in the ocean. Her movements are strangely consistent with mantle plume or hot spot theory. That is, a plume (column) of hot, molten rock from deep within the mantle creates a crustal hot spot at the earth's surface. As the oceanic plate moved in a northwesterly direction over the hot spot (plume), the underside of the plate was heated, cooked and magma came up through vents in the ocean floor, building what's called a Seamount. The seamount eventually grows and appears above the water line like the Hawaiian Islands. As they move beyond the plume, volcanism ceases and erosion takes over, eventually dismantling the island until it sinks back below the waves. The plate continues to carry what remains of the islands, above or below water, to a deep trench near Japan and another trench beyond, farther to the north. The trench is the entry point into a subduction zone where that part of the oceanic plate, islands and all, is driven down into the trench to the mantle where the plate is melted and sent back up as magma, at times erupting near or on the island of Japan. On the other side of the moving, oceanic plate new islands form in their place. The Hawaiian Islands seem to grow to the southeast as the plate moves to the northwest. Hawaiian legend and geology are strangely in agreement. The main island of Hawaii has the youngest rocks of the entire island chain—less than a million years of age. The goddess Pele lives on the southeast tip where the youngest rock has formed, some of it flows from Kilauea. And more is forming every day. The location of the hot spot below the moving plate remains fixed. It's the plate that moves and so hot spots can be traced as volcanism seems to move in the opposite direction of the plate. Yellowstone has taken its place over one such hot spot and will some day move beyond it, in a western direction at an inch or more a year. At that rate, we can expect the hot rocks to remain under Yellowstone for some time. Perhaps a million years from now, volcanism will move to an area east of Yellowstone thus proving the theory, which also states that hot spots may last up to a hundred million years, more or less. Watch out Chicago!

Hot spots report their presence in two ways. In some areas, the crust above the hot spot domes as the pressure below builds and there is no vent to the surface for the building magma. Some geologists have postulated that the continental divide is a result of such activity. The divide traces from the Yellowstone area, where a hot spot is known to exist, to northern New Mexico where one may also exist. Could it be that the doming at Yellowstone and in northern New Mexico exert such force between them to bring up the ground, forming a ridge, the divide, for hundreds of miles? Ground studies at Yellowstone do show that a certain area within the caldera rises and falls over a fixed period of time. The second type of behavior exhibited by hot spots is volcanism in the form of lava flows, usually of basalt. Basalt flows freely so these flows cover large areas. Aside from the studies that established asteroids as the cause for mass extinctions, such as those that killed off the Paleozoic Era fish and the Mesozoic Era dinosaur, hot spots and their resulting flood basalts may also have played a hand. The volumes of lava flowing onto the earth's crust can do strange things. However, sometimes the magma doesn't make it to the surface. If the magma has a higher silica content than basalt and remains below ground doming the earth, it mixes chemically with other rocks that reduce its basaltic content even more, creating a pasty, thick magma like rhyolite. Rhyolite does not flow freely so when it bursts from its underground source, a park like Yellowstone is created.

Some theorists maintain that the two hot spots, the one under Yellowstone and the other under northern New Mexico, run in a parallel direction. Actually, it's the continental plate that is moving in a westerly direction, over two hot spots in the mantle. As the plate moves, volcanoes appear as though they are moving toward the east. These two plumes could have been more involved than plate boundary activities and the Basin and Range Orogeny in raising the Colorado Plateau and the Rockies. And if you look at New Mexico's suspected plume, maybe the Valles Caldera was a victim of a hot spot versus the influence of the Jemez Lineament and the Rio Grande Rifting Center. For that matter, is the hot spot playing a role in spreading the Rio Grande Valley? Dome it up, it spreads. The plate moves west, the hot spots influence crust in an eastern-directed pattern. Plume theory geologists believe that many millions of years ago, an older hot spot may have existed under Wyoming. It may have lifted the Rockies back then. By calculating its speed and direction over time, plume theorists believe it is now sitting under Bermuda. The island sits about 17,000 feet above the sea floor. On its way, the hot spot made a pass under the southern Appalachian Mountains before heading out to sea. The Great Smoky Mountains may be the result as the doming effect bulged the range from below after many million years of erosion of their peaks. Another hot spot may have also been responsible for lifting the northern Appalachians. It came out of Canada. There were no active plate boundaries on the east coast of North America at the time. Geologists know the speed (an inch or more a year) at which the continental plate moves over a fixed point, the hot spot. The distances and directions coincide perfectly with the early action in Wyoming, then the Smokies and now Bermuda. And speaking of Wyoming, the Grand Tetons south of Yellowstone and Craters of the Moon National Monument just to the west in Idaho don't fit into plate tectonic boundary activity either. But, their time of uplift and eruption does match calculated hot spot positioning under the moving plate. Actually, and more acceptable to field geologists, the uplift of the Tetons does fit quite well within the Basin and Range mountain building episode. If it's a coincidence, it's a great one. The Tetons are Grand indeed! Don't get sidetracked in the Tetons. Yellowstone and its hot spot await our visit.

Grand Tetons

Hike Guide: The hike itself starts at a trailhead a mile below Fishing Bridge Junction and across the road from Lake Village. This area along the northern shore of Yellowstone Lake is currently being uplifted in the form of an oval-shaped dome above the magma chamber below. It rises an inch or two a year from magma and gas pressure probing the earth for a vent. The Fishing Bridge area is known as one of the best trout spawning grounds in the west. Pelicans feed on the trout during the summer season. Related to that feeding activity, the campgrounds in the Fishing Bridge area don't allow tents. Hard-bodied vehicles are required for overnights. Bear like trout also so this is a favorite hangout and a tent is no match for a bear that just had a bad day fishing. During my last hike at Elephant Back Mountain I sang songs all the way up and spoke to myself all the way down. You want bear to know you're in their territory. The secret to this hike is to get through the forest to the top where the views are spectacular. Take a seat, spend some time and imagine how this beautiful country was formed. And what may happen if the crust can no longer contain the magma chamber below. When magma chambers bow up the earth above, earthquakes often occur as the rock layers above the chamber are fractured by its gas charged bloating. If earthquakes were occurring, and in regular intervals, the park would be cleared of all visitors immediately because it would be Plinian-time again. Enjoy the hike (3 miles roundtrip) and watch for wildlife. The scenery and the absolute power of Yellowstone will take care of the rest.

Bison (keep your distance) with Yellowstone River running through Hayden Valley in the background.

The best approach to this moderate hike is to focus on the whole of Yellowstone versus specific places along the Elephant Back Mountain trail. At the summit on Elephant Back, the time of geologic thinking arrives as the view opens before you. First, think back to our discussion of the geologic construction of the southwest, particularly Arizona. You may recall that when Arizona started to form in the Precambrian Era, it was just a small chunk of crust that broke off from Wyoming, which was a west coast beach at the time. Arizona's oldest rocks date to not quite 2 billion years. Wyoming has rocks that date to 2.7 billion years, mostly visible along some highway roadcuts, particularly northeast of the park in the Beartooth Mountains, which are visible on the horizon to the northeast. Wyoming was the west coast of the young North American craton before the continent expanded to the west and south through accretion of plates and volcanic activity. The reddish to pink granites along highway roadcuts in the Beartooth were brought up to view by faulting of these mountains. This rock is not exposed along roadcuts in the park because it's still deep underground and covered by massive accumulation of volcanic rock—all trails are cut through thick layers of welded ash and lava flows. But the rock that makes up the Beartooth range is solid, old granite that lifted up through the earth to expose the basement of Yellowstone Country.

As you hike and take in the scenery, consider that Yellowstone has had many episodes of volcanism, some of the most active occurring near the end of the Laramide Orogeny, about 50 million years ago. Idaho, Montana and Wyoming were doted with volcanoes. Then came long periods of erosion. A mile or so underground, the magma chambers continued to build finally culminating in three catastrophic episodes of volcanic eruption that marked Yellowstone's current history. The first eruption about 2 million years ago, about the same time as the Valles Caldera eruption in New Mexico, was responsible for the first caldera which was pretty much removed by later eruptions. But this first event was no less violent than the next two. Geologists estimate that what came out of the ground, between 500 and 600 cubic miles of material, was close to 5,000 times the debris produced by Mount St. Helens. If you remember watching the news reports and pictures of the St. Helens eruption, a factor of five thousand seems beyond comprehension, except to maybe geologists and the Atomic Energy Commission. The second eruption came almost one million years later but was small compared to the first one and the final event. The third eruption, concurrent with the eruption at San Francisco Mountain in Arizona, was Yellowstone's great climax, about 600,000 years ago. Smaller eruptions and lava flows continued to about 70,000 years ago. Nearly 250 cubic miles of debris was thrown in the air by the most recent eruption creating much of the welded tuff that covers the park. As the magma chamber was vacated, like most Plinian eruptions, the roof caved in. The top of the chamber and all above it collapsed into a caldera, up to 47 miles wide in some sections. This caldera superimposed itself on the calderas created during the earlier eruptions. On the map, the caldera rim runs from the southwest boundary of the park right near its junction with Montana and Idaho, northeast to Canyon Village and around, down and through the center of Yellowstone Lake to the south of Lewis Lake. Compare this caldera with the 12-mile-wide Valles Caldera in New Mexico. And it contains one of the largest mountain lakes in North America. The sculpting of Yellowstone's volcanic landscape occurred during the final advances of ice during the Ice Ages of the Pleistocene. Many glacial features are evident in the mountains in and around the park.

The recommended hike, Elephant Back Mountain Trail, provides wonderful views of Yellowstone Lake and the majestic Absaroka Range that marks the eastern boundary of the park. The Absaroka Range trends south along the park's edge then bends southeast, almost as though it was pushed out of the way by the mighty Rockies that pour out of the center of the park like a great dragon. And just to the southwest, also part of the Rockies, the Grand Tetons. The Absarokas didn't burst out of the ground in Rocky Mountain fashion. They were born in volcanic frenzy during the Eocene Magma Gap, a time when volcanism slowed in the west. It marked the reawakening of many magma chambers initiated during the Laramide Orogeny a few million years before. The Absarokas spill into the Wind River Range which were pushed up by the Laramide event. The uplift of the Rockies occurred more than once, having been beveled by erosion, only to rise again. When the Pacific and North American plates were converging during the Laramide Orogeny, the Rockies were pushed up like a rug shoved against a wall. Then erosion took over, decapitating the peaks. The last episode of uplift, which most geologists contend was a result of the Basin and Range Orogeny but others say, may have more to do with hot spots than anything else. No matter where you look from the top of the Elephant Back trail, the huge Yellowstone Lake dominates the view right up to the foot of the Absarokas. The river that exits the lake at Fishing Bridge is still sculpting the Grand Canyon of the Yellowstone to the north. The volcanic rock of the canyon is truly yellow, tinted that way by hot fluids and metallic minerals in the rock. The canyon also contains more than one waterfall that rival Niagara Falls in shear power. Sitting on the summit of the trail, the eye takes in the beautiful mountains of the Rockies that certainly match the majesty of the Sierra Nevadas. Then to the north, the Grand Canyon of the Yellowstone comes close to anything the Grand Canyon of Arizona has to offer. And on top of all this scenery, it helps to remember you're sitting in the southeast corner of the rim of one huge caldera, which daily proves itself still active at the hot springs, geysers and other hydrothermal displays that vent the pressure building below.

Grand Canyon of the Yellowstone and the Lower Falls.

Other Points of Interest: I mentioned hot springs and geysers above. I should have mentioned fumaroles and mud pots. There are close to 10,000 hot water and gas-generated features in the park. Hundreds erupt regularly. Old Faithful Geyser was pretty regular, once an hour, until an earthquake interrupted the cycle. The road from Grant Village to Madison has the highest concentration of thermal features near the highway, including Old Faithful and other geysers, mudpots, gaseous fumaroles and hot springs. Continue on the road toward the north entrance at Mammoth Hot Springs, itself quite a thermal feature, and the road passes Obsidian Cliff. Obsidian is a black volcanic glass created when lava flows and cools fast. It hardens to obsidian rock so quickly no mineral grains are visible and the rhyolitic composition lithifies to translucent, even transparent, glass. The cliff shines as you drive by as long as the sun's in the right position. Fossil forests are another feature. Throughout the park, trees that were buried during eruptions starting 50 million years ago were covered with ash. The silica content in the ash replaced the organic matter of the trees and solidified to rock, called agate. These formations are similar to the Petrified Forest in Arizona. Many of the trees are still standing. You are not allowed to collect specimens of the rock in the park but outside, at Gardiner (north entrance), inquire at the ranger station for permission. You can pick up small samples along creeks in the area. Within the park, on the north side near Tower Junction and Roosevelt, there's a short trail to a petrified tree and southeast of the junction is Specimen Ridge, named so because of the petrified trees in the area. For one of the best wildlife viewing areas, particularly if you're interested in getting some great pictures of bison, travel south from Tower Junction and Roosevelt to Canyon Village and farther south to Fishing Bridge. Hayden Valley is a beautiful meadow that stretches in all directions around the road. Yellowstone River meanders through the valley. The last time I was at Yellowstone, bison were right near the road, just sort of ignoring the tourists who stop and cause all kinds of traffic jams. And there were two bald eagles feeding on fish down by the river. Another recommended hike would be below Canyon Village, where a trail follows the Yellowstone River toward Artist Point. Here you can view the Upper and Lower Falls. The Lower Falls are to me the most picturesque and the most interesting geologically. Waterfalls are created as streams or rivers cut into hard and soft rock. The hard rock remains, the soft rock is broken up and transported away. In the case of waterfalls, it's hard rock holding the cliff up for the falls, everything else is eroded and taken down stream.

Although we've been debating the effects of hot spots in the Yellowstone area, the Rockies and the Grand Tetons, forget the debate and visit the Tetons. Itself a national park, the geology is tremendous and there are many trails. Stop in Jackson Hole for trail information, maps and recommendations from the locals on where to go. Whether hot spots had anything to do with the uplift of the Tetons is still a matter of debate. Some laboratory geologists feel they have it answered in hot spots. But field geologists are not sure. They are the ones out in the wilderness with their eyes on the rocks and they tell a different story only seen in the rock strata. For our purposes, we'll go with the Basin and Range Orogeny, a great mountain building event where blocks of crust were driven skyward while adjoining blocks were dropped into deep basins. That's what happened in the Teton area. If you were to approach the Grand Tetons from the west, you'd notice a broad westward dipping slope that starts at the highest peaks of the Tetons. The slope is the backside of the block and it reaches up to where the rugged scenery of the east facing mountains begin. The north-south line of faults, called a normal fault, on the east face of the mountains sent the great block of the Tetons up while the valley east of the block dropped. The valley has since been filled with debris from the mountains. But 9 million years ago, when it happened, the earthquakes from blocks of rock rubbing by each other and fracturing must have been beyond description. You know these are young mountains. The rock in them is very old but they are considered young because they were uplifted only 9 million years ago. Their age is also obvious in the lack of foothills, benches and hills of debris that come out of older mountains. Debris piles up at the base of eroding mountains creating long slopes out to the basin. But these mountains are different. Most of the debris was carried into the basin. There hasn't been enough time for foothills to fully develop. You can almost walk right up to the base of the mountains and see where they came out of the ground in great spasmodic surges. This was and is Basin and Range mountain building at its best. And there's still movement along the west coast fault as the transform plate boundary, marking the San Andreas Fault, continues to slide and stretch the crust inland. The Grand Tetons may be worth the visit just to find a viewpoint and imagine the power of normal faults that seem anything but normal to the mind's eye.

On the Road to the Next Hike

Well, this is it. Our grand debut with the Cascades is at hand. The next stop is the Cascade Range that runs from northern California into Canada. Specifically, we are interested in Mount Lassen, Crater Lake and Mount St. Helens. Crater Lake is another twist on the caldera theme. The entire rim of the caldera is dramatically displayed because the two features that outline the rim are blue—assuming clear weather—a deep, blue lake within the caldera's walls and the blue sky that seems to act as a light reflector for the lake. The crater rim appears even larger than it is because no matter where you are the opposite crater walls are mirrored in the lake. Known as Mount Mazama before the eruption, this different caldera theme begs a visit. And as far as Mount St. Helens is concerned, there's the final act of our play across the great western volcanoes. And what a way to finish a road trip. Mount St. Helens is the perfect climax because it is the youngest of volcanoes, just over 20 years of age, and it's classic Plinian. At Helens, the hikes are the classroom because the trails are right on and through fresh signs of destruction and construction. We will begin with the southern-most Cascade volcanic mountain, Mount Lassen. At Lassen we'll focus on the Cascade Range in general, the evolution of the Cascades and we'll set the stage for our trips to Crater Lake and Mount St. Helens. But Lassen is interesting because of the beautiful trail on its west side and because it's a plug dome. We've discussed and seen plug or lava domes that tend to form outside a caldera's moat, around the ring fractures. Many of them are mounds to small hills. Dacite is a typical volcanic rock found in lava domes, such as the small dome now forming inside the Mount St. Helens crater. The big difference at Lassen is that this dacite dome is 10,000 feet above sea level, the biggest plug dome in the world. My mind has a hard time comprehending the size of the volcano that once existed in the Lassen area if this is just one of the plug domes. So let's start at Mount Lassen, spend a brief time there discussing the Cascades, take a hike and then on to our meeting with the great ones farther north.

7

Hiking the Cascade Range

Hike: Mount Lassen (Lassen Volcanic National Park)

An opportunity to explore the evolution of the Cascade Range on a scenic trail, then head north for the final act.

Location: Northern California—east of Redding, California from Interstate 5 on State Route 44 or come up from the south on State Route 36. You can enter from the south on State Route 36, near the town of Mineral, the park headquarters. Our approach is from the west from Redding on Route 44. We'll be camping and hiking at Manzanita Lake Campgrounds.

Hike Type and Length: There are three hikes near the campgrounds, which are not quite 6,000 feet elevation. One is the Emigrant Trail, north of the lake. Another is the trail east and up to Crags Lake. Our trail heads south from the end of the campground road toward Loomis Peak, paralleling Manzanita Creek. There is some up and down but the hike is moderate with beautiful views of Chaos Crags and the west side of Lassen. The terminus is about 6 miles from the trailhead so go as far as you feel comfortable, return the same way. At one point in the trail, it follows a beautiful meadow where I'd recommend spending some time studying the landscape and wildlife.

Elevation: Starting at 6,000 feet with a few hundred feet of elevation, up and down as you proceed south.

Precautions: There's a ranger station, near the lake, on the road to the campgrounds. Check on trail conditions and any other considerations before hiking. This is a moderate day hike so prepare according to how far you want to walk.

Planning Information: Contact the park directly at 530-595-4444. Ask them to mail you a copy of their newsletter Peak Experiences and the Lassen Volcanic Official Map and Guide. You can also download a file to PDF format describing the park and its geology. Below is the Lassen Park web site:
    http://www.nps.gov/lavo/
Another very good site dedicated to the park:
    http://www.lassen.volcanic.national-park.com/
And the USGS web site for Lassen:
    http://vulcan.wr.usgs.gov/Volcanoes/Lassen/Locale/framework.html

Geologic Setting: Let's use the Mount Lassen hike to set the stage for the Cascade Range in general. An understanding of the evolution of the Cascades is essential because this volcanic part of the west is somewhat different than anything we've seen. From here, we'll move on to Crater Lake and Mount St. Helens were the volcanic results of subduction zones are so evident and young. So far in our travels we've seen only one volcanic center that was a direct result of a subducting plate—the Chiricahua Mountains. The other volcanic features had more to do with hot spots, areas of crustal weakness, mid-crustal spreading centers and lineaments that represent fractured crust nowhere near a subduction zone. The Cascades, however, line up along the coast where the Pacific and North American plates are very active.

    Around 180 million years ago, during the Age of Reptiles, the young North American plate had broken away from a huge continental mass and began its voyage to the west. A spreading center grew in what is now the Atlantic Ocean, pushing the continental plate west. And as the Atlantic Ocean opened up on the east coast, the North American plate closed in on the Pacific plate to the west. Eventually the two plates collided, subducting the oceanic plate under the continent. Volcanoes grew along the coastline, which was much farther inland than it is today. The pressure also drove up early mountain ranges, such as the ancestral Rockies, as the two plate fought for dominance.

The Laramide Orogeny ended around 50 million years ago and things quieted in the west but the plates were still active. The tectonic plate boundary along the west coast changed from convergence and subduction to a transform boundary where the plates slide by each other. Apparently, the continental plate had swallowed a large section of the Pacific plate along with the oceanic spreading center that was pushing it eastward. With the cessation of subduction, the plates began to slide by each other, at the transform boundary. Where the plates met, the Pacific plate was moving northwest while the North American plate headed south at the boundary. Strike-slip faults were created, such as the grand one known to us as the San Andreas. As they slide by each other, tension builds as rock binds then releases, resulting in earthquakes. This activity was happening along the coast and was responsible for stretching the crust inland to the point that block faulting was initiated as the Basin and Range Orogeny began. Here's the big question: with the plates sliding by each other, why is subduction still occurring in the northwest thus affecting the Cascades?

Off the coast of northern California, the transform plate boundary takes a left turn and heads out to sea along another fault. North of that fault, in the ocean, two small plates formed with their own spreading centers, a few hundred miles off the coast. These spreading centers are pushing the plates against and under the northwest coast, forming relatively small subduction zones. Somewhere around 36 million years ago, in Oligocene time, volcanoes started to erupt along the coast as a result of subduction. In Miocene time, as the crustal stretching really got underway inland and the Basin and Range Orogeny was starting to throw blocks of crust up and down in the west, large composite volcanoes erupted and grew along the coast. At the time, the sea covered parts of the northwest so these volcanoes (volcanic islands) came out of the water. The volcanic mountains along the coast eventually came to be called the Western Cascades but are not the Cascades we see today which came much later and are known as the High Cascades.

The transform, slip and slide, boundary was very active to the south along the California coast. The Baja California peninsula was torn from Mexico and began to ride north on the Pacific plate, bringing with it parts of southern California. In the northwest, where that section of the plate headed out into the ocean, the combination of subduction by the small plates and stretching of the crust to the south opened huge cracks in the earth. Flood basalts (lava flows) poured out of the ground. The action moved inland. Flood basalts covered most of eastern Washington and Oregon, and parts of Idaho. Basalt plateaus, or basalt deserts, burned and covered the land. Some lava forced its way through the mountains and headed west, reaching the ocean. The topographic result is the dark colored (basaltic) Columbia River Plateau. Eventually the Western Cascades were folded and eroded to minor mountains along the coast. But inland, the flood basalts built much of the platform upon which the younger Cascades would grow.

A few million years ago, basaltic action increased thus adding to the footings of the Cascades. The area probably looked more like El Malpais or Capulin where shield volcanoes and cinder cones dominated. But as the magma chambers below gave up much of their basaltic lava, the composition changed to more silica-dominated andesite, dacite and rhyolite. The geologic time was the Pleistocene. We've seen in other hikes the activity that occurred during the Pleistocene, particularly at Valles Caldera, Mt. Taylor and San Francisco Mountain. The only difference in the northwest was that the Cascades were built as a result of subduction. Great composite or stratovolcanoes grew inland east of the old Western Cascades. Their base was basalt but as they grew, the lava composition diversified allowing for more explosive volcanism and the growth of very large stratovolcanoes. Geologists believe the entire volcanic Ring of Fire around the Pacific was active at this time.

Today's younger High Cascade Range parallels the old Western Cascades nearer the coast. The Northern Cascades, from northern Washington into Canada, is a bit different from the rest of the Cascades to the south. The Northern Cascades are composed mostly of old, twisted, tortured metamorphic rock. The metamorphic Northern Cascades are believed to have been islands of rock (exotic terrains) that floated onshore earlier in geologic time. When the Pacific plate was whole and subducting under the entire western coast, it carried large volcanic islands and slabs of oceanic and micro-continental crust with it. As the plate subducted, the load it carried was scraped off the plate and jammed hundreds of miles inland forming large mountains. The Northern Cascades metamorphic rock is believed to be the compressed remains of those islands of rock brought onshore as the coastline grew outwards from it original beach near Wyoming.

Each volcanic mountain in the entire stretch of the modern High Cascades has its own history. Most are volcanically related but each tells an amazing and unique story of eruption, destruction and in most cases, rebirth. The Mount Lassen area is part of a huge lava plateau that extends to the south and all the way north to Crater Lake in Oregon. The area of Lassen is also a laboratory for studying the effects of Cascade volcanoes and how the land recovers. They used these studies after the destruction at Mount St. Helens to plan its recovery.

Mount Lassen / View from the east side.

Hike Guide: There are hundreds of miles of trails at Mount Lassen and outside the park (national forest). Most can be found at the southern entry to the park and east of the main road through Lassen. There's even a trail to the summit of Mount Lassen that opens in early July. Our hike is in the northwestern section and starts at the Manzanita Lake campgrounds. Follow the campground road to the end to find the trailhead, which trends in a southeast direction, mostly paralleling Manzanita Creek. At about 6 miles, it ends in a swampy area that appears to be the source of Manzanita Creek. The trail will eventually disappear in moist ground. You'll know when it's time to turn around for the hike back. This trail is interesting because it presents features that are unique to Lassen. Here's what to look for and what Mount Lassen has to offer in terms of its location in the Cascades.

The Cascade Range provides a youthful perspective into volcanic activity and glaciation and how they relate. During the Ice Ages, all the peaks were glaciated. Now, as you travel north along the Cascades, only the higher elevations of the range are glaciated. Mount Lassen's small snow mass melts as the summer progresses. But when the major eruption occurred, the snow was there and as it melted, avalanches and mudslides caused much of the devastation. This is not unique to the Cascades but has taught geologists much about the effects of the heat of volcanoes mixing with ice and snow of glaciers. In many cases, the more destructive eruptions of Cascade volcanoes created an initial avalanche of mud, rocks and broken trees. Chaos Crags, a dome north of Lassen, displayed such behavior when a landslide blew down the north flank. The air lubricated slide reached speeds of 100 miles per hour. You can see the results, Chaos Jumbles, on the road east from the campgrounds. It was an event initiated by a steam blast within the dome of Chaos Crags. In many cases in a glaciated range, massive avalanches were followed by typical pyroclastic flows of burning clouds of ash, rock and gas. The flows followed the path already swept clean by the avalanche. The result of avalanches, mudslides and pyroclastic flows at Lassen can be seen along the road to the Devastated Area. First the avalanche slid down the east flank of Lassen and cut a path through the forest. Then a pyroclastic flow burned whatever was still standing, down the same path. Stop along the road at the Devastated Area to see the results. It's also a great place to get a picture of the snow covered summit of Mount Lassen. The view of the Devastated Area will be repeated throughout the Cascades. Mount St. Helens is no exception. There are two large areas of destruction north of the mountain, called the Blow-down Forest and Standing Dead Trees. On the west side of Lassen, where our hike is located, the steam blasted slide on Chaos Crags that created Chaos Jumbles dammed Manzanita Creek, forming the lake. The 1915 eruption of Lassen also affected the west side sending mudflows over the entire area around the lake. In the Cascades, glaciers and large slides play a major role in the destructive power of volcanoes. Glaciers also are responsible for much of the erosion of the high peaks.

Mount Lassen / View from west side along the trail.

As you hike from the campgrounds, Chaos Crags can be seen as the rugged ridge up to your left. The large mass of jagged rocks extends to the north from Mount Lassen, which is farther south and again to the left. Once you find Lassen, the highest peak to the left, Chaos Crags spills north of Lassen in jumbles and jagged blocks. As for Lassen itself, if you're eyesight is good or you have binoculars, you should see a dark tongue of rock draping over the west side of Lassen's summit. This tongue is actually a hardened lava flow of dacite. As with most highly viscous flows, they don't move far from the vent. The flow actually covered the east side at one point but was blown away during one of the eruptions. Then came the west side flow, almost 1,000 feet long and still visible at the summit. At first, it was thought to be mud but it stopped flowing soon after it came over the lip of the crater and hardened—not the type of behavior you'd expect of mud. Much of the rock along the trail is dark, almost glassy black, dacite that is the same composition of the tongue of dacite at the top.

Chaos Crags as seen from the trail.

In May 1915, Lassen came to life. It was once a vent that sat on the northeast flank of a larger volcano called Mount Tehama or Brokeoff Volcano. Brokeoff, which partially sat inside a caldera of an even earlier volcano, began its formation hundreds of thousands of years ago and eventually erupted in Plinian style creating its own caldera. The original volcano itself was huge and covered with glaciers. As you hike south, picture Brokeoff Volcano straight ahead, dominating the scenery. After its eruption, the caldera was eroded by glaciation and other factors to the point where it is difficult to see the outline of the caldera. Mount Lassen, one of many domes on Brokeoff, formed on its northeast flank near the end of the Ice Age, about 10,000 years ago. Again, during the hike, picture Brokeoff erupting and disappearing into a caldera. Then, the Lassen vent on its northeast side coming alive, sending up lava that eventually piled to 10,000 foot Mount Lassen. The highly viscous lava oozed out of the vent creating a pile that at times covered the vent. But the lava continued to ooze through as Lassen grew in size. It is now one of the largest plug domes in the world. During the most recent eruptions in 1915, it acted more like a composite volcano, spewing ash in the air and sending avalanches and pyroclastic flows down its flanks. This is not typical behavior for a plug dome, like the large one sitting in the center of Mount St. Helens crater. Before the final eruptions of Lassen, about a thousand years ago, Chaos Crags formed as another dome north of Lassen. The fractured boulders at its top are often found around dome vents as the lava oozes out, hardens, then cracks into large chunks as the lava continues to force its way out from under the hardened cover. Chaos Jumbles, on the valley floor below the Crags, is the result of a rockslide that was triggered by a steam explosion a few hundred years ago. On the trail, up to the left you can see the rugged Chaos Crags and to its left the slope of the landslide that covered much of the land north of the Crags.

Geologists believe that Mount Lassen and Mount Shasta to the north, both in California, are the most likely to reawaken in our time. Of course, that includes Mount St. Helens. What you see at Mount Lassen, will be repeated in grand scale at Crater Lake and Mount St. Helens. Again, Lassen is a dome so its violent behavior is atypical. Crater Lake and Mount St. Helens were and are composite volcanoes. So the destruction they created is expected but the similarities are striking. When Chaos Crags sent Chaos Jumbles sliding down its northwest flank it didn't stop when it reached the Manzanita Creek area. It's air lubricated slide continued up Table Mountain on the other side of the park road. As it climbed the mountain, it lost momentum and slid back covering the area in boulders. The same happened at Mount St. Helens. During the initial eruption, a huge avalanche carrying much of the north flank of the mountain along with a charging pyroclastic flow steamed into Spirit Lake. It picked up quite a bit of lake water and sloshed up a ridge north of the lake before losing momentum. The debris slid back into the lake and what didn't sink can still be seen floating along the lake's shores. What did sink, like Spirit Lake Lodge and its proprietor Harry Truman, are a testimony to the Cascade volcanoes and our need to take them seriously.

Other Points of Interest: This is northern California so there are many beautiful locations to visit. Most of this part of the state is national forest—hike anywhere, camp anywhere. Or, if you're looking for more civilized activity, you can travel south to San Francisco. Visit the big trees in the John Muir Woods National Monument or continue north of San Francisco along the Russian River, a beautiful drive. Or follow the coast highway. At this point though I have to admit I'm getting anxious to continue our hikes in the Cascades. We are only two states away from our final debut with Mount St. Helens; already I'm hearing her message and feeling her brooding in the clouds. And we can't miss Crater Lake on the way. There's a beautiful summit hike at Crater Lake and an almost surrealistic hike up to the Breach where the main blast brought down Mount St. Helens.

On the way to Crater Lake, up Interstate 5 near the Oregon border, stands Mt. Shasta. I've been there once and encountered many strange aspects to this mountain. Yes, it is a monster, a giant in California. It stands over 14,000 feet above all else and is one of the largest composite volcanoes in the world. And it's far from extinct. It may be considered dormant but geologists expect future eruptions since thermal studies show heat at the top in more than one vent. As for the strange aspects of Shasta, they don't relate to geology. A friend of mine hiked to a ridge near the top after spending a year planning his trip. He was most concerned about the weather at the top so he picked the time of year when the weather was most stable, temperate and forgiving. When I ran into him after the hike, he had two remarks about his trek to the top. The first had something to do with not having much fun on the way up—straight up and long. The second had to do with weather. It seems he and his hiking buddy spent three days in the tent waiting for the snow, sleet and rain to clear. He doesn't even mention Shasta anymore. But above all else he told me there was something kind of mystic about the mountain, a feeling he experienced from the very beginning of the hike to the end. He said it was uncomfortable. I did some research because I had considered attempting Shasta as part of this book. My findings convinced me to continue on to Crater Lake and Mount St. Helens.

First of all, Native People considered it a sacred mountain where a divine chief lived. The smoke they saw near the summit, relating more to a gaseous vent, was proof of the chief's existence. Aside from Indian lore, Shasta and the villages around its base are home to many fanatical cults. I could go through some of the names of these cults but suffice it to say there's at least one cult for each dreamer who thinks he may have god-like qualities. The innards of Shasta are believed to contain tunnels. Now I can see conduits for magma but the tunnels are questionable. Perhaps they relate to the belief, I almost said fact, that Shasta is a runway for UFOs. Maybe that's why the tunnels are there; like the subway system at Atlanta's airport that shuttle you between gates. No matter, the geology of Mt. Shasta is very interesting and consistent with the other Cascade volcanoes. As the interstate travels north, and as you approach Shasta along its west side, the view is of another high peak nearer the highway. Shastina (little Shasta) is a cone that formed on the western flank of Shasta. Shastina stands over 12,000 feet, itself one of the highest of the Cascade Range. So these two mountains are formidable structures along the highway. Shasta is a complex structure like most Cascade volcanoes. There were earlier large volcanoes at this site that have eroded away. The ancestor to Shasta formed over 600,000 years ago. Shasta is young. It started to grow in composite volcano fashion toward the end of the Ice Age. So, once again, the Pleistocene Epoch was an active period, particularly toward the end for Cascade volcanoes. Shasta also contains many vents and five well defined glaciers. Geologists believe that Shasta is actually a combination of maybe 3 to 4 composite volcanoes that grew at different times, erupted, were glaciated and eroded until Mt. Shasta superimposed itself on their remains. The summit crater formed around 6,000 BC and continued to erupt until about two hundred years ago. Since then there have been reports of smoke, mostly gas, circling one of the vents around Shasta's summit. Thermal studies show ground heating at what must be former vents near the summit. Any of these vents, even Shastina's, could activate without warning. Given its size and proximity to population centers, including those of the cults, a devastating slide could cause a major catastrophe. And like Mount St. Helens, a slide could open a vent initiating an eruption. You may want to pick up speed on Interstate 5 as you pass Shasta. Not for the sake of getting out of town before the action starts but because Crater Lake has so much to offer and is getting closer. The emotional rush you experience at Crater Lake as you approach your first overlook is similar to the feeling of awe at the Grand Canyon's rim. It's hard to imagine, hard to take in, because it looks more like a surreal picture, a postcard. It seems that only when you hear the wind, or the cry of a raven below the rim, does the view come in touch with reality.

On the Road to the Next Hike

As you drive north toward Crater Lake, remember that there's an active, subducting, oceanic slab below. If its angle is steep into the mantle, more magma is on the way up. If the angle flattens, like the Pacific plate once did causing it to travel great distances inland, the Cascades may go dormant but Idaho and Montana could be in for it. Nevertheless, it is still moving a few inches a year—enough to add to the beautiful scenery of the Western Cordillera.

Once again, the High Cascades are Pleistocene Epoch stories. Much happened before the Pleistocene that laid the foundation for the Cascades but it was the Pleistocene's habit of creating violent eruptions that built the High Cascades. Sixty million years ago, Oregon itself was covered by warm, shallow seas about the time of the Laramide Orogeny, ending around 50 million years ago. The dinosaurs had vanished in one great extinction. Mammals were active. There were patches of land, just above water level, that supported conifer forests. It was a temperate climate. Because of mountain building and volcanism initiated by the Laramide event, Oregon eventually came up out of the seas and the earlier Cascade volcanoes erupted. At one point, the ancestral Cascades were high enough to cut off moisture coming in from the west. The west slopes were wet, the east slopes dry, not unlike the current High Cascades. As the ancestral Cascades (Western Cascades) began a long period of erosion, the High Cascades early history started with flood basalts that came out of huge fissures in the crust, some fissures were miles in length. It was about 17 million years ago when eastern Washington and Oregon and western Idaho witnessed crustal extension (stretching), perhaps because it was on the fringe of the Basin and Range Province. Close to 300 fissures ripped open the earth's crust, sending very fluid basalt lava over the three states, all the way through breaks in the mountains to the Pacific. The Columbia River Gorge now displays hardened lava flows that are 2,000 feet deep in places. You'll drive over the gorge on the way to Mount St. Helens. These great basalt plateaus are the foundation for the High Cascade stratovolcanoes. It was on this dark (basaltic) foundation that 12,000 foot Mount Mazama started to grow over 500,000 years ago. From Mazama, Crater Lake would form, another Plinian eruption so typical of the High Cascades.

Hike: Crater Lake National Park (Mount Mazama)

A classic volcano story, with unmatched scenery along a summit trail high above the crater rim.

Location: The best approach is to enter Crater Lake from the south and exit to the north, in the direction of Mount St. Helens. State Route 62 from Interstate 5 at Medford, Oregon travels east to the south entrance. State Route 62 also comes up from Klamath Falls to the south entrance. Either way the scenery on route 62 is beautiful but the road is not a superhighway so take your time. Exiting the park at the north entrance takes you through the Pumice Desert. Driving within the national monument can be a challenge. In bad weather, fog cuts down on visibility sometimes to just a few feet. Another challenge is following some of the road signs. At the park entrance you'll receive a map and guide. During my last visit we entered from the north and wanted to travel down the east side of the rim drive to Mt. Scott. As the road approaches the rim drive a sign points to the west side rim drive; there's no mention of the east side. By looking at the map we made the correct turn. Keep the map close at hand.

Hike Type and Length: There are three hikes to be considered. Remember to call ahead to make sure the trails are open and the roads to the trailheads are open. One hike is to Garfield Peak, east of the Crater Lake Lodge, about 3-1/2 miles roundtrip and climbs about 1,000 feet. It is moderately strenuous. The other hike, Mount Scott, where we'll focus most of our attention, is even more strenuous but can be considered the premier hike in the park. The Mount Scott trailhead is on the east side of the rim drive. Follow the rim drive along the east side and look for a small pullout and the sign for Mt. Scott. A roadside signpost describes the trail. The trail is around 5 miles roundtrip and climbs about 1,500 feet. Of all hikes, this is the best in terms of scenery and finding points of interest. If you want to hike down to the lake level and take a boat ride, Cleetwood Cove trail on the north side of the crater is about one mile down and around 700 feet elevation change. The return is all uphill. Let's focus on Mount Scott where we'll sit at the top and review all that has happened to Mount Mazama and Crater Lake.

Elevation: Crater Lake Lodge is around 7,000 feet. The Garfield Peak trail is east of the lodge and climbs to 8,054 feet. The Mount Scott summit is 8,926 feet and starts around 7,600 feet. Cleetwood Cove is less than 1,000 foot elevation change but the difference with this hike is the first part is downhill, coming back is all up.

Precautions: Mid-July to mid-September, snow accumulations along the trail are not an issue. However, as well as following the usual hiking precautions, prepare for quick weather changes. Bring rain gear, warm clothes, food and water. Also, this is open country so a cell phone, in case of emergencies, may work at certain elevations. Contact the Visitor Center (phone # below) for trail conditions and weather. If it's raining and foggy as you approach the park, there's a pretty good change you'll see nothing once you reach the higher elevations of the crater rim. You can wait it out outside the park by camping or staying in a local hotel. The Diamond Lake resort has a nice, reasonably priced, hotel and restaurant not far from the north entrance. As with any national park, when you enter and purchase your pass, the receipt is good for a week so you can return when the weather clears.

Planning Information: First, call the Visitor Center at 541-594-3000 (or 3100). Ask them to mail you the Crater Lake official map and guide and Reflections, a great newsletter. You should also check on trail availability and inquire about lodging or camping (2 campgrounds within the park). Remember that you can camp outside the park and there are hotels in some towns. The Diamond

Lake resort on the north side is probably the closest and very nice. Access the following web sites for more info:

Crater Lake National Park:
http://www.nps.gov/crla/brochures/geology.htm

Cascades Volcano Observatory:
http://vulcan.wr.usgs.gov/

USGS Volcano Site and Crater Lake:
http://vulcan.wr.usgs.gov/Volcanoes/CraterLake/framework.html

Geologic Setting: Like Mount Shasta, there is a mystical and mythical air to Crater Lake. After the Paleo-Indians, the earliest Native People, traveled over the Bering Land Bridge into the New World, around 10,000 years ago, they experienced many cultural changes. Starting from a nomadic, hunter-gatherer, lifestyle they eventually chose a more permanent, sedentary existence. They were living in this area when a catastrophic eruption removed the top of the highest mountain. One day the summit was covered with glaciers about 12,000 feet above sea level. The next day, after much noise, fire and smoke, it was gone. So they were well aware of the crater that remains. Around 200 AD, the Mesoamericans traveled more than a thousand miles from Central America into Mexico, then up north through Arizona and New Mexico. Images in painting and pottery report the influence of these southern people. They affected the cultures of the nomadic people to the south and the village dwellers farther north. The Shamans, their cultural leaders, had a problem with Crater Lake and declared it off-limits. There were probably stories or pictures scratched into rocks relating the violence that tore off the summit of their highest mountain. They kept a safe distance from the crater that remained. Crater Lake was eventually discovered by gold prospectors. They must have thought they hit the "Big One" since the gold rush was active in northern California at the time of the discovery and the area topography and geology were so unique.

To begin with, Crater Lake is the result of two major events or episodes. The first episode is the construction of the great mountain volcano. The second is the destructive eruption that tore off the roof and dug the crater. Like other High Cascade volcanoes, this area had its share of eruptions and volcanoes before one grand mountain would superimpose itself on the remains of the others. Hillman Peak along the west rim stands 8,151 feet and is itself a composite volcano but very young (70,000 years). It was standing there as the main volcano was building long before the final climatic eruption. Other older composite volcanoes formed a line from Hillman on the west side all the way to Mount Scott on the east side of the crater. When and where did Crater Lake's recent history begin? Around 500,000 years ago (Pleistocene time), lava poured and ash spewed through several vents building an irregular shaped composite volcano now known as Mount Mazama. Many overlapping shield volcanoes and composite volcanoes, erupting during different intervals, added to Mazama's growth. Geologists estimate it once stood 12,000 feet and contained many vents and separate cones along its flanks. Some cones were from earlier volcanoes, others were active while Mazama was growing. The inner walls of today's crater, at the lower levels near the lake, report the early history of Mazama. Lava flows dominated Mazama's life, although there were periodic explosive episodes sending ash and pumice over the countryside. The oldest rock formations, which are mostly 400,000 year old lava flows of andesite, are exposed on Mount Scott (our hike). Mount Scott, across the crater from the much younger composite volcano Hillman Peak, is itself a former composite volcano, one of the many that added to Mazama's growth. As you travel around the lake, and take in the views from our summit hike, note that some of the crater's flanks and inner walls are composed of hard solid cliffs while other outcrops are lighter colored and eroded to slopes. These layers tell of the different episodes of eruption. Some of the dark colored cliffs are the hardened remains of lava flows. Some lighter colored cliffs are the tightly welded pyroclastic flows and the eroded slopes represent the less welded ash flows and ash falls. Think of Mount Mazama spewing ash and oozing lava from more than one vent for almost half a million years as the mountain increased in size and the landscape surrounding the mountain grew from the ash falls and flows. Then, the one great eruption decapitating the structure. The magma chamber had sent out a great volume of lava and gas that had kept the surrounding walls in tact. Eventually with the chamber mostly vacated of its support, the roof of the chamber collapsed and the mountain top followed.

You'll see on our hike that the crater walls exposed above water line are the visible, bisected remains of the volcano's history. During the collapse, which didn't take long, the top and insides of the mountain dropped like a cylinder head. Hardened lava flows may have sat there as part of Mazama's cone for a hundred thousand years or more—like the one we'll see at Llao Rock. When the magma chamber was vacated and the volcano collapsed, these remnants of past volcanic events were sheared in half and are now presented along the inner crater like pictures on a wall. The catastrophic eruption that created Crater Lake occurred about 8,000 years ago when some of the eruptions were so gas charged that frothy ash and pumice crossed and landed on eight states and a few Canadian provinces. On the road north out of Crater Lake, cars cross the Pumice Desert. Ash and pumice deposits there are 50 feet deep. As usual, geologists like to compare past eruptions to what was experienced in our time at Mount St. Helens. Mazama's climax was 40 times more powerful than Mount St. Helens, throwing 150 times more rock in the air. And another comparison—the main eruptive vent was on the north side of Mazama, sending ash north and east. Recall that Mt. Taylor, San Francisco Mountain and Mount St. Helens all directed their fury to the north and northeast. Volcanic activity at Crater Lake is at best dormant, the last small eruptions occurring about 5,000 years ago. But given that Mazama's cone-building eruptions took place over a half-million year period, 5,000 years doesn't seem like much of a lull. Crater Lake is actually part of a huge volcanic field, surrounded by shield volcanoes and cinder cones. The composition of much of the magma that built Mazama is mostly andesite, much like other Cascade composite volcanoes. Andesite is typically found near subduction zones. The volcanic activity of the High Cascades is a result of subduction of the oceanic plate below the continent. As the magma chamber underground sent up much of its andesite, more silica-rich magmas began to form and erupt. The composite volcanoes throughout the Cascades present similar behavior and composition. They were constructed on a basaltic plateau. The first eruptive phase in the cone building process was of magma mostly composed of andesite. As that magma was ejected, the conduit brought up the more silica-rich magma from deeper in the chamber. The more silica, the more viscous the lava, the harder it is to flow, the more explosive it becomes. Hence, the violent eruptions of dacite to rhyolite that were responsible for the final episodes of most Cascade volcanoes, particularly Mount Mazama.

Crater Lake's body of water, about 5 miles across and almost 2,000 feet deep, has an interesting history. There are no streams or springs to feed the lake. From the time the mountain collapsed, the crater immediately began to fill with water from snow and rain. The lake level grew even as smaller eruptions of lava and ash continued from ring fractures along the caldera rim and other vents. Wizard Island (a cinder cone), along the southwest wall of the crater, is one example of post-collapse activity. As you may recall from our other hikes, caldera activity after a volcano's collapse usually involves resurgence of domes within the crater, lava domes growing along ring fractures and lava and ash flows filling a moat between the resurgent dome and the ring fractures. This caldera was no different except that it was filling with water the whole time. The collapsed crater is itself almost 4,000 feet deep from bottom to crater rim so it must have taken the lake quite a long time to reach a point of equilibrium where yearly precipitation equaled evaporation and loss through fractures. The lake is almost 2,000 feet deep and the lake level fluctuates about three feet a year. It is the deepest lake in the United States, rivaling Yellowstone's deep mountain lake. The blueness of the water comes from its clarity and depth. It is so clear and deep that it absorbs most of the colors of the spectrum except blue, which it beautifully reflects. Glaciers also played a role in Mazama's life. The southeastern wall of the crater was cut and eroded by glaciers during the Pleistocene. On the rim just west of the lodge, there is evidence of glacial movement seen in striations and grooves in rock surfaces once covered by ice. Many of the land forms cut by glaciers were later filled in by lava flows. The construction and destruction of Mount Mazama and Crater Lake represent a typical and historical record seen in many Cascade Mountains. The combination of volcanic violence with glacial ice flows sculpted most of the scenery of the High Cascades.

Hike Guide: For any hike at Crater, bring a map like the Crater Lake official map and guide you receive when entering the park. You'll need a map or some reference to find volcanic structures we'll be discussing. During the hike we'll also review the growth and collapse of Mazama and birth of Crater Lake. As mentioned, we'll focus on the Mount Scott hike but many of these features can be seen from various hikes in the park.

Trail begins in bowl-shaped depression (glacial cirque) at base of Mt. Scott; note summit at upper left.

Mount Scott Hike (take the rim road to the east side of the crater and look for signs for the trailhead):

    If you enter the park from the north, the Mt. Scott trailhead is about 11.2 miles from the entrance and about 5 miles from Cleetwood Cove. The very beginning of the hike is rather flat and skirts a bowl-shaped depression to the left of the trail, at the base of the mountain. This bowl, a glacial cirque, was carved out by glaciers that affected many areas around Crater Lake. As the trail climbs, the best photo opportunities begin at about 1.5 miles. There are switchbacks nearer the top that provide beautiful views to the north where the spire of Mt. Thielsen, the Lightning Rod of the Cascades, can often be seen peering above clouds that form around Diamond Lake. Along the trail looking south, on a clear day you should see snow-covered Mount Shasta with the Shastina bump on its west side. And a bit closer, the almost symmetrical cone shape of Mount McLoughlin. As the trail nears the tower at the summit, it follows a ridge with views in all directions. You won't be disappointed.

Summit ridge of Mt. Scott with tower and Mt. Thielsen peering through clouds in distance to left.

Our discussion starts at the summit, so when you get to the top find a comfortable place to sit facing the lake. Look directly across the lake (west). Find Wizard Island below the west crater wall—a beautifully shaped cinder cone sitting in the lake. The island developed after Mazama collapsed. It grew underwater as the lake filled. Now find the Crater Lake Lodge (to the left), on the south rim. Garfield Peak is the mountain just to the left and between you and the lodge. Below it in the lake, another island and not visible from here, is Phantom Ship. Look farther to your left away from the lake. There are a number of drainages (in valleys) that flow away from the lake. Two of which, Sand Creek and Wheeler Creek, contain fossil fumaroles that are hardened gas vents (tubes) along the walls of the creek bed. Around the time of the collapse, late phase blasts of ash, pumice and scoria traveled down the south side of the mountain. The debris accumulated and as it started to weld together from heat and pressure, gas escaped from the super-heated pile through holes, eventually forming tubes. They weld tightly like cement because of the heat from the ash and gas. Over thousands of years, much of the surrounding rock was eroded and transported downstream, leaving the hard tubes, called fossil fumaroles. You'll have to hike to those locations to see the fumaroles. Or, as you enter or exit the park on the south side, Route 62 southeast toward Klamath Falls passes an overlook not far from the park entrance. The overlook sits above one of the drainages just mentioned. Fossil fumaroles can be seen cemented to the canyon walls looking like long cylindrical beehives. These fossil rock formations are typical in many volcanic environments where ash piled up and hot gas forced its way to the surface venting through what geologists call fumaroles. Some are still active at parks we've visited like Yellowstone and Valles Caldera.

Back at the Mt. Scott summit, some formations are not visible from your location but interesting nevertheless and best viewed from the west side. For instance, looking west from our summit but on the near crater wall (east side) is Sentinel Rock, just north (right) of it is Redcloud Cliff, then Cleetwood Cove on the north side, which you can see. Outcrops of a tightly compacted tuff, the Wineglass Welded Tuff, can be seen along the top of this whole stretch of crater wall. These pyroclastic flows are visible from Garfield Peak, not from Scott. Along the east side rim drive, particularly between Cleetwood Cove and the Mt. Scott trailhead, you'll notice red tinted road cuts and slabs of reddish to gray rock. These formations are part of the pyroclastic flows that blew from the magma chamber down the mountain's slopes just before the final collapse. The Wineglass Formation may represent the last flows that emptied the magma chamber, causing the volcano's demise.

I find Llao Rock, the bisected lava flow at the top of the cliff on the northwest side, to be one of the more interesting rock formations along the upper crater wall. On the northwest rim, halfway between Cleetwood Cove and Wizard Island you will see a large outcrop (cliff) of dark rock near the top. It has a rounded top and fins or appendages that sweep out to each side. That's Llao Rock. Llao was a god to one of the local Native American groups. When Mazama began its final eruptive phase before the caldera event, it blew ash over a large area along the north and east flanks. Then lava composed of a mixture of dacite and rhyolite oozed from the vent and flowed for over a mile. This flow was very thick, about 1,000 feet. After it hardened, the final eruption occurred and when the collapse followed, the lava flow was bisected. As you look at Llao Rock you'll note the darker rock near the top. Below it are ash deposits from much older eruptions but the dark dacite to rhyolite lava flow is quite obvious just below the crest of the hill. The ancient Indian god (Llao) who lived in the mountain was decapitated by the eruption but Llao Rock remains. Farther to the left sits a light brown ledge on top of the rim. It's known as Devils Backbone and is a dike that fed lava from the magma chamber to a vent on Mazama's west flank. Then to the left of it is Hillman Peak, just off the right shoulder of Wizard Island, another composite cone and fairly young at 70,000 years. Its internals were also exposed during the collapse.

Clouds hover over Watchman behind Wizard Island, then Hillman Peak and Llao Rock to far right.

Now let's focus on the north side of the crater. You may be able to see the trail down to Cleetwood Cove (shoreline) from the rim and the parking area across the rim road. You may even see the boat launch area at lake level. The upper crater wall at Cleetwood Cove is composed of the most recent lava flows, ash flows and ash falls deposited just before the cone collapsed. In fact, it collapsed as the lava was flowing. This lava is also composed of dacite to rhyolite that came from a different vent than the one that oozed the Llao Rock flow. Vents were forming around the mountain as the collapse began. Finally, looking north past the rim in the distance is the light colored Pumice Desert surrounded by green forest. One of the final eruptive events before the collapse spewed many feet of ash, pumice and scoria over the countryside to the north—in places ash and scoria piled up to 50 feet deep. That's the desert, the long plain that extends well into the distance. And beyond, on the horizon, is the sharp peak of Mt. Thielsen, hundreds of thousands of years older than Mazama, it was carved to its present shape by glaciers. A former composite volcano, the summit is a hard plug that capped its vent. It does have the appearance of the Lightning Rod of the Cascades and that's what it's called.

Mount Mazama and Crater Lake present another interesting tale in our travels to the great western volcanoes, particularly the Plinian behavior that creates composite volcanoes. Our first encounter with a caldera-forming Plinian eruption was at Valles Caldera in New Mexico. Valles Caldera presented, from the road and from the hills overlooking the caldera, the main structures that often result from a Plinian eruption: resurgent domes, lava or plug domes, ring fractures and moats. The next caldera we visited was at the Chiricahuas where we focused on the interesting rock formations. The caldera was not evident but the rock that resulted from the eruptions told an interesting story of Plinian eruptions. Now, at Crater Lake, we can look at composite volcanoes and a caldera from a different perspective. The inner walls of the crater, some hidden by the lake, report the episodes of eruption that created Mazama—the oldest activity reported on the walls near the bottom, the most recent at the top. The volcano's history is well displayed on the walls because the collapse that created the caldera sliced lava flows and tuff formations in half exposing their internals like pages of a book. As the roof of the magma chamber collapsed and the cone's summit followed, dropping into the void, Mazama's life-events were exposed on the walls that were left standing. It's like looking at the inside of a partially demolished building. During your hike, keep an eye on the crater walls. You'll notice differences in texture and form (cliffs and slopes) that tell geologists what happened, when and how.

From Garfield Peak trail: Wizard Island, Llao Rock, Mt. Thielsen.

As you look across the lake from Mount Scott, picture Mount Mazama as it stood before the big collapse, a highly irregular mountain with other peaks projecting from its flanks. Recall that Mazama was a patchwork of other volcanoes, some shield and others composite. The highest peak, Mazama's summit, was not centered over the lake. It stood above the southern end of the lake (to the left). The main vent was more centered over the lake and was constantly smoking due to gas discharging from the magma chamber a mile or so down. Just before the magma chamber was vacated and the collapse initiated, a huge column of gas and ash was blown into the air along the north side, forming a suspended cloud. The cloud's weight increased to the point where it was greater than the force that suspended it above the mountain. It eventually fell over the mountain in one huge burning cloud that drove at high speeds down the volcano's flanks. The flow was lubricated by heated gas pockets forming at the bottom of the moving mass of gas, ash and rock. The result is the Wineglass Welded Tuff. The Wineglass eruption probably had more to do with the volcano's total collapse than any other event. As the walls weakened and cracked, more vents were opened sending more ash into the air.

The mountain was in trouble, it was foundering. Burning clouds coming from various vents streamed down the flanks at great speeds covering 30 to 40 miles of ground well beyond the volcano—hence, the Pumice Desert north of the park. The entire countryside was on fire. Clouds of ash were drifting east in the jet stream. Burning clouds that shot down the flanks had set everything on fire except rocks, which were almost melted from the heat. After everything burned it welded together. As the countryside lay smoking, the volcano's top moved, cracked, waved and caved in, hollowing out a 4,000 foot deep crater. It must have been quite a site for the ancient people who were likely buried in ash, dead or alive. Hiking to the top of Mount Scott and taking in the serene beauty of the lake is one thing. But the mind's eye may never be able to visualize how it all came to be. This is just one story of the Cascades and what a magnificent view!

Garfield Peak Hike (trailhead is a short distance east of Crater Lake Lodge, to the right as you face the lake):

This hike is shorter and less of a climb than Mount Scott. Volcanic bombs, pyroclastic flow and lava flow formations are evident along the trail as well as some interesting pieces of dark glassy andesite. At the summit, the east wall of the crater is visible and presents some other interesting formations already discussed (Sentinel Rock, Redcloud Cliff and the Wineglass formation).

Cleetwood Cove Hike (north side on rim drive, parking is north side of road, trailhead is south of road):

If you want a close-up at lake level, take this trail. It is downhill going and uphill return. This trail presents the most recent pyroclastic and ash flows, the last before the great collapse. The boat launch is at the end of the trail.

Other Points of Interest: Crater Lake has many other features and activities, mostly available between June and September. Outside of those dates, snow changes the situation but when it snows the park is less crowded. Upon arrival, stop at one of the Visitor Centers. Steel Information Center is open all year while the Rim Village Center is only open June through September. During those months the two campgrounds are usually open, unless there's snow. Mazama Campground is the larger of the two. Lost Creek Campground is restricted to tents only. There are also ranger-led activities. Or you may want to take a boat trip. On the north side of the crater, only one trail leads from the rim to the bottom at lake level. Boat trips around the lake are launched at

Cleetwood Cove. The trip provides excellent views of the internals of the crater walls, with a stop at Wizard Island and a close encounter with Phantom Ship. Tickets for the boat trip are purchased at the Cleetwood Cover parking lot. When you decide to leave the park, follow the rim road to the north side and exit through the North Entrance Station. From there you can travel west to Interstate 5 on State Route 138 or go east to US Route 97 north, the more scenic route. Either way, point the vehicle north. Mount St. Helens is next.

On the Road to the Next Hike

When I last drove out of Crater Lake, I was in such a frenzy to get to Mount St. Helens I blew by everything on the road. If you have time and more patience than I do, please realize that you've only seen the southern section of the High Cascades. There are many other volcanic mountains on the way. For instance, Mt. Thielsen, Three Sisters, Mt. Jefferson and Mt. Hood all offer hiking trails for every taste. They range from easy day-hikes to very remote wilderness experiences. Back on the road, cross the Columbia River into Washington and you have Mount St. Helens, Mt. Adams and the big one, Mt. Rainier. If you want to visit Rainier, Packwood is a nice town to stop in for supplies. There are many hotels and some fine restaurants. As for Mount St. Helens, there are three approaches. A must see is the west side where you get the best views into the great crater from the Johnston Ridge Observatory. It's also the most crowded. The south side offers an opportunity to hike to the top of the rim overlooking the crater's insides. The hike requires a permit and some rock climbing ability. I think the east side is the best—less crowded, a nice camp site along the road in and the best trails. The ultimate east side destination is Windy Ridge, another must see. The town of Randle is northeast of Helens and a good place to stop if you're doing the east side. You can check in with the Ranger Station in Randle for trail and road conditions. Enough said. Time for our final debut with her majesty, Mount St. Helens, only 400 miles from Crater Lake.

Hike: Mount St. Helens

There is no way to describe or prepare for what you're about to experience at the foot of Her Majesty.
And I'd like to offer this hike to the independence of Harry Truman and the dedication of David Johnston.

Location: Southern Washington, northeast of Portland, Oregon. There are three approaches. The southern approach is by State Route 502 from Interstate 5 to Cougar, WA. The road passes the main park headquarters in Amboy. Route 502 connects with Forest Road (FS) 90. Hiking to the summit of the crater is possible from the south side. Basalt lava flows, just 2,000 years old, are another feature on the south side. These lava flow types are similar to what we've seen at El Malpais. The west side is the most active (visitors) and where most of the park facilities are located, such as the Visitor Center, Coldwater Ridge Visitor Center and the Johnston Ridge Volcanic Observatory. Take Route 504 from Interstate 5. From Interstate 5 it's a little over 50 miles to the end of 504. At the end of the road, you'll get the best view of the inner crater and the active lava dome. The other approach is from the north and east side at Randle, WA. Turn south off Route 12 at Randle onto Route 131 to FS 25, then FS 99 to Windy Ridge, about 36 miles, where our hike will start on the Truman Trail, #207.

Hike Type and Length: Although this is backpacking country, these are day-hikes. On the Truman Trail, #207, the length varies depending on which spur trail you want to take. Our hike will trend southwest from Windy Ridge to #216E and #216F, then west on #216. The total hike is about 6 miles roundtrip but there are many variations to the main theme. So we'll start you off on Trail #207 and you can improvise as you see fit. Our plan is to hike through the Pumice Plain and stand right at the location where the great blast was directed, the Breach through the crater wall. There's another interesting hike that provides nice views of the remains of Spirit Lake and another perspective of Mount St. Helens. Before reaching Windy Ridge, look for the Norway Pass trail marker on the right. One way covers about 3 miles but offers excellent views from high up and a close-up of the trees that were blown down during the initial blast. Since the countryside was wiped clean by the blast in the Truman Trail area, Norway Pass, which is on the other side of the lake, provides an appreciation of how the blast affected the forest.

Elevation: Elevation change on the Truman Trail can be up to 1,200 feet depending on which way you go. There are many spur trails that may interest you. Some trend south, along the east side of the mountain. The most interesting trails head west and provide great views of Spirit Lake and the mouth of the crater. Other trails will take you closer to Spirit Lake. Our trail travels between the mountain and Spirit Lake with fairly flat terrain and some up and down but not a lot of elevation change.

Precautions: Check with the monument Visitor Center and the ranger station in Randle, just east of town on US Route 12. The hike from Windy Ridge is not strenuous but it is far removed from civilization (36 miles) so prepare for a full day and bring plenty of water, food, rain gear and a map. This is the state of Washington, rain is not uncommon. Temperature swings can be expected. Below is what the park recommends:
1. Map and knowledge of the trail you're hiking. Let someone know your destination and your return time
2. Flashlight
3. Extra food
4. Extra Clothing
5. Sunglasses/ sunscreen/ hat for blast area (it's wide-open country with no shade)

6. First aid kit
7. Pocket knife
8. Waterproof matches, candles or fire starter
9. Water or the means to purify water (some areas are hot and dry in the summer)
10. Tarp, tent or emergency shelter

Planning Information: Planning is truly key to this trip. Do you want to camp or stay in a hotel? Where and how do you want to eat? The west side entrance has facilities but you can't camp and there are no hotels on Route 504. The east side has facilities in Randle and Packwood but the road to Windy Ridge is fairly remote. You can camp at Iron Creek, a fee-based established campground along the road to Windy Ridge, or camp in the National Forest. Check with the ranger station in Randle. Above all else, you must have a trail map. Here are some web sites and phone numbers for further information (ask about maps, such as the trail map put out by Gifford Pinchot National Forest):

Web Sites:
    Mount St. Helens National Park:
      http://www.fs.fed.us./gpnf/mshnvm/
    Gifford Pinchot National Forest:
      http://www.fs.fed.us./gpnf/
    Pyroclastic Flows at Mount St. Helens:
      http://volcanoes.usgs.gov/Hazards/What/PF/PFMSH.html
    USGS Volcanoes (Mount St. Helens):
      http://pubs.usgs.gov/gip/volcus/page20.html
    Volcano World (Mount St. Helens):
      http://volcano.und.nodak.edu/vwdocs/msh/
    Cascades Volcano Observatory:
      http://vulcan.wr.usgs.gov/

Phone Contacts:
    Gifford Pinchot National Forest (Randle - Cowlitz district) phone number: 360-497-1100
    Monument Headquarters: 360-449-7800
    Coldwater Ridge Visitor Center: 360-274-2114
    Johnston Ridge Observatory: 360-274-2140
    Main Visitor Center: 360-274-2100

Geologic Setting: I realize I have a tendency to refer to Mount St. Helens as Her Majesty. There's a certain atmosphere at her base that brings me to that position, without kneeling. Truth be told, she was named after a man. In the 18th century the mountain was named by a British naval explorer for his friend, Alleyne Fitzherbert, who held the title Baron St. Helens. I'll stick with Her Majesty because she is regal and, as I've already mentioned, this mountain is a woman through and through. She's unpredictable, volatile and above all patient. Her eruptive episodes are grouped into nine separate and distinct periods of activity, some lasting thousands of years others only hundreds. Between the eruptive episodes there were lulls of basically the same durations before firing up again. Each period has its specific rock and eruption types. But primarily, unpredictability characterized her behavior. The volcano also has had at least one bizarre episode, not unlike a woman but maybe more like a man. A few thousand years ago the eruptions changed several times in magma composition— from andesite to basalt, then to dacite and back to andesite again. Some geologists have suggested that perhaps more than one magma chamber fed the volcano. It was as though the magma chamber couldn't make up its mind. Do I throw up basaltic lava and just let it flow or do I need to let off some gas— more like a man? But patience ruled and unpredictability continued. What concerns geologists most is that Mount St. Helens has a distinctively violent history. When comparing the episodes with their length of activity it appears that Mount St. Helens may be in one of those active periods and if the past is any indicator, it could last a few hundred years. So future eruptions are more than likely and with the lava dome still growing in her crater, pressure below could put her in a volatile mood. Unfortunately, much of Mount St. Helens older eruptive evidence has been removed by glaciers and erosion at the end of the Ice Age. But her recent activity, going back more than 12,000 years is generally intact and stacked in volcanic layers from the mountain's base to its now truncated summit.

Mount St. Helens once stood 9,677 (evergreen and glacier-white) feet above sea level and was beautifully reflected in Spirit Lake. Harry Truman's lodge was near the lake shore and had such a view. Now the maximum height along her crater rim is 8,364 (dirty brown) feet above sea level, with a crater 2,000 feet deep. And as usual, geologists offer a comparison of her energy. All of 1,300 feet of mountain summit was removed solely by the power of the initial eruption. The energy released by the eruption can be compared to a Hiroshima-type bomb, not just one but more than 20,000 of them! Fly over

Mt. Rainier and drop that many atomic direct hits and maybe it too would look like Mount St. Helens.

From the western Pacific over to Alaska and south along the entire American coast, the Ring of Fire is the name given to a great horseshoe shaped circuit that marks plate boundaries of transform faults and subduction zones. The Ring of Fire is known for its current volcanic activity and earthquakes. Mount St. Helens, along with the other Cascade mountains and the San Andreas Fault, are our piece of the Ring. And although Helens was once called America's Fujiyama, because of its perfect shape and its white-over-green appearance, her position on the Ring of Fire changed that view on May 18, 1980.

Although some ash deposits from ancestral Mount St. Helens are dated to 40,000 years ago, the current Mount St. Helens didn't really start its eruptive behavior until the Ice Ages were ending, over 10,000 years ago. It seems there was a very early Mount St. Helens, even an ancestral Spirit Lake. But age, glaciers and erosion recycled them to the geologic bin. Current Mount St. Helens grew on top of the remains. Its cone was constructed and then destroyed over many episodes. What is left of the cone is young in geologic time. It started to grow in earnest 3,000 years ago and through repeated episodes of pyroclastic flows, lahars (hot mudflows), lava flows and ash deposits, layer upon layer was added until reaching its peak in the 1800s. One lahar dammed a river and created an earlier version of Spirit Lake a few thousand years ago. In typical Plinian and Cascade fashion, this last period ended with the creation of a lava dome in 1857. Then she rested until the spring of 1980.

The eruptions that marked Mount St. Helens reawakening were the first in the lower United States since the early 1900s when Mount Lassen dominated the news. This was an exceptional opportunity for geologists to experience and study in real-time a major geologic event. It was March 1980 when earthquakes started to rumble the area around the mountain base. Many were centered near the north flank—the first one registered a 4 on the Richter Scale, enough to shake food off store shelves. Over a two month period before the big event, scientists counted close to 10,000 quakes. Steam blasts were seen near the summit. Material ejected from a new vent consisted mostly of pieces of rock shattered by the blasts. Scientists viewed this activity as signals the magma chamber was filling and expanding—breaking surrounding rock, which caused the earthquakes. The steam explosions were probably the result of ground water coming in contact with hot rock and gas rising to the top of the chamber, bubbling up within the hot magma body. What was once a beautiful, snow-covered, green-treed mountain suddenly had a mood swing toward more volatile behavior. The snow-capped summit was coated by sooty material ejected from multiple vents, adding a dark pall to the peak. In April, geologists noticed a bulge on the north flank. As they measured its growth, the bulge continued to expand five feet per day. It stuck straight out from the flank to the length of a football field and with the continued earthquakes it was considered highly unstable.

On May 18, 1980, a 5.1 earthquake shook the bulge loose. As the mass started to slide downhill, taking that part of the north flank with it, pressure was released within the magma chamber. Shake a bottle of soda and pop the cap and you'll get an idea of what happened. The dissolved gases within the chamber were released as magma at the top of the chamber bubbled with froth. The eruption was imminent. As the largest known landslide in historic time was moving downhill, the fractured flank opened sending a huge burning cloud downhill chasing the slide at 200 miles per hour. As the mass of rocks, mud and trees flew over the topography, its path was broken up by hills into separate slides. Only a small lobe of the slide dove into the west edge of Spirit Lake. By this time, the super-heated, lateral blast of burning rock, ash and gas had overtaken the slide and flew past the lake and up the ridge behind the lake, flattening all trees in its path. As the landslide hit the lake, behind the hot blast, it pushed a huge wave of water almost 1,000 feet up the hills and ridges behind the lake. When it lost momentum, the lake water sloshed back into the lake carrying all the blown-down trees ripped from the ground by the hot blast. The landslide and the pyroclastic flow were fighting to see which could cause the most destruction. The pyroclastic flow itself was responsible for blowing down 230 square miles of trees. Outside the Blow-down Forest is the Standing Dead Forest, where the hot flow exhausted itself but managed to singe many acres of trees that are still standing but dead. The avalanche and the blast had also mounted the now-named Johnston Ridge, where the geologist David Johnston was recording the event. Close to 250 feet of avalanche debris accumulated at the base of the volcano while everything else lay smoldering from the burning cloud that had reached 1,100 degrees.

Cloud covered Spirit Lake / Pumice Plain in foreground with dead floating trees along far lake shoreline.

Rivers were flooded, some were dammed to form lakes as the avalanche covered 25 square miles. Mudflows assaulted the river drainages coming from the mountain and from Spirit Lake. The largest flow was along the North Fork Toutle River. It carried bridges, hundreds of homes, road surfaces and a few logging camps downstream. Other blasts and flows followed. As some pyroclastic flows hit bodies of water like Spirit Lake, the heated debris caused steam explosions. One boom from the first hot blast that hit the lake was loud enough to be heard in Canada. This was the typical avalanche and pyroclastic behavior of many glacier-covered Cascade volcanoes.

After the May 18 violence and short period of quiet, there were five more episodes of eruption. Not quite as devastating as the main event, they produced ash columns that soared up to 50,000 feet. And pyroclastic flows continued to fan out along the base adding to the ash and pumice ground cover. As the fury died down, lava oozed from the main vent within the crater forming a lava dome. The first mound of hardened lava that plugged the vent was blown away about a month later and the second was blasted from the crater at the end of the summer. Geologists observing the destruction of the lava domes noted that large chunks of the dome were tossed against the crater walls, shaking more rock and snow loose. As debris and water gathered in the crater, more muddy slides followed. At one point, a small glacial-fed lake appeared inside the crater. A third dacite dome that formed in the fall is still there and smoking from gas below. The dome itself has acted like a combination resurgent and lava dome. Some of the dome growth was from magma pushing the ground up (resurgent), while the rest of the lava seeped through the vent adding to the pile. As magma forced its way up, cracks formed in the hardened dome eventually breaking and sending lava blocks tumbling around the mound; others were hurled against the crater walls. The constant dome building has succeeded in creating a huge bump in the crater that is almost 1,000 feet high and a few thousand feet wide at its base. Steam and a bluish gas can still be seen rising from the dome located near the middle of the crater that itself is 2,000 feet deep and a mile wide. Again, typical Plinian processes at work. The question now is will the dome build another summit, like the original Helens or more like Mount Lassen, or explode into another episode of cone destruction. If it continues building, it may only take a few hundred years for Her Majesty to reach her former height and once again be considered the Fujiyama of America.

Hike Guide: The secret to this hike is to set your mind to a time and place that coincide with the sequence of events that occurred on May 18, 1980. Imagine Harry Truman, probably preparing his lodge at the shore of Spirit Lake for the summer season. Or, David Johnston sitting on a ridge north of the mountain—now the ridge is named after him. The young geologist was a volcano expert and was probably a bit chilly sitting on the ridge in the early morning of May, monitoring the volcano.

At the parking lot of Windy Ridge, take a few moments to study the landscape. Mount St. Helens dominates the left side, the Pumice Plain sweeps down from its base and to the right is Spirit Lake, or what's left of it. Note the grayish debris floating around the water's edge. What appears to be a crust floating along the shore is actually the trees that were ripped from the ground by the pyroclastic blast, carried by the avalanche then dumped back in the lake. There's a small tree-capped island farther out into the lake. Rangers giving presentations to visitors at Windy Ridge say the remains of Harry Truman's lodge sits at that spot at the bottom of the lake. The Johnston Ridge Observatory can be seen across the southern edge of the lake, on the hill in the distance to the northwest. As you look at Mount St. Helens, the jagged break in the north flank is obvious. The open wound is called the Breach. Imagine the mountain 1,300 feet higher, green and glaciated. Everything else from the mountain to the lake was green with trees. From the lake, if you were a visitor, you could see the snow-capped Mount St. Helens reflected in the blue water. Unfortunately, it is May 18, 1980.

Around 8:30 that morning the area was rocked by a 5.1 earthquake. The center of the quake was below the north flank of the mountain. The volatile magma below was pushing against the confines of the magma chamber, breaking its rock walls. One crack was powerful enough to cause the quake. The shaking was sufficient to loosen the bulge growing on the mountain flank. The north side of the summit began to move downhill as the bulge peeled off the mountain like an old scab. A huge landslide, moving slowly at first, picked up speed down the north flank, reaching almost 200 miles per hour. The slide would eventually move miles downhill, then miles uphill past the lake. Behind the west corner of the lake you can see two wide troughs that were probably gouged by the slide as it plowed back into the lake. Part of the slide mounted David Johnston's ridge-top lookout. As the slide started downhill, clouds of gas and ash appeared above the now fractured summit. The clouds gathered in size and weight, then collapsed into burning ash and rock fragments moving downhill after the slide at speeds up to almost 700 miles per hour. The fiery cloud that chased the avalanche must have magnified the terror for those who were in its path and watching. As it tore down the hill, it uprooted any tree still standing and carried most of them in its turbulent wind. Everything including dirt was scoured from the ground, leaving bare bedrock exposed. The devastation covered 150 square miles as it fanned out into a 180-degree arc. A vertical column of gas and ash rose 15 miles up into the sky, true to form in a Plinian eruption. This Plinian eruption column continued to grow as atmospheric currents moving east in the jet stream carried ash to the northeast United States and eventually around the world in less than two weeks after the initial event. Scientists calculate that the ash deposits from this preliminary phase amounted to more than 500 million tons, dropped over more than 20,000 square miles. By noon, a number of pyroclastic flows were observed streaming down the north flank, fanning out and scouring what was left of the land, which by this time was dead-bare earth and rock. These series of flows piled on top of each other like blankets forming the huge Pumice Plain covering an area more than 5 miles to the north. Weeks after the eruption, temperatures taken of the piles of mostly pumice and ash were in the neighborhood of 700 degrees Fahrenheit. In a short time, more than 60,000 acres of forest were down and more than 50 people were dead, including the geologist David Johnston and the innkeeper Harry Truman. The eruptions finally quieted the following day. But Plinian activity is rarely spent in one event. The mountain sat there with a smoking horseshoe-shaped crater, a smoldering devastated area that fanned out to the north, while magma continued to churn below as it still does today. The barren scenery between the mountain and the lake reports the piled remains of the shattered mountain summit, almost 600 feet thick in places. Now it's time to hike.

View of Mount St. Helens near the trailhead at Windy Ridge.

The Truman Trail #207 starts on the south side of the Windy Ridge parking lot. The beginning of the trail is a gravel (cinder) covered service road that is closed to traffic. A trail sign sits just beyond the road barrier. As you hike, listen for elk calls. I've been on this trail three times and have heard elk bellowing each time. They can usually be seen down in the valley to the left. Much of the road is surrounded by a light colored rock. White to gray with many holes and so light it floats, the rock is pumice and is found in most composite volcano environments. Pumice is the result of frothy magma that accumulates at the top of the magma chamber as dissolved gases percolate to the top, increasing the pressure within the chamber. Shattered lava, which hardens to pumice and fractured pumice (ash), are usually the first material ejected during the initial stage of eruption. In typical Plinian phases, ash and rock are mixed with gas forming a suspended cloud above the crater. The cloud, or eruption column, can climb miles into the sky. As the gas pressure from below is reduced, the support for the column of ash is lost and the cloud begins to sink around the mountain. Some of it fills the crater while the remains, now burning clouds, race down the volcano's flanks. These are the burning pyroclastic flows that created the scenery north of the mountain and are typical of the second phase of a Plinian eruption. As the second phase continues, pyroclastic flows are blown out laterally from the vent, while others sink under their own weight thousands of feet above the crater. A hiker can appreciate the silence along the trail, which would have been shattered by the burning pyroclastic flow entering the west edge of the lake. People in Canada heard the steam explosion. Although the summit did not collapse forming a caldera, a collapse is typical of phase three of the Plinian eruption sequence. Maybe a future Mount St. Helens will rebuild and collapse leaving a caldera like the ones we've seen at Crater Lake and Valles Caldera.

As we continue the hike, the scenery to the left and below the trail changes. The valley looks like it was carved by a glacier. In the spring and early summer, water from snow melt streams over waterfalls into the valley. One such waterfall reminds me of Yosemite Valley's Bridalveil Falls which itself was carved by a glacier. To geologists it's called a hanging valley. The glacier's gradual movement carved through a stream system, leaving the upper stream high while removing the rest of the stream drainage, resulting in a hanging valley with a waterfall. As you turn each corner along the trail and your view of Mount St. Helens improves, you're getting closer to a trail junction and a better view of the valley below. You'll appreciate the comparison to Yosemite. It's almost as beautiful. The gravel road eventually branches at a trail marker. The left dirt trail climbs a steep ridge. Continue on the Truman Trail (#207) which will start downhill still on the gravel road. At this point, with a view of what's ahead, decide which trail you want to take. At the bottom of the hill, you will have three choices. Continue toward the mountain and follow the trail (216E) that runs directly west right by the Breach, along the north base of Helens (our choice). Or, you can take trail 216D and 234 left, directly south along the east edge of the mountain's base. The third choice is to follow trail 207 (Truman) right, northwest toward the lake.

Continue downhill and at the trail junction we'll take the Windy Trail (216E). You're about 3/4 of a mile into the hike and now walking through a drainage that was carved by the avalanche and various flows. In fact, everything from this point is part of the devastated area where evidence of pyroclastic flows, mudflows and the Blow-down forest dominate the scenery. During the 1980 eruption, lahars (hot mudflows) rushed into rivers and drainages, carrying the mass of mud, trees and other debris downstream. Much of this muck ended up emptying into the Columbia River, adding 25 feet to the river bottom, which brought navigation to a halt.

As the trail approaches the crater, the destroyed north side (the Breach) becomes more obvious and ominous.

At about one mile, the trail moves up a ridge to great views of Spirit Lake and a better view of the crater fracture, the Breach. You'll also start to notice that the trail cuts across many ridges and drainages. In the drainages, note the different rock types. Some were part of the pyroclastic flows, others were blown out of the vent and crater during the eruptions while others were transported by mudflows and streams. At 1.5 miles, the trail branches at a marker. To the left the trail hugs the east base of the mountain. We'll continue to the west, right toward Loowit Falls, which you'll eventually see in the distance. At 2 miles the trail enters a creek bed with much vegetation and more interesting rock types. At 2.2 miles the trail again comes around another ridge to another breathtaking view of the Breach. You're now entering the direct path of the initial slide and blast that removed the mountain top and flank. This area is the Pumice Plain, which branches out all the way to the west edge of the lake and beyond. At this point you can improvise. You must stay on the trails but decide how far you want to go. One of the most amazing experiences in my life happened when I reached that exact northern edge of the fractured crater and stared into the Breach. You can't see the dome building within the crater but you do understand once and for all the true power of a Plinian eruption. Also, the eruptive history is beautifully displayed on the inner walls of the exposed crater, which is now open before you like a book. You can remain there for hours, doing 360 degree turns, taking it all in. In a way, nothing and everything makes sense. What was it down below that removed that wall of rock? No geology book ever written will describe it to my satisfaction. But it all makes sense when you stand there, look and listen to the message the volcano brings. And it's best seen and heard at the base of the throne of Her Majesty, Mount St. Helens.

The Breach.

Other Points of Interest: From Mount St. Helens north it's a hiker's paradise, with one wilderness after another: Goat Rocks, William Douglas, Tatoosh, Clearwater, Norse Peak, on and on. Mount Adams and the Mount Adams Wilderness sit directly east of Mount St. Helens and Mount Rainier National Park is north. Route 12 east takes you to the town of Packwood, a nice place to stock up with supplies or spend a night. From there it's a short ride to Rainier. The scenery on Route 12 is magnificent, particularly if you're driving east to west from Rimrock. Beautiful lakes surround the road at places and eventually Mount Rainier appears in front of you like a postcard. From Rainier north, wilderness continues as do the Cascade Peaks, including Mount Baker, all the way into Canada where Mount Garibaldi marks the northern terminus of the High Cascades. Also, Olympic National Park, with its own mountain types, overlooks the coast west of Seattle. But for me, it's hard to leave Mount St. Helens.

On the Road to the Next Hike

There are many more geologically significant and beautiful areas in the west. Mount St. Helens is one of the most striking and I hope the visit was meaningful. It is the final destination of our trek across the west but, above all, I hope you enjoyed the journey as much as, or more than, the final destination. However, there are many more areas to explore. The metamorphic rock environments that report North America's ancient history. And the sedimentary rock formations that contain signs of ancient, fossilized life. This volcanic trip, and its rocks, are just a beginning in a long, wonderful journey to find new ways to hike and new ways to absorb life and time that surround the trail.

INDEX

Anasazi Culture, 94
Andesite, 61
Asthenosphere, 33

Bandelier National Monument, 77
Basin and Range, 27
Basalt, 33, 52, 60
Batholith, 41
Big Bang, 19
Blow-down Forest, 198

Caldera, 28, 43, 46, 48
Canadian Shield, 71
Capulin Volcano National Monument, 52, 64
Cascade Range, 42
Cenozoic Era, 27
Central Highlands, 118
Chiricahua National Monument, 47, 120
Cinder Cone Volcano, 44, 50
Clovis People, 30, 51, 73
Coelophysis, 25

Colorado Plateau, 117
Composite Volcano, 43, 49, 54
Conglomerate, 134
Cordillera, 72
Core, 31
Crater Lake, 43, 179
Craton, 65, 71
Cretaceous Period, 25
Crust, 31

Dacite, 47, 61
Diabase, 60
Dike (volcanic), 57
Diorite, 61

Earth, 31
El Malpais National Park, 101
Exotic Terrains, 36, 39

Fault, 75
Folsom People, 30, 51, 74
Fumaroles, 84, 187

Gabbro, 59
Geologic Time, 21
Grand Canyon, 117, 152
Grand Staircase, 152
Granite, 33, 41, 61
Gypsum, 59

Harding Mine, 75
Hawaiian Islands, 30, 38, 49, 53
Hot Spots, 30, 38, 53, 156

Ice Ages, 28, 30
Igneous Rocks, 59

Jemez Mountains, 43, 79
Jemez Lineament, 67
Juan de Fuca Plate, 35
Jurassic Period, 25

Laramide Orogeny, 26
Lava Domes, 42, 58, 61
Limestone, 59
Lithosphere, 33

Magma, 8, 13, 33, 40, 59
Mammoths, 30
Mantle, 31
Marble, 59
Mesozoic Era, 25
Metamorphic Rocks, 59
Mid-Tertiary Orogeny, 28
Moat, 82, 84
Morrison Formation, 148
Mount Lassen, 167
Mount Mazama, 179
Mount St. Helens, 193
Mt. Taylor, 101

Nature Conservancy, 134
Navajo Sandstone, 26
Neck (volcanic), 57
North American Plate, 36
Nuee Ardente, 48

Obsidian, 63, 84, 93, 95

Pacific Plate, 36, 155
Paleozoic Era, 23
Paleo-Indians, 116
Pangea, 24
Pegmatite, 75
Permian Period, 23
Plate Tectonics, 35, 39
Plate Boundaries, 35
Plinian Eruption, 43, 46, 48
Plumes (mantle), 30
Pluton, 41
Precambrian Era, 21
Pumice, 34, 203
Pyroclastic, 42

Quartz, 61
Quartzite, 73

Resurgent Dome, 62
Rhyolite, 61
Ring Fractures, 49, 81
Rio Grande Valley, 79
Rockhound State Park, 133
Rocks, 59
Rocky Mountains, 72, 80

San Andreas Fault, 75
Sandstone, 59
San Francisco Mountain, 56, 139

Seamounts, 38, 156
Sedimentary Rocks, 59
Shield Volcano, 49, 52
Spreading Center, 25, 35
Standing Dead Forest, 198
Subduction, 26, 27
Sunset Crater, 139
Superstition Mountains, 57

The Breach, 201, 204
Triassic Period, 25
Tuff, 34, 42

Unconformity, 134

Valle Grande, 84
Valles Caldera, 62, 77
Volcano, 38

Weavers Needle, 58
Windy Ridge, 193

Yellowstone Park, 38, 154

Zuni-Bandera Volcanic Field, 107
Zion National Monument, 26

GLOSSARY

Accretion: Where tectonic plates collide (converge) at a subduction zone, crust, other (exotic) terrains, even island volcanoes from one plate are attached to the margin of the receiving plate.

Anticline: Deformed sedimentary beds of rock are bent to an upside down U-shaped formation, the result of tectonic compressional forces.

Asthenosphere: The dense, elastic ("without strength") zone in the upper mantle just below the lithosphere upon which tectonic plates move.

Basin and Range: During the late Miocene Epoch (about 8 million years ago), a period of major faulting occurred, where normal faults caused basins to fall and surrounding mountains to rise. The faulting was caused by tensional plate activity as the earth's crust was being stretched. The results of Basin and Range faulting are evident through out the Southwest, particularly Utah, Nevada and southern Arizona and New Mexico.

Batholith: When a large body of magma crystallizes below the surface, at depth where the magma cools slowly, plutonic igneous rock forms. The typical rocks that make up a batholith are granite, diorite and granodiorite. These massive rock formations are called batholiths when they appear as large mountain ranges exposed at the surface through erosion or faulting.

Big Bang: Scientists use this phrase to describe the event that caused the formation of our universe—the beginning of it all.

Breccia: The same as conglomerate but the rock fragments in the mix are angular versus the rounded pieces of a conglomerate.

Caldera: Large summit depression caused by the collapse of the magma chamber and flanks of a composite volcano, usually the result of Plinian eruptions.

Cenozoic: Geologic (recent) era dating from approximately 65 million years ago to the present—also called the Age of Mammals.

Conglomerate: A rock or rock formation made up of any other rock fragments from pebbles to boulders where the rock mix is uneven in size, well rounded and cemented together. If the fragments are angular, the rock is called breccia.

Cordillera: Chain of mountains, the Western Cordillera of North America is a combination of volcanic landforms and accreted terrains that attached to the continent as it was growing outward, then compressed by the Laramide Orogeny and faulted by the Basin and Range Orogeny.

Core: The super-heated, solid center of the earth.

Crust: Outer zone of the earth, above the mantle, composed of thin oceanic crust and thick continental crust.

Crystallization: The process where minerals crystallize to eventually form a rock. In igneous rock, crystallization during magma cooling creates the minerals, then the rock.

Dike: Igneous intrusion into existing rock layers where the intrusion is discordant—it cuts across layers of rock. When the surrounding rock is eroded away, the harder igneous rock, the dike, is exposed at the surface and appears as a thick dark sheet across the landscape.

Domes: Formed at volcanic vents, lava domes grow as thick lava oozes out and piles up above the vent often eventually plugging the vent (plug dome). If there is no vent, magma will dome the earth above to form a resurgent dome.

Exotic Terrains: Remnants of former continents that are often attached to the margin of a receiving plate when two plates converge at a subduction zone.

Fault: A fracture in existing rock where one or both sides of the fracture move in opposite directions. If the fracture has no movement, it is called a joint. Fault types are normal, reverse, thrust and strike-slip.

Ferromagnesian: Minerals of iron and magnesium composition. These minerals are often present in the igneous rocks that are low in silica such as basalt and are common in the oceanic crust.

Flow-banding: The tendency of mineral crystals like quartz or pumice in igneous rock (particularly rhyolite) to appear stretched (elongated). It occurs as the rock is hardening while it is still flowing or pressured by weight.

Hot Spot: Long-lasting heated locations at the earth's surface that cause either volcanic activity or doming of the earth above the hot spot. Mantle plumes rise from within the mantle to cause hot spots.

Igneous: One of three specific rock types formed from magma that hardens above or below ground. The other two rock types are sedimentary and metamorphic.

Island Arc: Line of volcanoes that form along plate margins in the ocean, where oceanic plates are converging and magma of basalt or andesite composition rises at the subduction zone to form volcanoes, sometimes above the water line.

Laramide Orogeny: Unique event of mountain building in the west, probably caused by the continued subduction of the oceanic plate under the North American plate. It lasted from 80 to 50 million years ago.

Lava: Magma or molten rock that makes its way to the surface while still in its semi-liquid state. It hardens to form volcanic rock at or near the surface. Underground it's called magma, at the surface it's termed lava.

Lithosphere: Earth's crust coupled with the uppermost section of the mantle to form stiff tectonic plates called lithospheric plates. Taken as a whole, the crust with the upper section of the mantle is called the lithosphere.

Maar: Huge steam-exploded hole or crater created when ground water comes in contact with magma or rocks heated by magma.

Magma: Molten (hot, semi-liquid) rock that forms underground and eventually hardens (crystallizes) above or below ground to become a rock type called igneous.

Mantle: Hot, mostly solid zone within the earth between the inner core and the outer crust.

Mantle Plume: Column of hot semi-liquid rock rising from deep within the mantle that causes hot spots under tectonic plates. At these hot spots, volcanic eruptions occur or the earth is domed by the magma.

Mesozoic: Geologic (middle) era dating from approximately 250 million years ago to 65 million years ago. Also known as the Age of Reptiles.

Metamorphic: One of three specific rock types that has been transformed from preexisting rock. Their texture and minerals have been transformed from heat and pressure underground to an entirely different rock from the original.

Monocline: Deformed sedimentary beds of rock that form a slope from the original horizontal plane and eventually flatten out to the horizontal.

Neck (volcanic): Hardened remains of magma that solidified within a volcanic conduit or vent and was left standing after the surrounding flanks eroded away.

Orogeny: A geologic term for mountain building, resulting from volcanic or tectonic plate activity.

Paleozoic: Geologic (old) era dating from approximately 550 million years ago to 250 million years ago. Also known as the Age of Fishes.

Paleo-Indians: The earliest ancestors of today's Native Americans. These hunters entered our continent through a land bridge over the Bering Strait during the Great Ice Age almost 15,000 years ago. Evidence of their existence in the southwest dates back to about 12,000 years ago.

Plinian Eruption: The most violent type of eruption usually associated with a strato or composite volcano. Plinian eruptions are characterized by up to four phases. First, a gas-charged ash column forms above the mountain followed by more violent, destructive eruptions and pyroclastic flows down the flanks. The third phase is climaxed by the magma chamber, depleted of its gas and magma, collapsing inward thus causing collapse of the volcano itself. The final phase is characterized by eruptions of pyroclastic material and gas along ring fractures that surround the caldera, the depression that remains after collapse.

Plutons: Large intrusions of magma originated at depth that rise toward the surface forming magma chambers. When it hardens (crystallizes) it becomes an igneous intrusive (plutonic) rock, usually granite or a type of granitic rock. Plutons often form large masses of rock called batholiths that are exposed at the surface through erosion or faulting, eventually becoming large mountain ranges like the Sierra Nevada.

Porphyry: A porphyritic rock is one that is generally dense but with other mineral crystals (phenocrysts) appearing unevenly in the rock matrix. These scattered minerals crystallized at a different time (rate) and manner than the more dense rock matrix.

Precambrian: The beginning of geologic time—ancient time. This geologic era dates from approximately 4.6 billion years ago to the Paleozoic Era.

Pyroclastic: Broken rock caused by volcanic eruption. Pyroclastic rock is formed from erupted pieces of magma and rock broken during eruption. If finely shattered it is called ash. Pyroclastic flow is a hot, turbulent mixture of gas and rock fragments. Pyroclastic flows are often termed Nuee Ardente, meaning burning cloud.

Regression: Term used to describe the retreat of water (such as a large sea) from land—the opposite of Transgression.

Schistose: A descriptive term for any rock where the rock texture or fabric shows a parallel alignment of specific minerals (like flaky mica) which form layers in the rock along which the rock may fracture. The rock schist is the prime example. The parallel alignment of the minerals, like mica or hornblende, into layers is called foliation.

Seamount: Mountains, the result of submarine volcanoes, constructed on the ocean floor from mantle plumes that feed magma through a vent eventually forming a volcanic island that grows above sea level, like the Hawaiian Islands.

Sedimentary: A specific rock type made up of sediments or debris from microscopic to large pieces of other rock. It can also be composed of the remains of plants and animals or chemicals precipitated from water.

Silica: Main element of the largest class of minerals, the silicates. Silica Dioxide is one such mineral called quartz. Minerals and rocks of the silicates group make up much of the continental crust. Two igneous rocks high in silica are granite and rhyolite.

Sill: Igneous intrusion into existing rock layers where the intrusion is concordant—the magma penetrates between the layers, versus intruding through them like a dike. Sills often form ledges when the surrounding rock is eroded away and the sill is exposed at the surface.

Spreading Center: The location where two plates move in opposite directions (divergent plate boundary). In the ocean the center is often referred to as a mid-ocean ridge while in continental crust it's referred to as a rift valley.

Stock: A small pluton that forms below the surface and is often fed by a large pluton.

Strata: Term used to describe layers of rock, mostly sedimentary, one formation on top of the other.

Subduction: When an oceanic tectonic plate collides with a continental plate, the oceanic plate is forced under the continental plate—a process called Subduction. The area where this activity is centered is called the Subduction Zone and occurs along the margin of plate boundaries. It can also occur where two oceanic plates meet.

Syncline: Deformed sedimentary beds of rock, they are bent to a U-shaped formation, the result of tectonic compressional forces.

Tectonic Plates: Continental and oceanic crust sit on, and are part of, large (lithospheric) plates, which are constantly moved by convection currents caused by heat from the mantle. The mantle below the crust is the source of such heat and the currents that boil up to move the plates over the upper section of the mantle called the asthenosphere. Where plates come together, they are convergent. Where they separate, they are divergent. And where they slide by each other, a transform plate boundary exists.

Transform Plate Boundary: Where two plates meet and slide by each other often causing earthquakes. An example is the boundary at the San Andreas Fault.

Transgression: Seas or bodies of water advance over land—the opposite of Regression.

Tuff: Rock solidified from hot pyroclastic material. Ash-fall and ash-flow deposits create tuff formations. If highly compacted, cemented, from heat it is termed welded.

Unconformity: A gap in the geologic record. Where two adjoining rock formations have a significant difference in age between them. The difference in their ages, which can be millions of years, marks a period at that location where there was either no geologic activity, such as sedimentary deposits or lava flows. Or what was there above the oldest layer, had been eroded away before the younger layer was laid down.

Vesicles: Holes in rock, such as basalt, formed from gas bubbles as the rock cooled and hardened. The holes may fill with liquids containing other chemicals that eventually crystallize as a mineral. When minerals fill the vesicles the rock is said to be Amygdaloidal. Basalt can often be identified by the presence of vesicles.

Volcanic Arc: A line of volcanoes created along the contact margin where an oceanic plate has been subducted under a continental plate. It is often referred to as Arc Volcanism and is sometimes confused with Island Arcs. In Arc Volcanism, the rock formed from the magma is usually granite, diorite, rhyolite or andesite. The volcanoes tend to form along the coast (continent margin) where the plates converge. The term Arc is used because, if seen on a map, the volcanoes appear to curve as they follow the contact margin of both plates.

Volcano: Surface structure caused by magma erupting from a vent in the earth.

SUGGESTED READING

Most of the reference material used for this book came from geologic web sites as well as papers and reports available through the US Geologic Survey and the Geological Society of various states. I attempted to synthesize the material into a less technical format, making it more comprehensible for the general reader. Geology books, papers and reports vary from highly technical to enjoyable reads. Most of the recommended works are generally understandable and enjoyable reads.

In this book, the Planning section of each hike suggests reference works and web sites that offer related material about the location and the trail.

Below are some of my recommendations:

SPIRIT of the AMERICAN SOUTHWEST, Geology/Ancient Eras and Prehistoric People/Hiking Through Time, by Tom Prisciantelli (Sunstone Press, 2002).

The Roadside Geology series is one of the best for the casual reader. Any work by Halka Chronic is highly recommended, including *Roadside Geology of Arizona* (Mountain Press Publishing Company, 1994) and *Roadside Geology of New Mexico* (Mountain Press Publishing Company, 1987). Ms. Chronic's area of interest is the plateau country of the Southwest. Another one of her excellent works: *Pages of Stone—Grand Canyon and the Plateau Country* (The Mountaineers, 2000).

For Yellowstone, *Roadside Geology of the Yellowstone Country,* by William J. Fritz (Mountain Press Publishing Company, 1985).

In my opinion, one of the best introductory books on geology is *Modern Physical Geology*, by Thompson & Turk (Saunders College Publishing, 1991).

If you want to hike the Cascade Range and learn more about its geology try *Fire Mountains of the West*, by Stephen L. Harris (Mountain Press Publishing, 1988).

If you want to get serious about Arizona's geology while enjoying some great hikes, try *Hiking Arizona's Geology*, by Ivo Lucchitta (The Mountaineers, 2001).

For technical papers, reports and books, contact the local Geological Society or the US Geologic Survey office for each state of interest. One of the most comprehensive reviews of Arizona's geology can be found in the *Geologic Evolution of Arizona*, by J.P. Jenney and S.J. Reynolds, Editors (Arizona Geological Society Digest 17, 1989).

Much of the reference material I used for the Valles Caldera hike came from these two field guidebooks:

    Field Excursions to the Jemez Mountains, Bulletin 134 (1996).

    Jemez Mountains Region (Sept 1996).

Although the above guidebooks can be technical, they are still very interesting and worth the read if you want to learn more about the Valles Caldera area. All states have geological societies and a chapter for the US Geologic Survey. For New Mexico related material, see the web sites below:

    New Mexico Geological Society web site:
        http://www.geoinfo.nmt.edu/nmgs/home.html
    New Mexico Tech (Geology and Mineral Resources) web site:
        http://www.geoinfo.nmt.edu/
    General volcano related material from the USGS:
        http://vulcan.wr.usgs.gov

My favorite author, who can assimilate any geological subject and reproduce it as a well-written novel, is John McPhee (Publisher: Farrar, Straus and Giroux). My two favorites:

Rising from the Plains (a great work on the evolution of the Rocky Mountains).

Basin and Range (you'll want to get on the interstate and spend some time in Utah and Nevada).

www.ingramcontent.com/pod-product-compliance
Lightning Source LLC
Chambersburg PA
CBHW022059160426
43198CB00008B/286